D1733342

RADICAL THEATRICS

RADICAL THEATRICS

PUT-ONS, POLITICS, AND THE SIXTIES

Craig J. Peariso

University of Washington Press ✳ Seattle & London

© 2014 by the University of Washington Press
Printed and bound in the United States
Design by Dustin Kilgore
Composed in ITC Century, a typeface designed by Tony Stan
18 17 16 15 14   5 4 3 2 1

All rights reserved. No part of this publication may be reproduced or transmitted in any form or by any means, electronic or mechanical, including photocopy, recording, or any information storage or retrieval system, without permission in writing from the publisher.

UNIVERSITY OF WASHINGTON PRESS
www.washington.edu/uwpress

Library of Congress Cataloging-in-Publication Data
Peariso, Craig J.
Radical theatrics : put-ons, politics, and the sixties / Craig J. Peariso.
    pages   cm
Includes bibliographical references and index.
ISBN 978-0-295-99411-6 (hard cover : acid-free paper) 1. Protest movements—United States—History—20th century. 2. Radicalism—Social aspects—United States—History—20th century. 3. Radicals—United States—History—20th century. 4. Political activists—United States—History—20th century. 5. Art—Political aspects—United States—History—20th century. 6. Performing arts—Political aspects—United States—History—20th century. 7. Street theater—Political aspects—United States—History—20th century. 8. Political culture—United States—History—20th century. 9. Counterculture—United States—History—20th century. 10. United States—History—1961–1969. I. Title.
HN59.P43 2014
303.48'4—dc23
                    2014025249

The paper used in this publication is acid-free and meets the minimum requirements of American National Standard for Information Sciences—Permanence of Paper for Printed Library Materials, ANSI Z39.48–1984.∞

To Larry and Sharon

CONTENTS

ACKNOWLEDGMENTS

THIS PROJECT WOULD NEVER HAVE BEEN FINISHED WITHOUT THE help of a number of colleagues, friends, and family members. From the project's origins to its current state, the input and support of the following have been invaluable. I owe particular thanks to Jonathan Katz, without whose advice a project of this breadth would have seemed unthinkable. His comments on early drafts of this work kept me focused and moving forward at a stage when it would have been all too easy to follow any number of false leads. Joseph Monteyne, John Lutterbie, Seth Clark Silberman, and James Rubin also provided valuable feedback on early versions of much of what follows, helping me to sharpen my thinking on a number of issues the work raises. More recently, the anonymous readers for the University of Washington Press offered thoughtful and incisive criticism, which in turn led me to further refine the arguments presented herein. To them I am incredibly grateful.

Archivists at numerous libraries have also played a key role in the completion of this work. Specifically, I would like to thank Terry Goldich and the staff at the University of Connecticut's Thomas J. Dodd Research Center. Their award of a Sigmund Strochlitz Travel Grant and their assistance in navigating the Hoffman family papers were vital in the earliest stages of my research. I would also like to express my gratitude to the archivists and staff at the New York Public Library, and at the Special Collections at Stanford University Library, for providing me with access to the International Gay Information Center Archives and the collected papers of Black Panther Party founder Huey P. Newton.

The list of colleagues and friends who have helped with various forms of professional, intellectual, and moral support over the years is far too long to include. There are, nevertheless, those whose omission would be unforgiveable. To my colleagues Zainab Bahrani, Francesco Benelli, Holger Klein, Matthew McKelway, Bill Hood, Caroline Earley, Kate Walker, Anika Smulovitz, Beverly Howard, Dominick Longbucco, Barrett Norman, Andy Goodman, and Michal Temkin-Martinez, I would like simply to say, "Thank you." Any attempt to formulate a specific debt I might owe you individually would only prove embarrassing. To Chad Laird, J. P. Park, Sarah Cartwright, Yvie Fabella, and Terry McLaughlin, I owe my gratitude not only for their friendship but also for their understanding and forgiveness in those times when the demands of this project—among other things—kept me from writing or calling as often as I would have liked. I must also thank Mike Hoglund and John Gold for their generosity and technical support; without their help, this work would have taken so much longer. Joel and Naomi Rosenthal, and Miranda Townsend and Jonathan Bayer provided me with homes away from home, playing an important, albeit unexpected, role in bringing this project into being. Similarly, Dave and Carol Hoglund may (still) never know just how much I appreciate their help and hospitality. And special thanks are due to my parents, Larry and Sharon, and my sisters, Stephanie and Katrina, without whom I would never have written a word.

I also owe thanks to Columbia University Press for allowing me to reprint "The 'Counterculture' in Quotation Marks: Sontag and Marcuse on the Work of Revolution" from *The Scandal of Susan Sontag*, edited by Barbara Ching and Jennifer Wagner-Lawer, 154–70, © 2009; and to Cambridge University Press for allowing me to use "'Styleless Style': What Photorealism Can Tell Us about 'the Sixties'" from the *Journal of American Studies* 47, no. 3 (August 2013): 743–57 (portions of both appear in revised form in the introduction). Taylor and Francis has allowed me to reprint "Formlessness as Figure: Guerrilla Theater and the Image of Utopia" from *Third Text* 17, no. 3 (Fall 2003): 261–71; and Cambridge Scholars Publishing has allowed me to use "Commercials for the Revolution: 'Movement Celebrities' and the Theatricality of Protest" from *Film and Television Stardom*, edited by Kylo Patrick Hart, 161–79, © 2008 (both of which appear in revised form in chapter 1). And Berghahn Books has allowed me reprint portions of "Representing Black Power: Handling a 'Revolution' in the Age of Mass Media" from *Media and Revolt: Strategies and Performances from the 1960s to the Present*, edited by Kathrin Fahlenbrach, Erling Sivertsen, and Rolf Werenskjold © 2014 (appearing in chapter 3).

Finally, I will offer my deepest gratitude to Sarah Hoglund, who for more than a decade has provided me with support and encouragement, regardless of context. Without her, nothing I do could ever be called complete.

RADICAL THEATRICS

INTRODUCTION

Stereotypes, Opposition, and "the Sixties"

IN 1970, DRAMA CRITIC ROBERT BRUSTEIN COMPLAINED THAT IN
America revolution had been reduced to a form of theater. What
had once appeared to be legitimate opposition to the morally bankrupt policies of the United States government had become little more
than costume drama. Groups such as the Weathermen and the Black
Panther Party, he wrote, "certainly have the ability to transform their
rhetoric into violent action, and are now suffering the consequences
in even more violent official retaliation." Nevertheless,

> both actions and rhetoric are an extension of theatricality, and proceed
> through the impulse to impersonation. When the Weathermen lock arms
> down a Chicago street, chanting "We love our uncle, Ho Chi Minh" . . . or
> when the Panthers, in paramilitary costumes, have their pictures taken
> serving breakfast to ghetto children, then the link with public relations
> and play acting becomes obvious. Indeed, the alleged murder of an
> alleged Panther informer in New Haven bore sufficient similarities to the
> plot of a recent movie . . . to make one suspect that life was imitating art.[1]

Shortly after the appearance of Brustein's essay, journalist Robert
L. Gross of the *Miami Herald* stated the argument in even starker
terms. "Posing is the key," Gross wrote. "Revolution has become
the giant put-on of the era."[2] To many, these arguments would have
seemed preposterous. How, in the face of mass protests, police
riots, shootouts with authorities, threats against heads of state, and

even bombings, could anyone think of trivializing the political conflicts taking place in the United States by referring to them as mere
"theater"? The answer, according to Brustein, lay in the guaranteed
right to free political speech. By allowing individuals to "speak their
minds," American culture had succeeded in replacing direct action
with "radical verbal displays."[3] It should have come as no surprise
therefore that no matter how loudly these "revolutionaries" called
for meaningful action, their cries seemed to fall upon deaf ears.
Stripped of its efficacy by the putative tolerance of contemporary
American society, political activism appeared to be more caricature
than rebellion.

But what if the "verbal displays" Brustein lamented represented, in
their very theatricality, a form of resistance that neither he nor Gross
recognized? This book argues that the political work of individuals
such as Eldridge Cleaver, and organizations such as the Youth International Party (Yippie) and the Gay Activists Alliance (GAA) may in
fact mark the emergence of a different approach to political dissent.
Rather than dismissing these individuals and organizations for having missed the point of Black Power, the counterculture, or the gay
liberation movement, I suggest that they may instead be understood
as efforts to negotiate the challenges of presenting radical politics
at a time when, as Brustein and others pointed out, the possibility of
opposition appeared to have been historically foreclosed. To reframe
these political tactics, I place the visual and verbal media games of
Cleaver, the Yippies, and the GAA next to the contemporary social
and cultural analyses of a number of their critics, each of whom
was, in his or her own way, perplexed by the crisis of theatricality
that Brustein described. Black Panther Party founder Huey Newton,
documentary filmmaker Norman Fruchter, countercultural theorist
Theodor Roszak, and film critic Parker Tyler—all politically progressive, these authors worried at length over the damage that activists
like Cleaver, the Yippies, and the GAA might do to the various causes
they advocated. At the same time, however, each author recognized
that the way in which the dominant social order seemed only to
thrive on images of opposition also jeopardized the very possibility
of meaningful dissent, at least as traditionally performed. Faced
with this predicament, each one argued in his own way for the
importance of what one might call a nonrepresentational politics,

that is, the enactment of a "real" alternative in the present.[4] Thus, to give but one example, in contrast to the media games of Abbie Hoffman, which seemed only a juvenile provocation of authority, Roszak celebrated the "authentic" sexuality, the "free love," as it were, of the counterculture.

But was it really so simple? Was there really nothing more to the Yippies' media mythmaking than childish pranks? Had Cleaver really mistaken his rhetoric of armed revolution for an actual uprising? Had the GAA, by employing media "zaps" to call for gay rights, turned the fight for gay liberation into a modest proposal for social reform? Put differently, one might ask, as many did, if each of these individuals and organizations had "sold out" their particular struggles, allowing a legitimate, systemic critique to be co-opted. When approaching their work in terms of the aesthetic, the very aspect that so bothered Brustein, those acts that seemed so thoroughly compromised begin to look quite different. After all, as others have noted in discussions of contemporary art and culture, it was in the 1960s that the very oppositions that had structured so much thinking about politics, the avant-garde, and so on—radical/compromised, alienation/assimilation, outside/inside—became far less stable than had been previously assumed.[5] Thus, for example, the artist's desire to "detach" himself or herself from society and mass culture in an effort to focus solely on his/her chosen medium, so famously described in 1939 by critic Clement Greenberg, appeared to have withered. In place of the hermetic practices of the "avant-garde" there emerged a new generation of artists willing to truck with the objects and images of popular culture.[6] Beer cans, comic books, Coca-Cola bottles, pin-up girls— all surfaced, seemingly untransformed, in the work of artists such as Jasper Johns, Roy Lichtenstein, Andy Warhol, and Mel Ramos. Whether this changing cultural/political perspective was grounded in the collapse of colonialism, as Michael Hardt and Antonio Negri have argued; the transition to "late capitalism," as proposed in Fredric Jameson's classic essay; or any other constellation of historical conditions and events, it is nevertheless clear that, in writing the history of "the sixties," any attempt to oppose "real" politics to its co-opted imitation will most likely run into serious difficulties.[7]

At the same time, however, these more recent discussions of the collapse of clear political oppositions tend to view this as cause for hope or lament. In the case of Hardt and Negri, for example, the end of any notion of a position that truly stands outside of or removed from the dominant political and cultural formation has given rise to a sense of the "common"—both the collectively produced experiences, languages, and affects that have been expropriated or privatized for the good of the neoliberal "free market," and the shared experience of life in this economic era. Recognizing the true significance of the common, they argue, will be the necessary first step toward the creation of a truly humane, and truly democratic social order. For Jameson, in contrast, the breakdown of any clear notion of opposition has brought us to an impasse, one in which our ability not just to speak politically but even to determine our position and thus orient ourselves in relation to the current crisis has been critically impaired. Faced with a world in which our sense of history has been largely erased, one in which events, images, styles, and so on, seem to stretch out before us simultaneously, interminably, we have become overwhelmed, caught up in the effective "schizophrenia" of the "hysterical, or camp sublime."

I am neither so optimistic, nor so anxious. Instead, in the pages that follow I would like to begin to think of this sense of collapse itself as something of a historical phenomenon, while maintaining, at the same time, a sense of the conflict, the antagonism, that was, nevertheless, always present. For that is the fascinating irony—one might say contradiction—that seems to have driven the individuals and organizations discussed herein: the sense that all conflict has been evacuated, stripped of its true significance, even in the face of profound bloodshed, oppression, and exploitation. Something had to be done, and yet, as all antagonism seemed to be neutralized as a simple matter of differing opinions, as the real seemed to have given way to an endless series of images, no one could say just what that something was. On this note, I would like to make clear that my goal in revisiting and reinterpreting the work of the Yippies, the GAA, and Cleaver is not to suggest that the late 1960s marked the point in American political history at which grassroots organizational efforts had to be left behind in favor of the politics of imagery and media performance. The reader should not be left feeling, in the end, as if s/he has to choose between being an "old-fashioned" protester and a mythmaker. This kind of simple, contrarian reversal of calls for "real" politics would hardly be worthwhile. It is not my intention to offer a set of simple oppositions between competing political strategies, fetishizing one as "progressive" and dismissing the other as passé. That is precisely the type of argument I hope to problematize. For as the thinkers and activists discussed in the following chapters demonstrate, the politics of mythmaking was not so much an effective solution but an exploration of what seemed a disavowed paradox at the heart of much contemporary thinking about political activism, namely, that all calls for "direct" action proceeded according to formal conventions determined largely by the media. This book, in other words, is not a story of "good" ironic performance's victory over "bad" grassroots organizing—and, by extension, a hopeful gesture toward the inevitable end of domination in all its forms—but an invitation to consider the difficulties that face political movements in our time and the historical moment in which a number of individuals and organizations seemed to engage those difficulties in an unexpectedly self-conscious manner.

Paying particular attention to the problem of political representation, of politics *as* representation, this book seeks to read "the sixties" anew, drawing on the theoretical frameworks developed more recently in fields such as visual culture and performance studies, among others, to rethink the practices employed by those claiming to act in the name of an existentialist-inspired "personal authenticity." In the chapters that follow it will become quite clear that without the work of authors such as Peggy Phelan, Craig Owens, Sue-Ellen Case, Judith Butler, Homi Bhabha, José Muñoz, Matthew Tinkcom, and others, this project may never have been conceived. As Jonathan Dollimore points out, however, these more recent debates over the prospect of a performance-based politics are possible only "because theoretical insights have already been struggled towards by thinkers, writers, activists, and others in specific historical and political struggles where the representative structures of oppression have been massively (if still only ever contingently) in place."[8] With this in mind, I have chosen to focus less on the writings of contemporary theorists than on the works of writers and thinkers of the period. For this reason, three authors in particular will provide the historical and conceptual framework for much of what follows: Herbert Marcuse, Susan Sontag, and Jacob Brackman. In the years between 1964 and 1971, each of these writers attempted to theorize the political ramifications of what they saw as a social and cultural order that had rendered personal authenticity meaningless. Throughout the 1960s Marcuse attempted to describe the historical, dialectical relationship between the flourishing of personal liberty on one hand, and the death of "real" opposition on the other. In works like *One-Dimensional Man* and "Repressive Tolerance," he argued repeatedly that "technological society" had succeeded in reconciling desire with the commodity form. From sex to works of art, virtually all of the forms that had once expressed individual dissatisfaction with society had been colonized, circumscribed by a social order that sought to eliminate opposition through a spurious tolerance.

Marcuse's argument concerning "one-dimensional" society's conquest of "higher culture" leads to a reconsideration of the contemporary writings of Susan Sontag, who, in her essays on art and camp, struggled repeatedly with notions of authenticity and theatricality in the context of American culture. Not unlike Marcuse, whose influence she openly acknowledged, Sontag wanted desperately to foster what she called an "erotics of art," a form of direct experience that would distance the viewer from an era dominated by an overwhelming tendency to separate form from content, and to understand "Being-as-Playing-a-Role."[9]

Finally, I will turn to the work of film critic Jacob Brackman, whose 1971 text *The Put-On* constituted an attempt to comprehend the rapid proliferation of what Sontag called the "Camp sensibility." Where in 1964 Sontag had written that practices of camp were almost the exclusive province of "homosexuals," by the late 1960s, according to Brackman, the popularization of these practices had made it difficult to take *any* statement at face value. The put-on, a mode of inauthentic self-presentation based in the performance of stereotypical identities, had become the basis for an almost standardized form of (mis)communication. By placing these analyses next to one another and using them to reframe the political careers of Cleaver, the Yippies, and the GAA, this book demonstrates that the very theatricality decried by Brustein, Gross, and others might be read not as an indicator of utter political impotence but as a series of critical inflections of the increasingly problematic language of "real" politics.

Rather than attempting to separate the political from the aesthetic, I seek here to investigate the extent to which a great deal of sixties activism revealed each to be unthinkable without the other. For Brustein, political activism in the United States had reached a dead end because the United States lacked the "adequate machinery for the redress of grievances and for social change."[10] As a result, those who found themselves marginalized by the dominant social order could do little more than stage "ineffective" or minimally disruptive demonstrations. Political opposition had been successfully channeled, he argued, because rather than squelching differing opinions American society had welcomed them. Dissent had been smothered by an overwhelming permissiveness. Unlike earlier periods, when an author may have suppressed a work to avoid provoking the authorities, playwrights in 1970 were "more likely to shelve their works for fear of displeasing the revolutionary young." Consequently, "Anti-Vietnam war plays have become a cliché, and black dramatists indict white audiences weekly from the stages of establishment theaters."[11] It was in no way surprising, that is, to see a play like *Hair* go from Joseph Papp's experimental Public Theater in the East Village to Broadway within a mere six months. Nor was it any longer unusual to find that groups such as El Teatro Campesino and the Black Revolutionary Theater, both of which were founded as guerrilla theater troupes in 1965, had by the end of 1970 earned critical acclaim, bookings on conventional stages, and upper-class, white audiences. Simply put, it had become virtually impossible to provoke theater-goers' outrage—a problem lampooned in Brian DePalma's 1970 film *Hi Mom!*, where well-dressed white men and women are frightened yet exhilarated when painted black, berated, and abused by black radicals in whiteface during the performance of a play called *Be Black, Baby*.[12] For Brustein, like many others, it was one thing to stage "*actos*" for United Farm Workers picket lines, or to compose something like street happenings for young black actors, or even to condemn the war in small, off-Broadway venues. But when productions of *La Conquista* drew praise from white theater critics, or when LeRoi Jones and the Black Arts Repertory Theater School accepted government funding, one could not help but suspect that something was amiss.

El Teatro Campesino performance featuring Don Sotaco, 1966. Photo by John A. Kouns. Photo courtesy of the Reuther Library, Wayne State University.

Brian DePalma, *Hi Mom!* © 1970, MGM.

In the end, however, for Brustein, more disturbing than the effects of this permissiveness in the theater were its consequences in the realm of politics. Though they claimed to be wary of any false sense of liberation, militants and radicals quickly latched onto these "extended verbal freedoms" all the same. Given the mass media's hospitality toward radical ideas and opinions, the result of this "muscle-flexing and tub-thumping" was "not revolution but rather theater." When, for example, Student Nonviolent Coordinating Committee spokesman James Forman, or Sonny Carson of the Congress of Racial Equality interrupted church services and community meetings to demand racial justice, reparations, and so on, "then we know that the incidents have been staged for the newspaper reporters and television cameras, and should, therefore, be more properly evaluated by aesthetic standards than by political criteria."[13]

According to Brustein, these performances, however "revolutionary" they might have appeared, served only to obscure the "real" issues. The only hope for change, he argued, was to be found in moderation, in "conceding that *revolution* in America is a stage idea, and turning away from these play actors of the ideal . . . writing off the radical extremes of the current younger generation, and trying to cultivate the genuine warmth and decency that this generation still retains."[14]

Like many at this time, Brustein borrowed a great deal from the contemporary writings of Herbert Marcuse. For Marcuse, by the late 1960s, traditional political actions—petitions, marches, sit-ins, and so on—had been rendered almost entirely ineffectual. In his 1966 essay "Repressive Tolerance," for example, despite a few closing comments regarding possibilities for qualitative change, Marcuse's tone conveys an unmistakable despair. The "abstract tolerance" of American liberal democracy—abstract "inasmuch as it refrains from taking sides"—offered nothing, he claimed, but a mockery of "true" tolerance.[15] Although contemporary cultural and social institutions allowed all sides of a given debate to be heard, "the people," called upon to evaluate contrasting positions, had been rendered incapable of making crucial distinctions between differing points of view. The tolerance that was said to have made individuals "free" had in fact subjugated them. They were able only to "parrot, as their own, the opinions of their masters."[16] What appeared to be tolerance was little more than a mirage.

James Forman at Riverside Church, 1969. Photo by AP.

The mass media, of course, were instrumental in perpetuating the myth of a thoroughly democratic political culture.[17] The press no longer played the role of the "fourth estate" but functioned instead to legitimate the existence of concrete social inequity. This was the result not of some conspiracy but of the "'normal course of events' . . . and . . . the mentality shaped in this course."[18] A general acceptance of inequality meant that restrictions on the media had become virtually unnecessary. In the media, "the stupid opinion" could be "treated with the same respect as the intelligent one, the misinformed may talk as long as the informed, and propaganda rides along with education, truth with falsehood."[19] This apparent objectivity could be afforded because nothing was at stake. Indeed, the potential persuasiveness of the "intelligent," "informed" opinion had been preempted. Value judgments, Marcuse argued, had been placed on all opinions prior to their articulation. But what made the mass media so harmful was the assumed naturalism of their representations. When combined with the unspoken bias of the dominant culture, he wrote, "such objectivity is spurious—more, it offends against humanity and truth by being calm where one should be enraged, by refraining from accusation where accusation is in the facts themselves."[20] The media's "objectivity" had succeeded only in isolating the vast majority of the public from its "political existence." Individuals had been stripped of any sense of the potential social importance of their actions. "Real opposition" had been replaced by "the satisfactions of private and personal rebellion."[21] One could do or say virtually anything without posing a significant threat to the status quo. "The publicity of self-actualization," as he put it, "encourages nonconformity and letting-go in ways which leave the real engines of repression in the society entirely intact."[22] Actual rebellion had been replaced by formulaic expressions. In the name of self-fulfillment individuals had allowed themselves to be nullified, subsumed within a social order that only worked against their best interests.

As some readers will have recognized, Marcuse had lain the groundwork for this theory of "repressive tolerance" in his 1964 book *One-Dimensional Man*. There he asserted that contemporary society was "irrational as a whole." It was a "society without opposition," one in which citizens submitted to the "peaceful production of the means of destruction, to the perfection of waste, to being educated for a defense which deforms the defenders and that which they defend."[23] Marcuse never denied that difference endured in this society, but the oppositionality necessary for dialectical thought, and thus for any meaningful, radical transformation, had essentially vanished. "The manifold processes of introjection seem to be ossified in almost mechanical reactions," he wrote. "The result is, not adjustment but *mimesis:* an immediate identification of the individual with *his* society and, through it, with society as a whole. . . . In this process, the 'inner' dimension of the mind in which opposition to the status quo can take root is whittled down. . . . The impact of progress turns Reason into submission to the facts of life, and to the dynamic capability of producing more and bigger facts of the same sort of life."[24] Contemporary society had eradicated virtually any trace of its underlying contradictions. Difference, promoted only to enhance the illusion of inclusiveness, had ceased to be meaningful. One of the ways in which this could be seen most clearly, Marcuse believed, was in the liquidation of oppositionality from the realm of "higher culture."

In one-dimensional society, the elements of "higher culture" that had once enabled it to stand against the dominant social reality had been expunged. This was not because the content of art had somehow been "watered down," but because artworks had been reproduced and distributed on a mass scale. Rather than delivering the potential liberation that Walter Benjamin saw in its mechanical reproducibility, mass culture, according to Marcuse, had done just the opposite. It had succeeded in its conquest of individual consciousness by claiming to have delivered the happiness to which it once only alluded. Unlike the "true" work of art, whose *promesse de bonheur* was invariably, necessarily deferred, the products of mass culture presented themselves as the real fulfillment of individual desires. One-dimensional culture thus appeared to have eliminated the social strictures that had produced the work of "higher culture" as a necessary form of sublimation in the first place. Art had once been meaningful precisely because it was in some important way removed from the demands of profitability. But one-dimensional society had rendered this mode of culture obsolete by blending "harmoniously, and often unnoticeably, art, politics, religion, and philosophy with commercials."[25] It brought these different cultural practices, along with the individuals responsible for them, into alignment with their common historical denominator: the commodity form. Sublimation no longer seemed necessary, therefore, for the desires of the individual appeared to have been accommodated within the social order they contradicted. They had been reconciled with the society that once worked to exterminate them. The utopian promise of art had been superseded by suggestions of a utopia achieved within mass culture. In this context, the modern artist's statements of alienation were transformed, becoming little more than advertisements for the status quo.

Susan Sontag, writing at roughly the same time, placed the blame for this problem squarely on the shoulders of the critic. In the nineteenth and twentieth centuries, she argued, the relationship between the critic and the work of art had reached an impasse. Simply put, critics no longer felt compelled to respect art's objectivity. "In most modern instances," she wrote, criticism simply rendered works of art "manageable, conformable."[26] By interpreting aesthetic works the art critic implicitly assumed that form and content were somehow distinct, thereby doing violence to the work itself; interpretation, as Sontag put it, "violates art."[27] In response to this critical aggression modern artists had actively thwarted any and all attempts at interpretation by appealing directly to the senses. These artists looked to "elude the interpreters . . . by making works of art whose surface is so unified and clean, whose momentum is so rapid, whose address is so direct that the work can be . . . just what it is."[28] Among the examples Sontag listed of this new, more insistently present work were the Theater of Cruelty of Antonin Artaud, the Happenings of Alan Kaprow, the novels of Alain Robbe-Grillet, and the films of directors such as Michelangelo Antonioni, Jean-Luc Godard, and Robert Bresson. The value of these works, in her estimation, was that they defied translation. They forced one to acknowledge the work's "pure, untranslatable, sensuous immediacy . . . and its . . . solutions to certain problems of . . . form."[29] Yet directness was not the only means of forestalling the incursion of interpretation. In fact, Sontag argued, certain forms of *in*directness could achieve the same end. In contrast to the brute materiality of the Theater of Cruelty, Pop Art had used "a content so blatant, so 'what it is,'" that it too defied any attempt to translate/domesticate the work of art. Upon introducing this idea of Pop Art's indirectness as a potential form of immediacy, however, Sontag ran head-on into the very same historical dilemma that so vexed Marcuse, namely, that claims to aesthetic "immediacy," whether direct or indirect, were inherently reconcilable with the demands of consumer capitalism.

That Sontag eventually stumbled over this problem should come as little surprise, for the urgency with which she pressed for a critical "erotics of art" was based, primarily, in the reformulation of psycho-analysis advanced by Marcuse and Norman O. Brown in the 1950s. Brown and Marcuse, Sontag wrote, were two of the first thinkers to give some indication of the "revolutionary implications of sexuality in contemporary society."[30] Like them, Sontag believed that Freud's theories of sexuality were deeply, inherently political. In *Eros and Civilization*, published in 1954, Marcuse had argued that Freud's belief that human culture is necessarily repressive amounted to little more than a defense of the status quo. The repression Freud saw as integral to any orderly and efficient society was, for Marcuse, "surplus repression," the subordination of individual desires and impulses to the demands of industrial capitalism. The corrective to this surplus repression was to be found, he argued, in revisiting and recovering the developmental state of "polymorphous perversity," in which eroticism was not restricted to the genitals. By re-eroticizing and accordingly reconfiguring the entire human organism, we might release the body from the type of instrumentality demanded by industrial society.[31] Similarly, in his 1959 text *Life Against Death*, Brown called for the reunification of mind and body. Unlike "revi-sionist" American Freudians, he believed that psychoanalysis held the key to healing both society and the individual. This would be achieved not through the reeducation of the mind, but through the recognition of the mind's dependence upon the body. If the primacy of the body could be acknowledged, and an androgynous mode of existence accepted, Brown believed that the neuroses resulting from sexual differentiation and "genital organization" could be overcome. As Sontag summarized his argument, "The core of human neurosis is man's incapacity to live in the body—to live (that is, to be sexual) and to die."[32] Much like the theory of art presented in *Eros and Civi-lization*, Sontag's "erotics of art" was to constitute a move toward this re-eroticizing of the individual. For Sontag, that is, the attempts to reeducate the senses found in the works of Artaud, Kaprow, Antonioni, and others were not just aesthetic obligations but social imperatives. Through the direct experience of these works and their material refusal to submit to the demands of "critical" thought, she believed that individuals could be transformed. But the "Surrealist sensibility" that functioned through these works had also given rise to the "cooler" works of Pop artists like Andy Warhol. Like Surrealism, both of these newer forms sought to "destroy conventional meanings" and to create new ones through the use of "radical juxtaposition."[33] For Sontag, however, where Kaprow and Artaud had actively challenged viewers' senses and sensibilities, Pop Art had ultimately looked only to entertain them. Warhol, therefore, was merely the legatee of those surrealists who made it fashionable for the French intelligentsia to frequent flea markets. The particular form of "disinterested wit and sophistication" in which he specialized may have stymied critical interpretation, but it nevertheless failed to acknowledge the more urgent task facing the artist, namely the personally and socially "therapeutic" work of "reeducating the senses."[34] Simply put, Pop Art was plagued by its dependence upon the more insidious form of the Surrealist sensibility known as camp.

The "Camp sensibility," in Sontag's phrasing, was not a way of changing the world through aesthetic experience but rather "of seeing the world as an aesthetic phenomenon."[35] Unlike the corrupted aesthetic Marcuse saw in mass culture, in which everyday images and objects presented themselves as truly fulfilling, the camp sensibility found in the world an image of failure. In her "Notes on Camp," published in 1964, Sontag wrote that camp was "the love of the exaggerated, the 'off,' of things being-what-they-are-not. . . . Camp sees everything in quotation marks. . . . To perceive Camp in objects and persons is to understand Being-as-Playing-a-Role."[36] Unfortunately for Sontag, the "Camp sensibility" proved exceedingly difficult to pin down for this very reason. Following a few introductory remarks on the necessity of understanding camp as a sensibility, she literally reversed her position. "Not only is there a Camp vision, a Camp way of looking at things," she wrote, "Camp is as well a quality discoverable in objects and the behavior of persons. . . . It's not all in the eye of the beholder."[37] To access the "Camp sensibility," it seems, Sontag felt it necessary to work backward from "campy" objects—things such as Tiffany lamps, the *National Enquirer*, Flash Gordon comics, and the famous Brown Derby restaurant in Los Angeles. By looking to "the canon of Camp," she believed it would be possible to extrapolate those characteristics that appealed to—and conditioned—"the Camp eye."[38] Through a brief survey of these objects, she surmised that camp could not be overly serious, overly important, or overly good: "Many examples of Camp are things which, from a 'serious' point of view, are either bad art or kitsch."[39] The camp object was one that proclaimed, whether naively or consciously, its own silliness, extravagance, or artificiality. It was an object in which form and content failed to coalesce. Like Baudelaire's concept of the "significative comic," the camp object was "visibly double."[40]

But it was the relation of camp's practitioners—as opposed to its objects—to another of Baudelaire's concepts that Sontag found more worrisome. As she understood it, camp amounted to the reformulation of dandyism for the world of mass culture. Its intimate ties to mass culture, however, had effectively expunged the dandy's "quintessence of character and . . . subtle understanding of the entire moral mechanism of this world."[41] In place of this character and understanding was mere "aestheticism." Camp's affected pleasure in the imperfections of the everyday was thus nothing more than the latest moment in the "history of snob taste."[42] More importantly, though, camp had only taken hold at a moment when "no authentic aristocrats in the old sense exist . . . to sponsor special tastes."[43] In the absence of a true upper class "an improvised self-elected class, mainly homosexuals," had come to serve as the "aristocrats of taste."[44] Camp's appreciation of the mundane, its celebration of the art of the masses, could never have been mistaken for a truly populist—or even avant-garde—project. Rather, it was precisely the opposite.[45] Unlike "true" artists, those who appreciated camp were virtually incapable of developing any deeper understanding of the world. Rather than providing a challenge to critical thought, they had merely inverted its standards.

Once again, though, for Sontag, the most profound challenge to critical thought would proceed through the senses rather than the intellect. It was for this reason, among others, that when faced with camp she experienced a "deep sympathy modified by revulsion."[46] In one sense, the "Camp sensibility" actively thwarted any attempt at easy interpretation—hence her decision to approach the phenomenon through a series of "notes" rather than attempting to fix its meaning in an essay. Yet, at the same time, the paradoxical immediacy of campy objects appeared to hold no social or political promise. To the contrary, camp seemed to render the notion of sensuous immediacy virtually nonsensical. As she observed, "Camp . . . makes no distinction between the unique object and the mass-produced object. Camp transcends the nausea of the replica."[47] Camp's emphasis on surface and the presentation of self as performance, in other words, was not an attempt to foreground the tensions that might be contained within those surfaces and performances but a clever way of accepting, or even celebrating, them. The camp sensibility delighted in images rather than interrogating them. Her accusation of "aestheticism," therefore, opposed camp not to reality but to the modernist notion of the work of art as a vehicle for critique.

Moreover, what made camp so repugnant was that its effects were virtually inescapable, so much so that Sontag feared her own attempt to define the "Camp sensibility" would result only in "a very inferior piece of Camp."[48] In spite of her efforts to avoid this fate by approaching camp obliquely, through a series of notes, her attempt to distinguish camp from non-camp ended in failure all the same. This is because in her search for the "contemporary *Zeitgeist*," as Fabio Cleto has argued, Sontag linked camp "through a paradoxical combination of 'aristocratic' detachment and 'democratic' leveling of social (and cultural) hierarchies, with the dandification of the . . . masses producing 'the equivalence of all objects,' and the transcending of the romantic disgust for the replica, be that the parodic repetition or the infinite technological reproducibility of an original which no longer holds its epistemic privileges."[49] Sontag, in other words, presented postwar America as a culture plagued by a series of crucial indifferences regarding foundational concepts such as originality, objectivity, and aesthetic quality. The revulsion Sontag felt in response to the camp sensibility may have been rooted in a wish to reinstate the work of art in all its sensuous immediacy, but, as Cleto suggests, it was the obsolescence of this type of immediacy to which camp alluded. Camp thus revealed the social aspirations of formalist criticism to be a farce. The sociohistorical conditions that had given birth to camp as a phenomenon had left nothing untouched. Everything, to

paraphrase Sontag, had been placed "in quotation marks"—not by
camp but by the historical conditions of its emergence. As a result,
the grounds from which critique might proceed seemed to have
crumbled beneath her feet. Camp was not the opposite of modernist
artistic practice but an indication of its collapse. The circumstances
that Sontag saw giving rise to the "Camp sensibility" were thus the
same as those that had allowed, in *One-Dimensional Man*, for the
apparent reconciliation of art and society. These were the same
conditions, moreover, that Marcuse believed had brought about the
"repressive desublimation" of human sexuality.

In *One-Dimensional Man*, Marcuse argued that desublimation,
as it existed in contemporary culture, was truly injurious to the
individual. It "weaken[ed] the necessity and the power of the intellect, the catalytic force of that unhappy consciousness . . . which
recognizes the horror of the whole in the most private frustration
and actualizes itself in this recognition."[50] Where the work of art had
once served to register one's dissatisfaction with the social order—
an idea that served as the cornerstone of modern art criticism—the
technological society's ultimately enslaving reconciliation of art and
mass culture had left the individual incapable of recognizing his or
her own unhappiness. Any sense of emancipation one felt within
one-dimensional society was nothing more than that society's "conquest of freedom." And, much like the artist, whose statements of
alienation had become easily assimilable, those who attempted to
flout the rules of this social order succeeded only in strengthening
its grasp: "Zen, existentialism, and beat ways of life, etc. . . . are no
longer contradictory to the status quo. . . . They are rather the cer-
emonial part of a practical behaviorism, its harmless negation, and
are quickly digested by the status quo as part of its healthy diet."[51]
Rebellion had been reduced to a set of signifiers so that it might
become the ultimate in conformity. Even sexual perversion, which
in *Eros and Civilization* was said to be essentially irreconcilable
with a society that attempted to subjugate all activity to the logic
of labor, had been successfully co-opted. One could "let go," as it
were, while leaving the "real engines of repression" entirely intact.
Asking the reader to compare "love-making in a meadow and in an
automobile, on a lovers' walk outside the town walls and on a Manhattan street," Marcuse explained that in the former situations, "the

environment partakes of and invites libidinal cathexis and tends to be eroticized. In contrast, a mechanized environment seems to block such self-transcendence of libido. Impelled in the striving to extend the field of erotic gratification, libido becomes less polymorphous, less capable of eroticism beyond localized sexuality, and the latter is intensified."[52] The body's increased sexualization had precluded its true re-eroticization. Perversion, desublimated only to be safely compartmentalized as a leisure activity, no longer upheld the possibility of the erotic as an end in itself. Yet the nausea of the replica, to paraphrase Sontag, seemed to have been transcended.

I will explore the relationship between eroticism and liberation in Marcuse's thought in greater detail in the next chapter. For now, I want only to stress that, while Marcuse had not abandoned all hope for a radical, total revolution, the source from which that revolution might spring was difficult to identify. Art, sexuality, alternative ways of life: nearly all forms of opposition had been rendered easily assimilable. Compelled nevertheless to designate a source of potential social transformation, he turned to what he called the "substratum" of the technological society, "the exploited and persecuted of other races and other colors" who lived "outside the democratic process." Given their direct and "immediate" relationship to the failure of American political institutions, the way in which their plight seemed to emblematize the failure of those very institutions, their opposition to authority was "revolutionary even if their consciousness was not. . . . it is an elementary force which violates the rules of the game and, in doing so, reveals it as a rigged game. . . . The fact that they start refusing to play the game may be the fact which marks the beginning of the end of a period."[53] For Marcuse, in other words, the experience of racial oppression provided the critical distance necessary for true critique. Writing in the early 1960s, he praised civil rights activists for their courage. The power of their willingness to "face dogs, stones, and bombs, jail, concentration camps, even death," he wrote, lay "behind every political demonstration for the victims of law and order."[54] By the time "Repressive Tolerance" appeared, however, his perspective had changed slightly. There he wrote that "the exercise of political rights (such as voting, letter-writing to the press, to Senators, etc., protest demonstrations with a priori renunciation of counterviolence) in a society of total administration serves to strengthen this administration by testifying to the existence of democratic liberties which, in reality, have changed their content and lost their effectiveness."[55] The turn in Marcuse's thought clearly reflects the public transition from the nonviolent civil rights movement of the 1950s and early 1960s to the openly confrontational politics of Black Power, but the potential catalyst for a true historical transformation remained in the oppositional strategies of "other races and other colors." Although the willingness to face dogs, stones, bombs, and so on was no longer sufficient, in the face of a virtually totalizing system of repressive tolerance, racial minorities apparently maintained an element of purity and authenticity otherwise lost. Race, in other words, had supplanted perversion as the true lever of social change. Perhaps Marcuse believed that its "indelible" visibility, an enduring reminder of the persistence of concrete inequality, served to render race ultimately unassimilable. Or, given his reference to the "immediate," "elemental" character of racial opposition, one might read in this attempt to posit a source of revolutionary consciousness a patronizing reverence akin to that of Norman Mailer's "White Negro." But whatever the justification, the racial identities that Marcuse saw as perhaps the last hope for radical opposition were, like the forms of "non-conformity and letting go" he dismissed, far less "immediate" than he assumed. In fact, as Jacob Brackman argued, the figures of the "assimilationist" civil rights activist *and* the militant black liberationist, along with the rhetoric of Zen, existentialism, and beat ways of life, had already been appropriated and redeployed by the practitioners of a satirically campy mode of miscommunication known as "the put-on."

The put-on, a seemingly playful, aimless conversational misdirection, was not necessarily new. What was new, and troubling, was its inescapability. Although it had once been only an in-group, "outlaw form," over the course of the 1960s the put-on had become virtually ubiquitous. What was previously "an occasional surprise tactic—called 'joshing' around the turn of the century and 'kidding' since the twenties," Brackman wrote, had been "refined into the very basis of a new form of communication."[56] From Warhol's *Brillo Boxes* to the maddeningly nonsensical cat-and-mouse interviews given by Bob Dylan, some unsuspecting "victim" was being confounded by a put-on almost everywhere one looked. As Warhol told Gretchen Berg in a 1966 interview ironically titled "Andy Warhol: My True Story," "I never like to give my background and, anyway, I make it all up different every time I'm asked"[57]—this, one presumes, was how Andy "put his Warhol on."[58] Similarly, the unapologetic fusion of high art and pop culture one found in his paintings, sculptures, and events such as the *Exploding Plastic Inevitable* left one uncertain whether this work was truly progressive, or if museums and galleries had simply been reduced to little more than glorified supermarkets. The put-on had thus necessitated a fundamental shift in the way audiences approached the latest works. Viewers had come to assume that a great deal of contemporary work sought to engage them not in some type of purely sensual communion but in an elaborate "con game." In response, Brackman suggests, critical arguments seemed to shift from determining what qualified as a "good" work to what constituted a "real" work. In this situation, of course, when a critic dismisses "something that others have considered good, he is no longer simply challenging the merits of a specific work; he is telling the public that his colleagues have been taken in by fraud, that they are hoodwinked in their notions of what constitutes art, that none of us really knows for sure anymore what is real and good."[59]

Illustration by Sam Kirson for Jacob Brackman, *The Put-On* (Chicago, 1971), 52.

To be sure, if this had remained the problem of a few art critics, it would most likely have merited relatively little discussion. What made the unavoidability of the put-on interesting was precisely the fact that it was not merely the problem of determined formalists. The put-on's cynical irony had tainted virtually every interpersonal exchange. One did not simply reenter the realm of sincerity by stepping outside of the gallery. And, quite interestingly, this proliferation of the put-on had begun, according to Brackman, with Sontag's attempt to define camp. Her "disjunct essay in *Partisan Review*," he wrote, "was read by tens of thousands, but its reverberations affected the culture consumed by hundreds of millions."[60] Whether the popularization of these ideas was actually rooted in the appearance of Sontag's "Notes" is debatable. After all, Erving Goffman had begun to speak of self-presentation as a type of performance in 1959, and Pierre Bourdieu, writing in France in 1965 of the poses commonly struck in pictures, asserted that the photographic representation of society could only ever be "the representation of a represented society."[61] Nevertheless, for Brackman it was clear that what had once been preserved within the "classy preconscious" of American culture had, in the second half of the 1960s, surfaced as a part of the popular consciousness. In the process, critical judgment had been "clog[ged]" and aesthetic standards "scuttle[d]."[62] Although Sontag "had been describing a method of appreciation, her rules were embraced as principles of manufacture."[63] Long before Madonna "struck a pose" and introduced a mass audience to voguing, the put-on had popularized the theatrically queer sensibility of camp. In the process, Brackman argued, that sensibility had been turned into a series of pointless, cruel jokes.

The cruelty of these jokes lay in their conscious effort to render virtually all communication suspect. While the "Camp sensibility" more passively viewed being as playing a role, the "put-on artist" intentionally evoked the citational aspect of every statement. For this reason, "conversation with a put-on artist is a process of escalating confusion and distrust. He doesn't deal in isolated little tricks; rather, he has developed a personal style of relating to others that perpetually casts what he says into doubt. The put-on . . . is rarely climaxed by setting the truth straight."[64] Unlike irony, the put-on worked through the exchange of disinformation. The content of the ironic utterance or gesture, according to Brackman, was essentially fixed;

it expressed the opposite of that which was said or done.[65] Strictly speaking, therefore, misunderstanding marked the failure of irony. The put-on, on the other hand, "inherently *cannot* be understood."[66] The "put-on artist," speaking from no fixed position, refused only to be pinned down. Always one step ahead, through a potentially infinite series of evasions s/he foregrounded the indeterminacy of her/his statements, leaving interlocutors utterly confounded. Most importantly, however, specific examples would nearly always assume one of two forms: "relentless agreement" or "actualization of the stereotype."

Relentless agreement required the put-on artist to assume her/his opponent's position. In this situation, Brackman explains, "the perpetrator beats his victim to every cliché the latter might possibly mouth," thereby pulling the rug from beneath the "victim's" feet.[67] For example, when a "straight . . . but enlightened man, evincing his enlightenment," asked a young gay man to explain the roots of same-sex attraction, the young man might sound almost apologetic, responding, "Why, of *course* it's a *sickness*, there's no *question*. Take me. My father was *weak, hen*pecked. It's psycho*log*ical. My mother wouldn't let me wear long *pants* till I was fourteen. And then the A*r*my. Well, *you* know. It's better than *an*imals. My analyst thinks I'm progressing toward a real ad*just*ment."[68] In contrast, the method of actualizing stereotypes was, at least on its surface, more openly hostile. There, "the perpetrator personifie[d] every cliché about his group, realize[d] his adversary's every negative expectation: He [became] a grotesque rendition of his presumed identity."[69] In conversation with a "benevolent progressive," to use another of Brackman's examples, a "militant Negro" might say, "Don't make your superego gig with me, ofay baby. Your graddaddy rape my grandmammy, and now you tell me doan screw your daughter? . . . don't offer me none of the *su*preme delectafactotory blessings of equalorama, 'cause when this bitch blows you gonna feel the black man's machete in the soft flesh of your body, dig?"[70] For Brackman, however, regardless of the perpetrator or the form, the result of gestures and actions such as these was always the same. The put-on made it impossible to determine just where the put-on artist stood. Rather than eventually revealing her/his "true" position, the put-on continued indefinitely, ultimately suggesting the impossibility of *any* "true" position. Both

sides of the presumed debate were thus exposed as clichés or performances in themselves, and the entire conversation was set adrift.

It is fitting, then, that at the center of Brackman's attempt to define
the put-on, much as in Sontag's efforts to discuss camp, one finds a
fundamental ambivalence. The put-on was naïve, or even politically
regressive, Brackman argued, because it proceeded from the basic
assumption that the forms of dominant culture could be used against
themselves. In spite of its ability to denaturalize existing social positions and relations, the put-on nonetheless remained ultimately reconcilable to that which it destabilized. No matter how "subversive"
the put-on might seem, if the "victim" failed to recognize the joke,
his or her assumptions were not thrown into question but reinforced.
Its exasperating (rather than insurrectionary) confrontations were
thus inherently limited. And because of these limitations, Brackman
wrote, the put-on was most frequently "employed against the most
sympathetic elements among the enemy."[71] Rarely was it used for any
purpose other than to confound an individual who might otherwise
be persuaded by rational arguments. Police officers, for example,
would often be treated with "careful deference," while a "friendly
probation officer or social worker" would be "put on mercilessly."[72]
The threat of "real" retaliatory violence, according to Brackman,
inevitably caused the put-on artist to lose her/his nerve. For this
reason, as far as he was concerned, the put-on was not revolutionary but theatrical. The progression of one-dimensional society thus
appeared to have been completed. "Resistance," taken in by its own
ruse, had been successfully colonized.[73]

Much as Brackman would have liked to dismiss the put-on as
nothing more than simple cynicism, however, he was forced time
and again to acknowledge the potential oppositionality of these
misdirections. At one point he wrote, "Even though it's really a
defensive weapon, the put-on almost always provides an offensive for
the questionee, representative of the smaller, more helpless faction,
making his group appear In and the larger, more powerful group of
the questioner appear Out."[74] The put-on could also be a means of
empowering the weak insofar as it tricked the powerful into engaging the essential inadequacy of their own terms. Thus, as a political
identity, the "militant Negro" may have been a site of opposition, but
not in the sense that Marcuse proposed. The critical edge of this

character/caricature lay not in its existence outside the grasp of dominant culture but in its exaggeration of that culture's stereotypes. Brackman's analysis therefore pointed to a dilemma overlooked by Marcuse. The political pronouncements of "other races and other colors," believed by Marcuse to be the site of a potentially powerful opposition, were, according to Brackman, recognized to be thoroughly stereotypical. Rather than simply dismissing these identities for that reason, however, the logic of Brackman's argument points to the ways in which these stereotypes may have presented a different form of resistance, one that began from a sense of the historical impossibility of transcendence, and thus looked to seed resistance in acts of interpretation.

Looking back on the political activism of the late 1960s with Brackman's analysis in mind, any number of actions begin to appear different or less settled than they once did. Consider, for example, the work of the Women's International Terrorist Conspiracy from Hell, or WITCH, a loose organization that eventually split from New York Radical Women in the winter of 1968–69. After participating in the bra burnings outside of the Miss America pageant in Atlantic City, New Jersey, the previous summer, Robin Morgan and friends chose to embody, quite literally, stereotypical notions of feminists as evil or unchristian, dressing in black robes and pointed hats (among other things) to place a hex on Wall Street. That Halloween, to "liberate the daytime ghetto community of the Financial District," she later wrote,

the Coven, costumed, masked, and made up as Shamans, Faerie Queens, Matriarchal Old Sorceresses, and Guerrilla Witches, danced first to the Federal Reserve Treasury Bank, led by a High Priestess bearing the papier-maché head of a pig on a golden platter, garnished with greenery plucked from the poison money trees indigenous to the area. Bearing verges, wands, and bezants, the WITCHes surround the statue of George Washington on the steps of the building, striking terror into the hearts of Humphrey and Nixon campaigners nearby, who castigated the women for desecrating (with WITCH stickers) the icon of the Father of our Country (not understanding that this was a necessary ritual against a symbol of patriarchal, slave-holding power). The WITCHes also cast a spell rendering the hoarded gold bricks therein valueless—except for casting through windows.[75]

Using the Republican and Democratic campaigners as their "straight men," as it were, the WITCHes lampooned both popular clichés about feminism and the dominant forms of American political debate. Was either Humphrey or Nixon really the solution . . . to any of the problems that faced the United States? The fact that supporters of each one considered New York's Financial District a good place to unearth sympathetic voters certainly suggested otherwise. But beyond this, and more importantly, the action also posed serious questions about the assumed means of addressing what seemed an exceedingly stubborn political impasse.

As Brackman suggested, examples like this are in no way uncommon. The chapters that follow thus present three case studies of political uses of the put-on, illustrating the perceived social utility of the gap between saying and meaning that so preoccupied the film critic. Chapter 1, "Monkey Theater," will address the group that made perhaps the most obvious and elaborate use of the put-on, the Yippies. In the wake of the riots at the Democratic National Convention in 1968, a number of activists felt a great deal of anger toward Yippie leaders Abbie Hoffman and Jerry Rubin. Seemingly caught up in their own status as "movement celebrities," these "leaders" appeared incapable not just of speaking for the movement they called their own but of "speaking truth to power" in any significant fashion. As Todd Gitlin, once a leader of the Students for a Democratic Society, put it twelve years later, "Deprived by resentful constituents of the chance to use the media legitimately as political amplification," Hoffman and Rubin were cut off from their supposed base.[76] Shunned by fellow radicals, the Yippie spokesmen were left to perform ever more outrageous visions of political opposition for viewers they could never hope to influence. This chapter reconsiders the ways in which the Yippies were seemingly co-opted, asking if Hoffman and Rubin were indeed so blinded by their celebrity status that they might have believed that nominating a pig for president was a "revolutionary" act. Were their threats to taint Chicago's water supply with LSD or to develop a pernicious new sex drug that could be administered to unknowing victims via water pistol anything other than irresponsible publicity stunts? What could it have meant for Hoffman to claim, following the riots in Chicago, that he hoped to fashion himself as a combination of Fidel Castro and Andy Warhol, or to write "FUCK" across his forehead—a move that he initially said would keep anyone from taking his picture—for a studio shoot with fashion photographer Richard Avedon?[77] Through an analysis of the Yippies' various media myths, one begins to see that their tactics may not have been designed simply to provoke the authorities but also to transform the futility of opposition decried by Marcuse, Brustein, Brackman, and others into its own historically specific form of technologically mediated transgression.

Chapter 2 looks to the Gay Liberation Front and the Gay Activists Alliance, two organizations that formed in New York following the Stonewall riots of 1969. At first glance, it may seem an odd choice to include the gay liberation movement in the current discussion. After all, not only were activists like Hoffman, Rubin, and Cleaver accused on more than one occasion of homophobia or antigay bias, but, as so many historians have pointed out, in the wake of the Stonewall riots an authentic visibility became one of the guiding concepts in the struggle for gay and lesbian liberation. Oppression would never end, it was said, if gay men and lesbians refused to "come out," to show their families, their friends, and the rest of the world who they "really" were. While it is true that the gay liberation movement held a different relationship to visibility than the counterculture, by revisiting these calls for visibility and authenticity in light of the Gay Liberation Front's efforts to be included within the constellation of progressive causes and organizations known at the time as "the Movement," the complexities and contradictions of that relationship will begin to emerge. Although, as so many historians of gay liberation remind us, groups like the GLF often took great pains to distance themselves from "queens and nellies," transsexuals, transvestites, and those lesbians who seemed "too butch," a reconsideration of radical post-Stonewall gay and lesbian politics reveals the extent to which a certain type of drag was nevertheless highlighted within these very same organizations. This reinterpretation of gay radicalism will give rise to a reevaluation of those organizations like the GAA that were often dismissed as "regressive," "reformist," or simply "naïve" for their willingness to engage the mass media and their refusal to abandon practices like camp and cross-dressing. In the end, I argue that it is perhaps more productive to view the practical and ideological divisions within the gay liberation movement not as a

case of radicalism versus reformism but, much like the debates outlined in the first chapter, as a struggle over the relationship between
politics and performance, "direct action" and aesthetics. In this sense
I will, as historian John D'Emilio has urged, put "gay" back into the
sixties.[78] Unlike D'Emilio, however, who sees returning to the history of gay and lesbian activism as an opportunity to resuscitate a
positive model for current political struggles, I will instead read gay
liberation as one of a number of indicators that there was something
quite queer, in the broadest possible sense, about a great deal of late-
1960s activism.

My final case study in chapter 3 looks to the political career of
"militant Negro" Eldridge Cleaver. Often seen as the personification
of what Michelle Wallace so famously dismissed as "Black Macho,"
Cleaver signifies to many the misguidedness of both the major figures
of the Black Power movement and the white activists who seemed to
accept him as the quintessence of personal and political authenticity.[79] Critics have repeatedly rejected Cleaver's political persona as
regressive because of his tendency to enact the very stereotypes of
hypermasculinity that had been used to oppress black men since
the end of the Civil War. Cleaver spoke repeatedly of the equivalence
between black liberation and the reclamation of black masculinity,
and, conversely, the "counter-revolutionary" nature of same-sex
desire. When confronted, for instance, by an "Infidel" who claimed
that black men would always be subservient to white males because
the "stem of the Body, the penis, must submit to the will of the Brain,"
he responded not with a rational argument but an "erect . . . strong
. . . resilient and firm" cock: "When I gave it that squeeze, a wave of
strength surged through my body. I felt powerful, and I knew that I
would make it if I never betrayed the law of my rod."[80] In response
to this type of rhetoric, contemporary feminists accused Cleaver of
being blind to the role women had played—and would continue to
play—in any movement working toward the total transformation of
society.[81] More recently, Cleaver has come under fire from authors
such as Kobena Mercer, Isaac Julien, Leerom Medovoi, and E. Patrick
Johnson for his insistence on equating masculinity and heterosexuality.[82] Medovoi, for example, explains that for Cleaver, "Black gay
men, because they threatened the simple association of black masculinity with hypersexual virility," had necessarily been "politically

stigmatized as decadents, race traitors, or 'false' men."[83] In hopes of reopening the discussion of not only Cleaver but of Black Power politics more generally, this chapter reads Cleaver's invocation of the "law of [his] rod" first in terms of the set of practices Henry Louis Gates, Jr. has labeled as "Signifyin(g)," and second in relation to the question of, as R. A. T. Judy puts it, "nigga authenticity." Is it possible that Cleaver, who repeatedly lamented the black male's social reduction to nothing more than brute physicality, was less interested in redeeming some essential black masculinity than in adopting the pose of "black macho"?[84] To reassess the potential value of Cleaver's political career, I argue, it is necessary to look closely at his enactment of a violent, hypersexualized version of black liberation, from his infamous critical attack on novelist James Baldwin in the essay "Notes on a Native Son" to his threat to kick California State superintendent of public instruction Max Rafferty's ass. By placing Cleaver's political actions and pronouncements within the history of the Black Power movement and alongside a close reading of the essays collected in *Soul on Ice*, I look to demonstrate that those actions that have for so long seemed only offensive may in the end have been rooted, at least in part, in a surprisingly subtle understanding of the politics of race, representation, and commodification.

Finally, in the short concluding afterword, I suggest the continued importance of aesthetic considerations to our analysis of contemporary politics. As so many retrospective texts and exhibitions have recently reminded us, the late 1960s occupy a special place in the American historical imaginary. The object of nostalgic reverence for many on the political left and of outright scorn for those on the right, talk of "the sixties" still has the power to provoke a heated reaction over forty years later. It is curious, therefore, to find that the events and ideologies of that decade are so often treated as all but settled in contemporary politics.[85] The 1960s were, for example, the years in which modern imperialism offered one last great surge in Southeast Asia, and individuals, in response, attempted to suppress their differences and to identify with an allegedly revolutionary "class" that would end not only colonial aggression/oppression in the developing world but also poverty, discrimination, and exploitation in the United States and Western Europe. The decade effectively ended (or devolved, depending on one's critical and political predilections) with the failure of both of these efforts. The United States suffered an embarrassing defeat in Vietnam, and various groups, insisting on the validity of differing subject positions, broke away from "the movement" to draw attention to individualized forms of oppression and liberation. After 1968, as we so often hear, the form of oppositional politics began to change dramatically.[86] In this short concluding essay, therefore, I look to problematize this apparent closure. Considering the ways in which the political tactics of the late 1960s, far from simply disappearing, actually became something like the standard form for grassroots politics, I argue that the difficulties confronting contemporary "opposition" are not altogether different from those that gave birth to the ironic performances of that decade. From the more recent grassroots actions of groups and movements like the Yes Men and Billionaires for Bush, and, now, Occupy/Occupy Wall Street, the echoes of the put-ons I describe, and their sense of the aesthetics of politics more generally, can be heard throughout our own, supposedly distinct, era. The reframing of the late-1960s radical left I offer herein is an attempt to complicate our relationship to that period in American history and culture. What lessons could the Black Panthers, the Yippies, or the Gay Activists Alliance hold for groups currently working for equal rights, to end the war in Afghanistan, to combat global warming, or to deliver power to "the 99 percent"? Given these ongoing struggles and the (hardly coincidental) attention paid to the late 1960s in the last ten years, these questions seem perhaps more urgent than ever.

I am, of course, not the first or only one to believe that the time may be right for a reconsideration of the methods of late-1960s activism. Since the beginning of the Iraq war in 2003, or, rather, since the United States government's explicit articulation of its intent to invade Afghanistan and then Iraq in 2001 and 2002, interest in the grassroots political tactics of that period has understandably surged. Yet even before these unilateral military actions were on the table, there was still a great deal of scholarly and popular interest in the relationship in that decade between grassroots politics and media representation. Todd Gitlin, Tom Wells, Doug Rossinow, Julie Stephens—a number of authors in the 1980s and '90s returned to the question of activism and media coverage in an attempt to determine just what we might learn from the struggles, triumphs, and failures of "the sixties."[87]

These reappraisals, and others, were part of what has been described as a larger shift in writing about 1960s grassroots politics, a move away from simplistic divisions between politics and culture toward a more nuanced understanding of the mutual influences of, say, the New Left and the counterculture.[88] Much as these authors have made an effort to not simply dismiss culture in favor of "real" politics, however, their generosity appears not to extend to engagements with the mass media. The media's commercial character, its propensity to turn all opposition into simple spectacle, they suggest, ultimately renders protest impotent. The mass media may have "made" the New Left, in Todd Gitlin's phrasing, but the inevitable allure of fame that accompanied the media's attention proved irresistible. For this reason, Gitlin and others conclude, media coverage and "real" opposition are best seen as mutually exclusive. Although willing, in other words, to acknowledge the cross-pollination of politics and culture, arguments such as these remain rooted in a basic assumption that true opposition must transcend the boundaries of a given social order: one must either provide a carefully reasoned argument exposing society's failure to live up to its own promises, or literally enact an alternative.

As it should by now be clear, this assumed choice between transcendence and "selling out" is, and was, not as clear-cut as it may seem. Thus, in the last ten years, authors such as Marianne DeKoven and T. V. Reed have begun to move beyond this basic position.[89] DeKoven returns to the work of Marcuse in a thorough and quite fascinating reading—one that has exerted tremendous influence on my own engagement with his work—and highlights the often self-contradictory language used to describe the utopian political visions of groups like Students for a Democratic Society. Reed, on the other hand, stresses the role of song in the civil rights movement, and the theatrical strategies adopted within, among others, the movement for Black Power. Both authors explore cases in which aesthetics and politics intertwine, thus calling into question familiar assumptions regarding the political value of asserting an authentic personal identity and the necessity for "true" critique to originate from a position excluded by the dominant order. In the end, though, neither fully takes on the relationship between the "emergence of the postmodern," strategies of political performance, and the mass media. This is precisely what makes the work of media historian Aniko Bodroghkozy so interesting. While many analyses could be said to sacrifice either an understanding of the media for an emphasis on history or an understanding of history for an emphasis on media, Bodroghkozy looks to situate television coverage of political demonstrations and protests within a larger discussion of the popular fascination with youth culture in the late 1960s.[90] This is an incredibly rich avenue of inquiry, and Bodroghkozy does a great deal to distance herself from the analyses of authors like Gitlin, arguing that the Yippies' understanding of the mass media may have been far more sophisticated than earlier authors assumed. But her account stops there, leaving the reader to wonder just what the subtleties of Yippie media theory may have been, or why Bodroghkozy insists on separating this "self-conscious" form of protest from what Sontag labeled the "Camp sensibility."

But the one effort to reassess "the sixties" that is most closely related to my own is David Joselit's *Feedback: Television Against Democracy*. Joselit offers a nuanced reading of the cultural significance of television in postwar America, paying particular attention to the way in which it seems to blur the distinction between commodity and network, the way it presents, in effect, the network *as* a commodity. Along the way, Joselit offers examples of activists seeking to make use of television and film as weapons in the struggles for Black Power or against the Vietnam War. These examples demonstrate, he argues, in contrast to so many who have written on grassroots politics in the late 1960s, that easy oppositions between the media and "real" dissent underestimate the sophistication of these activists and, more importantly, leave later generations facing a political dead end. As a fellow art historian interested in the televisual (re)presentation of political positions, I find Joselit's ambition, his hope for a thorough reconsideration of art history's scope, incredibly exciting. The practice of art history, he suggests, should not be approached as a simple matter of cataloging objects, as it is also, or primarily, a concern with the history of taste, aesthetics, and representational conventions. For this reason, he writes, "If we . . . rethink our critical vocabularies and allow them to migrate into areas of vital concern . . . [we] will find ourselves with much to contribute to the social and political debates of our time."[91] As promising as Joselit's proposal sounds, however, one finds in *Feedback* a number of moments in which his own attempts to shift the terms of existing debates through art historical intervention appear to fall short. In spite of his urgings to rethink the simple opposition between "real" politics and television, for example, he nevertheless falls back, at times, on a very similar distinction. Chiding those who stubbornly cling to the notion of an "outside" in the face of the "closed circuits that fashion our public worlds," he rather puzzlingly asserts that neither "the modernist aesthetic tactic of revolution nor the poststructuralist technique of subversion (which in any event are two sides of the same coin)" can provide an adequate response, "unless one is prepared to wage actual political revolution and to pay its price of massive violence (something those with subversive on their lips might well remember)."[92] Perhaps moments like these should come as no surprise, given that Joselit's title pits, quite literally, television *against* democracy, an incompatibility or mutual exclusivity suggesting that, ultimately, his arguments may not be so far removed from those of Gitlin and others. Moreover, Joselit at times recapitulates, however unconsciously, Marcuse's most questionable assertion—both factually and politically—by posing a stark contrast between the media-based actions of white artists and activists and those of their "informationally disenfranchised," that is, nonwhite, counterparts. Activists like Hoffman and artists like Warhol, as complex as their engagements with the media may have been, nevertheless "presume[d] the possession of an intelligible identity," forgetting that "such self-possession was not a universal privilege."[93] In contrast, Joselit argues, a film like Melvin Van Peebles's *Sweet Sweetback's Baadasssss Song*, by virtue of its status as an independent, nonstudio production starring the "Black Community," offers an example of a less-compromised, more authentic version of media politics.

As I have already indicated, and as the chapters that follow will make clear, when we write the put-on back into the history of the late 1960s, this distinction between those whose actions have been rendered image and those who have been denied that "privilege" becomes far more difficult to maintain. No one was exempt from the system of representation and commodification. Like the "militant Negro," the "hippie," and the "homosexual" in Brackman's examples, Cleaver, Hoffman, Rubin, the members of the GAA, and the "queens

and nellies" so frequently condemned within the gay liberation movement seemed on some level to recognize the inseparability of politics
and performance. This, I argue, is why they appeared to recite time
and again the very terms they claimed to dispute. For this reason it
may be more fruitful to read Cleaver's "shit talking," Hoffman's "monkey theater," and the GAA's "zaps" not as mere symptoms of personal
neuroses or indications of a thoroughly co-opted or misguided radicalism, but as put-ons, campy repetitions of political personae that
were, in themselves, little more than repetitions of normative conceptions of opposition, whether in the form of black masculinity, youth
culture, or same-sex sexuality. My goal, in other words, is not so
much to determine precisely what it meant for Cleaver to denounce
Baldwin, for the Yippies to threaten Democratic Party delegates with
seduction, or for Sylvia Rivera to wear women's clothes. Rather, I
propose that we should read these actions as performances, analyze
them in relation to the forms of nonconformity they recited. Just why,
we should ask, did the members of the GAA smile when reminding
New York mayor John Lindsay during the taping of his televised talk
show that it was "illegal to blow anything in New York"? Why would
Hoffman and Rubin have wanted to lead thousands of young people
into Chicago for what many said would almost certainly end in a
police riot? Why would Cleaver have so willingly embodied the image
of black male "supermasculinity" he claimed to detest?

Again, my aim is not to demonstrate that these performances
offered a practical counterpoint to, or advantage over, the misguid-
edly "authentic" statement of political commitment. This would
be merely to rephrase the opposition between political purity and
co-optedness that practices like the put-on attempted to expose as
effectively meaningless. On the contrary, to understand the legacy
of the 1960s it is essential that we begin to perceive these two modes
of political speech as inextricable. What emerges from the parodic
performances outlined herein is the sense of a historically specific
form of transgression, simultaneously earnest and campy, claiming
to present thoroughly oppositional identities while demonstrating
the incredible difficulty of that very enterprise. Where Marcuse and
Sontag had hoped for a form of true eroticism or aesthetic practice
capable of distancing the individual from the instrumental logic of
capital, these stereotypical personae may in fact have been a series of

attempts to lead viewers to recognize the impossibility of achieving that distance—whether through racial or sexual difference, an unfettered Eros, or any other ostensible mode of opposition. By reading these enactments of acceptably unacceptable "radicalism" as put-ons, rather than misguided attempts to articulate "real" opposition, we can begin to recognize the perceived urgency of the "impulse to impersonation" condemned by Brustein. In so doing, we may come to see this radical theatricality as a signifier not of the failure of identity politics but of the politics of failed identities.

1. MONKEY THEATER

IN A 1970 COMIC STRIP TITLED "ABBIE HOFFMAN'S CHARM SCHOOL," Paul Laikin and Jerry Grandenetti lampooned Hoffman, the Yippie "leader" and media darling, for appearing to revel in his ironic celebrity status. The strip depicts Hoffman guiding students through a course in the etiquette of activism in an age of media saturation, telling them, for example, that when protesting, what one yells at the "pigs" is of great importance: "No more four-letter words. Remember, you're on TV and they'll bloop you out. We must use different kinds of obscenities suited to the medium. Obscenities that will really shock the TV viewer. Like, for example, instead of yelling 'You filthy pig!' at a State Trooper, we yell 'You have bad breath!'"[1] Later, Hoffman tells the class that throwing rocks at the police

> is also out this year. They don't dig that jazz anymore. The same goes for beer bottles, Molotov cocktails and Clorox jars. Makes 'em get mad and they start retaliating. What we gotta throw is something like, deadly. Are you ready for this? Garbage! Man, like, garbage is really groovy. . . . One important thing about garbage—since TV is covering all this, we can't just throw any kind of garbage. We gotta throw colorful garbage. Like ferinstance, tangerine peels are wild because they're a bright orange. Leftover meat bones are also groovy, if they are a nice brown. Likewise, with grapefruit skins you get a crazy yellow. Only lay off egg shells as they're too white, and coffee grinds which are too black. Remember, we play to color TV![2]

"Throwing rocks is also out this year. They don't dig that jazz anymore. The same goes for beer bottles, Molotov cocktails and Clorox jars. Makes 'em get mad and they start retaliating. What we gotta throw is something like, deadly. Are you ready for this? **Garbage!** Man, like, garbage is real groovy. The only thing though, chances are you won't find much garbage on the spot, so what you have to do is bring your own. Just empty your refrigerators before you start out!"

"One important thing about garbage—since TV is covering all this, we can't just throw any kind of garbage. We gotta throw **colorful** garbage. Like ferinstance, tangerine peels are wild because they're a bright orange. Leftover meat bones are also groovy, if they are a nice brown. Likewise, with grapefruit skins you get a crazy yellow. Only lay off egg shells as they're too white, and coffee grinds which are too black. Remember, we play to color TV!"

Paul Laikin and Jerry Grandenetti, "Abbie Hoffman's Charm School," *Sick Magazine*, September 1970.

Finally, with the police moving in to adjourn the class and administer beatings, Hoffman feels compelled to tell his students what to do "when the pigs start closing in on you." Faced with the threat of real violence, however, he loses his studied cool, breaking off midplatitude to shout, "RUN LIKE HELL BABY. . . . When they start closing in, it's every man for himself!"[3] And, almost predictably, as the police carry Hoffman away he reminds his students that they should "call my agent at the William Morris Agency" for the time and place of their next meeting. While not as nuanced as some of the arguments concerning Hoffman's political work, Laikin's and Grandenetti's cartoon nonetheless spoke to the anger that a number of activists felt toward "movement celebrities." Seemingly co-opted by their own stardom,

Paul Laikin and Jerry Grandenetti, "Abbie Hoffman's Charm School,"
Sick Magazine, September 1970.

these "leaders" appeared incapable not just of speaking for their own
constituents but of speaking meaningfully of opposition at all.

But what if the point of Hoffman's activism—or media mythmaking,
as he called it, indicating the extent to which his approach to political
action was inseparable from the creation of falsehoods and tall tales—
was not so much to use the media as a means of broadcasting "real"
revolutionary views or "correct" revolutionary ideology as to turn the
apparent futility of opposition into its own form of historically and
technologically mediated resistance? To answer this question, I would
like to look closely in this chapter at Hoffman's political actions, and
at the arguments of a number of his critics. I will look, specifically,
at the work of Emmett Grogan, founder of the San Francisco–based
guerrilla theater group known as the Diggers, and Theodor Roszak,
the author who in 1968 coined the term "counter culture," defining it
explicitly in opposition to "extroverted poseurs" like Hoffman. Finally,
I will turn to the criticisms of activist and independent filmmaker Norman Fruchter, who in 1971 argued that Hoffman had only betrayed
the youth culture for which he claimed to speak. For each of these
commentators, Hoffman's version of political activism was ultimately

counterproductive because of its relation to the mass media. Quite interestingly, however, the arguments of Roszak and Fruchter, like those of Robert Brustein, were each based primarily in a reading of the works of one of Hoffman's mentors, Herbert Marcuse. Drawing on Marcuse's works of the 1950s and '60s, these authors dismissed Hoffman for his apparent faith in the media's ability to aid in bringing about revolutionary social change. Hoffman's willingness to engage the media, they argued, merely indicated the extent to which he had mistaken images and performances for reality. By looking at the ways in which Hoffman courted the media, however, one might argue, to the contrary, that his antics took Marcuse's work more seriously than any of these authors recognized, and that, in turn, his media mythmaking may have been most radical precisely when it seemed to these authors most compromised.

While Brustein, as I have explained, depicted contemporary calls for "revolution" as little more than hubris and delusion, a number of activists had intentionally embraced theatricality in hopes of exploiting what appeared to be a historical inability to distinguish between aesthetics and politics. The Diggers, for example, were a loosely organized offshoot of the San Francisco Mime Troupe, conceived in 1966 by Emmett Grogan, Billy Fritsch, and Peter Berg as a type of performative resistance to the commercialization of the "hippie" counterculture. In opposition to the Haight Independent Proprietors (HIP), a group of merchants looking to capitalize on San Francisco's reputation as the epicenter of the emerging youth culture, the Diggers served free food in Golden Gate Park, offered free "crash pads" for those who had nowhere to sleep but on the street, opened a free store that gave away anything from clothing and shoes to money and marijuana, and attempted to establish a free medical clinic with the help of local doctors. These services were necessary, the Diggers believed, because the HIP's reckless promotion of San Francisco's counterculture had brought on not a "summer of love" but a throng of runaways. There was simply no way of accommodating this swarm of homeless, penniless young men and women. The free food, clothing, and shelter the Diggers' sought to provide, therefore, were largely designed to avert a potentially disastrous situation.[4]

What is important about the Diggers' Robin Hood–style charity work—items they offered for free were often stolen from stores, delivery trucks, and so on—is the way in which they described their "social work" as a form of theater. In 1966 Berg wrote that the group's actions were in fact a new form of dramaturgy.[5] The Diggers were not, he insisted, simply offering food, clothing, and shelter, but performing a utopian future. In the essay "Trip Without a Ticket," Berg argued that the Diggers' brand of activism was, simply put, "Ticketless theater": "It seeks audiences that are created by issues. It creates a cast of freed beings. It will become an issue itself. . . . This is theater of an underground that wants out. Its aim is to liberate ground held by consumer wardens and establish territory without walls. Its plays are glass cutters for empire windows."[6] For Berg, the significance of the Diggers' guerrilla theater lay in its ability to bring about real change in real time. By collapsing the distinction between theater and everyday life, it allowed individuals to become "life-actors." Rather than performing predetermined roles that ended with the play, actors and audience together would use their skills and imaginations to bring an alternative reality into existence. If individuals could realize this capability, Berg argued, virtually anything was possible. Social change would no longer be something that required plans and strategies; it would simply happen: "Let theories of economics follow social facts. Once a free store is assumed, human wanting and giving, needing and taking, become wide open to improvisation."[7]

Frustrated not only with the marketing of "hippie" culture but also with the plodding, ineffectual political work of the Students for a Democratic Society (SDS), the Diggers took their "ticketless theater" to Denton, Michigan, in the summer of 1967 to disrupt SDS's "Back to the Drawing Boards" conference. The seminal organization of the student New Left, SDS had planned their annual conference hoping to bridge a widening gap between the organization's founders, who were no longer students, and its younger "prairie power" members, who had taken on active roles in local offices throughout the country, and who were far more amenable than their predecessors to the ideas of the counterculture.[8] As the conference opened with Tom Hayden delivering the keynote speech, Grogan, Fritsch, and Berg burst through the door. They seized the microphone, accused SDS's members of being more concerned with maintaining organizational structure than bringing about real social and political change, and angered the "straight" SDS'ers with their macho posturing.[9] SDS was no longer the "New Left," the Diggers suggested; the Diggers were. "You'll never understand us," Grogan told them. "Your children will understand us." Then, exposing perhaps the most obvious political blindness of much of the counterculture and New Left, he called the men in the room "faggots" and "fags," shouting "You haven't got the balls to go mad. You're gonna make a revolution?—you'll piss in your pants when the violence erupts."[10] For the Diggers, SDS was, in every sense of the term, impotent. In spite of the organization's stated desire to reassert the social and political significance of the individual, their refusal to abandon the form of a rigidly organized political movement had done just the opposite.[11]

As former Digger Peter Coyote has written, "Ideological analysis was often one more means of delaying the *action* necessary to manifest an alternative."[12] Guerrilla theater offered a way of moving beyond the inevitable difficulties of "participatory democracy" through immediate, direct action. As Grogan told the members of SDS, "Property is the enemy—burn it, destroy it, give it away. Don't let them make a machine out of you, get out of the system, do your thing. Don't organize students, teachers, Negroes, organize your head. Find out where you are, what you want to do and go out and do it."[13] Guerrilla theater, unlike grassroots politics, would bring about an alternative future simply by enacting it in the present. Why waste time organizing and compromising, they asked, when it was possible to "find out . . . what you want to do and go out and do it"? For the Diggers, guerrilla theater was not, as Brustein argued, a series of meaningless gestures carried out simply for effect, but the next logical step in the search for personal and political authenticity.

As one might have guessed, the Diggers modeled their guerrilla theater, at least in part, on Antonin Artaud's "Theater of Cruelty." According to Artaud, to be rescued "from its psychological and human stagnation," theater must refuse to be governed by any set of preexisting texts. "We must put an end to this superstition of texts and written poetry," he explained. Artists "should be able to see that it is our veneration for what has already been done, however beautiful and valuable it may be, that petrifies us, that immobilizes us."[14] As Jacques Derrida so famously described it, the Theater of Cruelty was designed to present "an art prior to madness and the work, an art which no longer yields works, an artist's existence which is no longer a route or an experience that gives access to something other than itself."[15] According to Artaud, the notion that theater would defer or subjugate itself to some preexisting text or language was ludicrous. The theater was to be its own concrete language, "halfway between gesture and thought," whose only value lay "in its excruciating, magical connection with reality and with danger."[16] While the Diggers may not have adopted Artaud's terminology, they nonetheless believed that guerrilla theater, like the Theater of Cruelty, could only ever exist prior to representation.

The form of representation that concerned the Diggers most, though, was not the theater's re-presentation of a written text or the psychological reduction of the therapist but the forms of mechanical reproduction that would allow their actions to be diluted and assimilated by dominant culture. Guerrilla theater was "free" because it could only ever exist in its enactment; it could be neither repeated nor commodified in the form of an image. Any attempt to reproduce guerrilla theater was destined to fail, therefore, because each performance, like those of the Theater of Cruelty, could exist only once, as an original. It was this obsession with the singularity of performance that led the Diggers to refuse to act as spokesmen not only for the counterculture but for themselves as well. When questioned about their actions, each one would refer to himself either as "Emmett Grogan," "George Metesky," or, more simply, as "Free."[17] To provide their own names would make them both legally and authorially responsible for their actions. As Grogan told the members of SDS assembled in Michigan, "I'm not goin' to be on the cover of *Time* magazine, and my picture ain't goin' to be on the covers of any other magazines or in any newspapers—not even in any of those so-called underground newspapers or movement periodicals. . . . I ain't kidding! I'm not kidding you, me or anyone else about what I do to make the change that has to be made in this country of ours, here!"[18]

Seeing the Diggers for the first time in Michigan, Hoffman was inspired by these ideas of direct, theatrical action. Describing his encounter with Grogan, Fritsch, and Berg, Hoffman insisted that he understood just what the Diggers meant. When he returned to New York, he began calling himself a Digger. He burned money, and opened a Free Store on the Lower East Side of Manhattan with

Jim Fourratt, a political activist and former student at the Actor's Studio.[19] But there was something fundamentally different about the version of guerrilla theater that Hoffman practiced, something that truly upset the Diggers. Not long after the New York Free Store opened, the Diggers contacted Hoffman and demanded that he stop using their name. Grogan even went so far as to publicly denounce Hoffman, saying that he had simply stolen and bastardized the Diggers' ideas.[20] What Grogan failed to recognize, however, was that, for Hoffman, what made guerrilla theater powerful was less its potential to bring about an alternative reality in the present than its ability to create startling, open-ended images.

The friction between Hoffman and the Diggers seems to have begun with one incident in particular. In August of 1967 Hoffman designed a piece of guerrilla theater to be performed at the New York Stock Exchange.[21] With a group of friends and reporters from local underground papers, who were there to both participate in and report on the action, Hoffman arrived at the Stock Exchange early in the morning dressed in full "hippie" regalia and requested a guided tour of the building. Security guards initially refused entry to the group, assuming, quite correctly, that they were there only to make trouble. When the guards attempted to block the door, however, Hoffman began shouting accusations of anti-Semitism, saying that their fear of hippies was only an excuse, that the real reason they were trying to turn him away was because he was Jewish. Embarrassed, the guards relented and allowed the group to pass. The guards' suspicions were confirmed, of course, when in the middle of the tour, upon arriving at the observation deck from which visitors were able to watch the stockbrokers at work, members of Hoffman's group pulled dollar bills from their pockets and tossed them onto the floor of the Exchange. Chaos erupted as the brokers stopped what they were doing and scrambled to pick up as many of the bills as they could. As Marty Jezer, one of the reporters in Hoffman's group, later wrote, "The contrast between the creatively dressed hippies and the well-tailored Wall Street stockbrokers was an essential message of the demonstration. . . . Hippies throwing away money while capitalists groveled."[22]

Jerry Rubin, who had met Hoffman only days before the demonstration, recalled, "Police grabbed the ten of us, dragged us down the

stairs, and deposited us on Wall Street at high noon in front of aston-
ished businessmen and hungry TV cameras. That night the attack
by the hippies on the Stock Exchange was told around the world—
international exposure!"[23] In spite of that exposure, however, just
what had happened inside the Stock Exchange was immediately
shrouded in myth. No two accounts were the same. No one—including the participants—seemed to be sure how much money had been
thrown, or just who had participated. When reporters asked Hoffman for his name, he told them that he was Cardinal Spellman, the
Roman Catholic leader who had recently offered public support for
the war in Vietnam; when asked about the number of demonstrators
involved in the action, he simply said, "We don't exist," and burned a
five-dollar bill for the camera.[24] The opportunity to play games like
this with reporters was just what Hoffman had hoped for in designing
the action. He and Fourratt had even contacted various media outlets
the previous evening and urged them to be at the Stock Exchange to
witness the commotion that morning. Hoffman believed that these
events, when presented in the form of a newspaper article or a story
on a television newscast, would be transformed into "blank space,"
one of the most useful weapons in any activist's arsenal. Blank space,
he wrote, was "a preview. . . . It is not necessary to say that we are
opposed to ___. Everybody already knows. . . . We alienate people.
We involve people. Attract-Repel. . . . Blank space, the interrupted
statement, the unsolved puzzle, they are all involving."[25] Rather than
simply telling people what to believe, actions like the one at the
Stock Exchange would give them an opportunity to draw their own
conclusions, to insert themselves into, or implicate themselves in
the meaning of what they saw or heard. If one could use the media
to broadcast those images to greater numbers, so much the better.
Thus, where the Diggers looked to make themselves unrepresentable,
Hoffman saw mechanical reproducibility as integral to the work of
political opposition.

   In part, this was because, at approximately the same time as his
encounter with the Diggers in Michigan, Hoffman had begun reading
the work of media theorist Marshall McLuhan. McLuhan, unlike the
Diggers, praised television as the technological form that would give
rise to new and radically different social forms. The way in which
television presented information to the senses would drastically and

Hoffman and Rubin burning a five-dollar bill at the Financial Center in New York, August 24, 1967. Photo by AP.

irreversibly alter the forms of human interaction. Unlike the "hot" printed word, television was a "cool" medium. It offered viewers the opportunity to insert themselves into its stream of information. As a result, McLuhan argued, it would bring together vastly different cultures in a new "global village." As he put it in perhaps his most succinct formulation, "The medium is the message": regardless of its ostensible content, what viewers would ultimately take away from television programming was an entirely new way of engaging the world around them. Drawing on these ideas, Hoffman began to believe that media mythmaking could be used as a form of political activism. Thus, refusing to privilege the direct, personal contact that the Diggers so valued, Hoffman saw television coverage of political demonstrations as not just inevitable but valuable. Seeing viewers as active consumers of the images that entered their homes, rather than as passive receptors, allowed him to conceive of television as a potential instrument of social transformation.

At the same time, however, Hoffman's belief in television as a revolutionary medium differed from McLuhan's in one important respect. McLuhan believed that the social forms produced by television would be the result of a fundamental alteration of the senses: "It is the medium that shapes and controls the scale and form of human association and interaction."[26] The instantaneous quality of televisual imagery would lead viewers to perceive the world in spatial rather than temporal terms, and thus to engage every facet of their lives in an altogether different way. Just how television's potential should be used, however, McLuhan never made clear. In fact, the closest thing one finds to a prescription in *Understanding Media* smacks of totalitarianism: "We are certainly coming within conceivable range of a world automatically controlled to the point where we could say 'Six hours less radio in Indonesia next week or there will be a great falling off in literary attention.' Or, 'We can program twenty more hours of TV in South Africa next week to cool down the tribal temperature raised by radio last week.'"[27] Exposure to media could effectively "program" cultures to "keep their emotional climate stable," he suggested, not unlike the way in which trade could be manipulated to maintain "equilibrium" in market economies. Obviously, Hoffman wanted just the opposite. It was the stable emotional climate of the United States, the "equilibrium in the commercial economies of the world," that he found so troubling. Playing on McLuhan's elision between two senses of the term "cool," Hoffman wrote, "Projecting cool images is not our goal. We do not wish to project a calm secure future. We are disruption. We are hot."[28] Thus, while he looked to McLuhan's work for the idea that television might play a role in bringing about a new "global village," Hoffman's idea of how television would be used to bring that village into existence differed greatly. For Hoffman, the medium and the message were far from inseparable. Although he sought to use television to broadcast his message, that message, ultimately, was a critique of the images television offered.

According to Hoffman, televisual images of the counterculture would never revolutionize society by "cooling off" a potentially dangerous situation. Rather, he argued that they would work by establishing a figure-ground relationship with other images on TV. As he put it, "It's only when you establish a figure-ground relationship that you can convey information."[29] Footage of "monkey theater," as he came to call his own version of guerrilla theater, would necessarily interact with, and stand out against, the background formed by more predictable scenes. If these images were outrageous enough, Hoffman believed, viewers would be unable to ignore or dismiss them, regardless of what commentary might be offered to frame or explain them. For this reason, he considered nightly news coverage of monkey theater to be something akin to an "advertisement for the revolution." Images depicting hippies tossing money onto the floor of the New York Stock Exchange would convey information much like the most persuasive images on television: commercials. Discussing the news program *Meet the Press*, Hoffman wrote, "What happens at the end of the program? Do you think any one of the millions of people watching the show switched from being a liberal to a conservative or vice versa? I doubt it. One thing is certain, though . . . a lot of people are going to buy that fucking soap or whatever else they were pushing in the commercial."[30]

Advertisements were figures standing out from the ground that was the regularly scheduled program. They were designed to be quick, to the point, and to capture the viewer's imagination. To function like an advertisement emerging from the middle of a newscast, therefore, protestors would have to distance themselves from any form of rational debate. Engaging in calm, orderly discussions about substantive issues was the manner of politicians, and, not coincidentally, of organizations like SDS. To Hoffman, any attempt to achieve political change in this fashion seemed doomed to failure: even if one managed to be included in nightly news broadcasts, the chances that what one *said* would change anyone's mind were slim. No one "switched from being a liberal to a conservative or vice versa" after watching *Meet the Press*. Showing, for Hoffman, was completely different from saying—but not in the way that the Diggers had insisted. To be effective, guerrilla theater had to be flattened out, treated, quite literally, as an image: "What does free speech mean to you?

To me it is an image like all things."[31] Attention to the form of one's actions was necessary not because those actions had the potential to bring about a new reality, or because one wanted to "speak truth to power," but because political opposition had become inextricable from practices and modes of representation. For this reason, monkey theater would assume a very specific form. After all, the actions of private citizens only received national attention when they were in some way sensational. Monkey theater, then, would have to be literally spectacular. In looking to make protest newsworthy, that is, the appearance and mannerisms of those who had already been deemed newsworthy would have to be adopted. Monkey theater would have to speak reporters' language. As Pierre Bourdieu would argue thirty years later, "You have to produce demonstrations for television so that they interest television types and fit their perceptual categories."[32] Monkey theater, in other words, would have to look like a "revolution"; it would have to conform to television reporters' conception of an uprising.

Following the events staged at the Stock Exchange, Rubin, captivated by Hoffman's media savvy, invited him to aid in the organization of an upcoming demonstration sponsored by the National Mobilization to End the War in Vietnam (Mobe). David Dellinger, the head of the Mobe, had enlisted Rubin's help that summer, after Rubin's bid to be elected mayor of Berkeley, California, had failed. Although he lost the mayoral race, Rubin's knack for publicity and his ability to appeal to young people seemed, to Dellinger, just what the Mobe needed. Dellinger was seeking to bring vast numbers of protestors to Washington, DC, in October for a national antiwar demonstration. He asked Rubin to take charge of the project, hoping that Rubin would be able to deploy the creative political tactics for which he had become known in Berkeley on a national stage. By appealing to those youths who might otherwise have been reticent to take part in one of the Mobe's more conventional actions, Dellinger hoped to assemble the largest antiwar demonstration to date. With Hoffman and Rubin composing the script, however, what was initially conceived quite literally as the antiwar movement's March on Washington became instead another work of monkey theater.

The event, as they saw it, might begin with a march, but that march would end south of the Potomac in a massive act of civil disobedience on the grounds of the Pentagon. Dellinger protested, explaining that authorities would simply have to block the bridge leading out of Washington and their plans would be ruined, but Rubin and Hoffman were undeterred. It was essential that the demonstration engage the Pentagon, Rubin explained, for it was "a symbol so evil that we can do anything we want and still get away with it." Thus, *Our scenario:* We threaten to close the motherfucker down. This triggers the paranoia of the Amerikan government: The Man then organizes our troops for us by denying us a place to rally and march. Thus just-another-demonstration becomes a dramatic confrontation between Freedom and Repression, and the stage is the world."[33] To announce the event, Rubin and Hoffman called an official press conference on August 28. As Rubin explained, their performance was to "grab the imagination of the world and play on appropriate paranoias," ensuring that no one would be able to ignore or forget their threats and promises in the weeks leading up to the protest.[34]

They assembled an appropriate cast of characters. David Dellinger and Bob Greenblatt were there as official representatives of the Mobe. Comedian and civil rights activist Dick Gregory was also invited, as were, Rubin recounted, "a Vietnam veteran, a priest, a housewife from Women Strike for Peace, a professor, an SDS leader," and "Amerika's baddest, meanest, most violent nigger—then H. Rap Brown," who, "whether or not he even showed up at the Pentagon, would create visions of FIRE."[35] As menacing as Brown may have seemed, however, it was Hoffman who stole the show. He wore an old, unbuttoned army shirt and introduced himself as Col. Jerome Z. Wilson of the Strategic Air Command, telling reporters that he had recently deserted because of "bad vibrations." On the day of the protest, he said, Washington's famed cherry trees would be defoliated, the Potomac River would be dyed purple, and marijuana, which had already been surreptitiously planted on the lawn of the Pentagon, would be harvested. Moreover, he explained, as a grand finale, demonstrators would stand side by side, holding hands and chanting in a circle around the Pentagon. The importance of the circle, he explained, was that a ring of humans joining hands would cause the Pentagon to rise from the ground, and would force the evil spirits inhabiting the building to fall out. The war-mongers were to be vanquished by a demonstration of countercultural "love" and "spirituality."

Of course, Hoffman never believed that protestors would be able to levitate the Pentagon. On one hand, the claim was about numbers: the idea of the number of bodies necessary to form a circle around the Pentagon would in itself make the upcoming demonstration seem enormous. On the other hand, the exaggerated and farcical reference to a kind of mystical spirituality emblematized a number of stereotypes regarding hippies and the counterculture. Describing his motives for the claim, Hoffman wrote, "The peace movement has gone crazy and it's about time. Our alternative fantasy will match the zaniness in Vietnam."[36] The outlandishness of this alternative fantasy would allow neither reporters nor viewers to ignore it. It would be so incredible, in fact, that it would stand in relief against the background of daily news footage from Vietnam, which, though often horrific, had become commonplace. Against this ground, Hoffman would attempt to broadcast a figure of "revolution."

In the days following the press conference, the story of the Pentagon's potential capture by hippies practicing a type of angrily joyful mysticism took on a life of its own. The Washington, DC, police department issued a formal statement saying that they were prepared, should the demonstration get out of hand, to use Mace to temporarily blind protestors. In response, Hoffman issued a statement of his own, claiming that hippie scientists had developed a new sex drug called Lace. "Lace is LSD combined with DMSO, a skin-penetrating agent," he announced to the press. "When squirted on the skin or clothes, it penetrates quickly to the bloodstream, causing the subject to get sexually aroused."[37] For those who doubted his claims, Hoffman and friends staged an orgy. Reporters were told to meet at his apartment for proof of the drug's existence. Upon their arrival, Hoffman delivered an introductory speech "full of mumbo-jumbo," and then asked a number of "test subjects" to proceed with a "demonstration." "The subjects shot themselves with water pistols full of purple Lace, took off their clothes, and fucked. Then they put their clothes back on, and the reporters interviewed them."[38] Within days the media was abuzz with rumors and questions about the new sex drug. As Hoffman later said, "People suspected the Lace demonstration was a put-on, but then again. . . . Hippies, drugs, orgies: it was perfectly believable."[39] Hoffman knew that in some sense the viewing public saw the counterculture as little more than a hypersexualized form of youthful rebelliousness. But rather than attempting to correct that impression, he seemed to delight in reinforcing it. Not surprisingly, his willingness to enact these negative stereotypes for the mainstream press drew the ire of more than one critic. In his 1968 text *The Making of a Counter Culture*, Theodor Roszak lambasted Hoffman for promoting a debased version of "cultural revolution." For Roszak, Hoffman's association with the counterculture was nothing more than the result of a series of misunderstandings. The "true" counterculture, he believed, would never have "performed" for the media. To the contrary, for those who understood and shared the counterculture's dissatisfaction, the media merely offered proof of the soullessness of contemporary society.

For Roszak—and, he argues, for members of the true counterculture—the media were ultimately symptomatic of the larger problem facing America in the mid-twentieth century, the problem of "technocratic" thought. The flood of information that confronted people in their daily lives had qualitatively transformed experience. Individuals had been subordinated to technology, categorized as sets of facts subject to specialized knowledge, and thus alienated from themselves: "In the technocracy everything aspires to become purely technical, the subject of expert attention."[40] Individual desires had been commodified and subsumed within the technocratic social order. Life, as a result, had come to seem like a parody of itself. For the first time in history it had become possible for people to believe that "*real* sex . . . is something that goes with the best scotch, twenty-seven-dollar sunglasses, and platinum-tipped shoelaces."[41] At the same time, though, this technocratic society carried within it the means of its own dissolution. The advanced education necessary to produce specialists in various technical fields had also equipped students with the ability to think critically about the sociohistorical conditions that necessitated such specialized knowledge. Recognizing the relationship between this highly specific knowledge, on one hand, and their own intense psychic and social alienation on the other, many of those who were to become the technocracy's future leaders began to rebel. According to Roszak, therefore, if one hoped to understand the counterculture it was essential to understand the work of Herbert Marcuse, for it was precisely this psychosocial alienation that Marcuse had, in the mid-1950s, so cogently diagnosed.

In *Eros and Civilization*, first published in 1955, Marcuse had argued that the solution to the alienation of the individual was to be found in the reclamation of the state of infantile sexuality that Freud labeled "polymorphous perversity." According to Freud, during infancy, the barriers that separate normative sexuality from perversion—the interdiction of bestiality, incest, homosexuality, and so on—are absent. The taboo that most interested Marcuse, though, was that which restricted erotic experience to the genitals. Unlike Freud, who saw this as a necessity of the individual's biological development, Marcuse claimed that this barrier's existence was firmly rooted in concrete historical circumstances. By condensing and restricting sexuality to the act of intercourse as such, Marcuse argued, social mandates had succeeded in relegating erotic experience to the realm of leisure. Eroticism, in other words, was transformed into something that was acceptable only at certain moments and in certain locations, an activity that could fit within the demanding schedule of the industrial worker. According to Marcuse, this particular process of socialization, necessary to reproduce the individual as a means of production, must therefore be described as "surplus repression." That is to say, the form of repression that Freud presented as necessary to the basic development of the individual was, according to Marcuse, intimately linked to the forms of heteronomy that characterized modern capitalism. Thus, for Marcuse, the elimination of surplus repression would play an absolutely central role in the liberation of the individual. The "unrepressed development" of the erotogenic zones of the body, he argued, "would eroticize the organism to such an extent that it would counteract the desexualization of the organism required by its social utilization as an instrument of labor."[42] In *Eros and Civilization*, in other words, Marcuse's concept of liberation was inseparable from a certain notion of anamnesis. It was the remembrance, or re-membrance, of the entire body as potentially erotically charged that guided his utopian project. As he put it, "if work were accompanied by a reactivation of pregenital polymorphous eroticism, it would tend to become gratifying in itself without losing its work content."[43]

By extension, he also believed perversion to function as a living symbol of utopia. Appropriating Stendhal's famous aphorism regarding the work of art, Marcuse wrote, "The perversions seem to give a *promesse de bonheur* greater than that of 'normal' sexuality.... The perversions ... express rebellion against the subjugation of sexuality under the order of procreation, and against the institutions which guarantee this order."[44] The continued existence of perversions in the face of their interdiction constituted a sign of potential liberation. They "uphold sexuality as an end in itself.... They are a symbol of what had to be suppressed so that suppression could prevail and organize the ever more efficient domination of man and nature."[45] For Marcuse, writing in the 1950s, perversion, unlike art, seemed to suggest a form of rebellion that could not be assimilated into the dominant culture in any positive form. Where art ultimately legitimized a given social reality, true perversion was said to be capable of relating to that social reality only as a site of failure.

For Roszak, this belief in the liberating potential of Eros lay at the heart of the counterculture. These youths sought to re-eroticize the individual, and, in so doing, to free human sexuality from the demands of instrumentality. At the same time, however, this was also one of their most frequently misunderstood demands. To their elders, these longhaired, shabbily-dressed hedonists appeared to be something akin to "an invasion of centaurs," a violently perverse "anticulture" seeking nothing other than to destroy society in the name of sensual indulgence.[46] According to Roszak, the media had only further exacerbated these fears. They had reduced the counterculture to a caricature, enabling it to be assimilated as an image of the "way out": "Dissent, the press has clearly decided, is hot copy. But if anything, the media tend to isolate the weirdest aberrations *and* consequently to attract to the movement many extroverted poseurs."[47] The individuals singled out by the media bore only an external resemblance to the counterculture. The "technocratic realism" of "CBSNBCABC" focused solely on appearances, and was therefore unable to make the distinction between the "true" counterculture and those "extroverted poseurs" that happened to turn up in the same places.

Not surprisingly, Hoffman was the "extroverted poseur" Roszak had in mind. By performing his "cultural revolution" for the media, Hoffman had succeeded only in promoting himself as a new form of celebrity; he represented not the counterculture but the "foul-mouthed whimsy of a hip a-politics."[48] It should have shocked no one, therefore, to find *Mademoiselle* magazine describing Hoffman as a "new type of sex symbol," and calling him "the Rhett Butler of the Revolution."[49] For Roszak, this would merely have confirmed the spuriousness of Hoffman's form of opposition. The "true" counterculture, Roszak believed, sought to redefine sexuality through the liberation of Eros. Thus the men of the "real" counterculture would never have staged orgies for reporters, and would never have been considered "sex symbols." In fact, as Roszak argued, they had cultivated a certain "feminine softness." Where the Diggers called upon misogynistic and homophobic rhetoric in hopes of avoiding the powerlessness that plagued traditional organizations like SDS, the men of the "true" counterculture, Roszak believed, were markedly *un*masculine. And for this they were to be celebrated. "It is the occasion of endless satire on the part of critics," he wrote, "but the style is clearly a deliberate effort on the part of the young to undercut the crude and compulsive he-manliness of American political life. While this generous and gentle eroticism is available to us, we would do well to respect it, instead of ridiculing it."[50] The goal of the liberation of Eros was not the intensification of sexuality but its fundamental transformation. Machismo, therefore, was to be abandoned for "true" eroticism. For Roszak, this is what separated the counterculture's version of "free love" from the debased sexuality of the technocracy. But because technocratic knowledge dealt only in surfaces, this was for many one of the most difficult aspects of the counterculture to comprehend. The media could thus present the counterculture as simultaneously violently aggressive and hopelessly ineffectual, or, to put it another way, threateningly hypermasculine and laughably effeminate. Nevertheless, for Roszak, it was this essential "softness" that distinguished the authentic counterculture from someone like Hoffman, whose testosterone-driven, egomaniacal self-promotion merely played upon the public's misconceptions for personal gain. Yet, to many Americans, Hoffman's sexuality, not to mention that of the Diggers, seemed just as ambiguous as that of any other member of the counterculture.[51]

In his book *Homosexuality in Cold War America*, Robert Corber explains this difficulty not in terms of a utopian eroticism but as a function of the postwar crisis in American masculinity. In the 1950s, he explains, masculinity had in many ways come to be equated with supportiveness and domesticity rather than ingenuity and independence. In the years following World War II, American men had begun to define themselves through patterns of consumption—something once expected only of women—rather than professional achievements. At the same time, however, to reach "the levels of consumption necessary for sustaining economic growth," forms of homosocial bonding had to be discouraged.[52] Thus, Corber writes, those most likely to be seen as "objects of suspicion in the intensely homophobic climate of the postwar period were not those who participated actively in the domestic sphere or who submitted passively to corporate structures—modes of behavior that in another context might have marked them as insufficiently masculine—but those who refused to settle down and raise a family."[53]

Those who rebelled against the restraint of consumer society, and were thus depicted as somehow more effeminate, had not cultivated a "feminine softness"; rather, they had deployed a regressive, outmoded form of masculinity. Sexuality, therefore, had not been transformed in Roszak's account of the counterculture so much as it had been romanticized, fetishized as *the* source of liberation. The sexuality of Roszak's counterculture appeared ambiguous not because it was a living symbol of liberation but because it was, in the end, a product of nostalgia.

Hoffman's Lace "demonstration" thus drew self-consciously not only on popular stereotypes of the counterculture but also on the myth of "free love" as liberation propagated by "proponents" of the counterculture like Roszak. Hoffman embodied the most hackneyed clichés about the counterculture, drawing attention to and satirizing those clichés while using them to raise the dramatic stakes in the coming showdown between protestors and the United States government. Once again, as Rubin explained, these publicity stunts were about turning "just-another-demonstration" into "a dramatic confrontation between Freedom and Repression." And in this sense, they got precisely the results they had wanted. As much as Hoffman's imagistic treatment of the counterculture unnerved Roszak, his antics were even more disturbing to those in power, though obviously for different reasons. In the weeks following the press conference and the Lace "demonstration," a number of government officials, including President Lyndon Johnson, became increasingly anxious about Hoffman's claim that demonstrators would levitate the Pentagon. Their concern, of course, was not that a circle of chanting human beings might actually raise the building. If demonstrators were to circle the Pentagon, however, it would render the building effectively inaccessible, either bringing all operations taking place inside virtually to a halt, or compelling officials to forcibly remove protestors from the grounds. News of the Johnson administration governing by force at home while attempting to spread "peace" and protect "democracy" in Southeast Asia would obviously have been a political disaster. In a battle of images, in other words, Hoffman and Rubin had backed the government into a corner. The tension would be defused only in the final days leading up to the demonstration, when, with Johnson threatening to deny march permits and to turn away all buses headed for the District of Columbia that weekend, Dellinger and other Mobe leaders were forced to negotiate.

To be sure, Johnson was not the only one pressuring Dellinger to concede. Leaders of other antiwar groups, such as SDS, Women Strike for Peace, and the Socialist Workers Party, along with activist-celebrities such as Dr. Benjamin Spock, threatened to withdraw their support from the march if Dellinger could not convince Rubin and Hoffman to soften their rhetoric. But in spite of these last-minute efforts to alter the demonstration's tone, it was too late. Hoffman and Rubin had already captured the imagination of America's youth, and thousands flocked to Washington for what the two "organizers" had promised would be the most exciting demonstration in recent memory. As Norman Mailer wrote in his novel about the Pentagon protests, *The Armies of the Night*, "Tens of thousands travel[ed] hundreds of miles to attend a symbolic battle."[54] Mailer described/romanticized "a hippie got up like Batman," another "dressed like Charles Chaplin," and still others dressed as "Martians and Moonmen and a knight unhorsed." Onlookers were thus treated to a scene that "fulfilled to the hilt our General's oldest idea of war which is that every man should dress as he pleases if he is going into battle, for that is his right, and variety never hurts the zest of the hardiest workers in every battalion." Their props and costumes, shabby as they may have been, demonstrated that "the aesthetic at last was in the politics."[55]

Hoffman's and Rubin's media tactics had mobilized the most creative elements of the counterculture. For Hoffman, however, placing "the aesthetic in the politics" was more than a matter of propaganda.

Rather, the image itself had become the primary site of battle. The distinction between the political and the aesthetic could no longer be taken for granted; calls for "real" politics had to be taken with a grain of salt. Hoffman rather cleverly illustrated this point when he urged his fellow activists, "You are the Revolution. Do your thing. . . . Practice. Rehearsals come after the act. Act. Act. One practices by acting. . . . There are no rules, only images."[56] This passage, which begins with what seems to be yet another Digger-inspired argument for the transformative power of guerrilla theater, concludes by alerting the reader to the doubled meanings inherent in many of its key terms. If, as Hoffman claimed, there were only images—if he *wrote* these thoughts only because, as he put it, he had "no idea how to make a movie"[57]—then what did it mean to speak of revolution as practice, or of practice as "acting"? It was precisely this play that guided Hoffman and Rubin in planning the Pentagon action and, later, their most famous (non)demonstration, which took place in Chicago during the Democratic National Convention in the summer of 1968.

Following the Pentagon action, a number of organizations began preparations for a series of massive demonstrations surrounding the Democratic National Convention. The Mobe, for example, announced that it would organize and sponsor a large-scale march that would conclude at the Chicago amphitheater where the convention was to be held. In light of the difficulties surrounding the demonstration in Washington, though, the Mobe's leaders were no longer so eager to capitalize on Rubin's and Hoffman's appeal. Likewise, the two mythmakers were pleased to sever their connections with the Mobe. Emboldened by their success in drawing so many participants to the Pentagon, they believed that, freed from the constraints imposed by the more conservative antiwar organizations, they might (dis)organize a truly grand work of monkey theater. With the help of a number of friends and fellow activists, they began developing plans for a large concert similar to the Monterey Pop Festival. A concert staged in spatial and aesthetic opposition to the Democratic National Convention, they believed, would allow them to provide a counterpoint not only to the official proceedings of the Democratic Party but also to the more staid, traditional demonstrations of groups like the Mobe. The concert would be more than a protest; it would be promoted as a celebration, an affirmation of life in the face of the "Party of Death."

Hoffman and Rubin trusted that large numbers of young people could be convinced to make the trip to Chicago to hear their favorite bands, and the news that tens of thousands had gathered in opposition to the prowar Democratic Party would energize and mobilize an entirely new constituency, one seeking an alternative to politics-as-usual. At a New Year's Eve party in 1967, Rubin, Hoffman, Fourratt, Nancy Kurshan, Paul Krassner, and Hoffman's wife, Anita, began to discuss plans not so much for the concert itself but for creating the festival as a media phenomenon. In hopes of maximizing their exposure, the group concocted a mock organization to serve as the event's mythical sponsor. Punning on the basic idea of an international youth festival, Anita Hoffman proposed calling this pseudo-organization the Youth International Party. With such an official-sounding title, she explained, the media would have virtually no choice but to take the group seriously. Furthermore, those who were in the know, so to speak, would get the joke, recognizing that "party" could be understood in more ways than one. To their supporters, therefore, they should be known not as the YIP but as "Yippie!"

As always, to rally support they would need the media's help. Hoffman later explained that when it came to publicizing the Youth International Party, "Reporters would play their preconceived roles: 'What is the difference between a hippie and a Yippie?' A hundred different answers would fly out, forcing the reporter to make up his own answer; to distort."[58] In March, the Yippies held their first official press conference to announce their plans for the "Festival of Life." The Mobe had already made public its own plans to hold peaceful protests in Chicago, but the Yippies promised to go much further. They vowed to present America with a vision of "the politics of ecstasy." America's youth, they claimed, would be transformed, radicalized by the Youth International Party's message. Everyone under the age of thirty would "rise up and abandon the creeping meatball."[59] Just what this meant was anything but obvious, and for the Yippies, that was precisely the point. "Yippie!" would become news not by issuing statements of theoretical or tactical precision but by playing on Americans' fears and preconceived notions regarding the emergent youth culture. "The straight press thought that 'creeping meatball' meant Lyndon Baines Johnson and that we wanted to throw him out of office," Rubin wrote. "We just laughed. . . . Where would we be without LBJ?"[60] In fact, "rise up and abandon the creeping meatball" was, in itself, meaningless. It was nothing more than a waggish turn of phrase, an empty signifier onto which each listener could project his or her own interpretation: "Everybody has his own creeping meatball—grades, debts, pimples. Yippies are a participatory movement. There are no ideological requirements to be a Yippie. . . . Yippie is just an excuse to rebel."[61] To further agitate and intrigue the public, Rubin and Hoffman announced that the group would stage an enormous, intentionally ill-defined "YIP-in" at Grand Central Station less than one week later.

The publicity worked. On the night of the YIP-in, nearly three thousand young men and women filled Grand Central's main terminal, blocking nearly all routes of passage. It was, as YIP's name suggested, a party: balloons floated through the air, and people danced and shared popcorn with bemused commuters. Not unlike tossing dollar bills onto the floor of the New York Stock Exchange, the YIP-in caricatured the seemingly obvious distinction between generations and cultures. And for its participants, whether or not they understood this, the event seemed a success. Everyone appeared to be enjoying themselves. The tone of the evening changed in an instant, however, when the police charged into the crowd swinging nightsticks. The officers claimed to be pursuing members of an anarchist group known as the Motherfuckers, who had begun dismantling the large clock atop the information booth. Yet in spite of their stated intentions, the scene was nothing less than a police riot. No attempt was made to clear the station in any systematic fashion; participants were beaten with billy clubs; and Don McNeill, a reporter covering the YIP-in for the *Village Voice*, was thrown through a plate glass window.[62] After more than an hour of brutal violence, the officers retreated, leaving nearly a thousand revelers behind. Clearing the station, it seems, was less of a priority than the assertion of police authority. The next day, when many expected the Yippies to hide in embarrassment, Hoffman and Rubin issued an "official" statement to the press accusing the police of "animalistic behavior," "brutality," and "creephood."[63] The Yippies, that is, responded to the officers' posturing with their own. As Brustein would suggest two years later, "violent official retaliation" had become, like the Yippies' version of "revolution," another form of theater.[64]

After the YIP-in, Hoffman, Rubin, Fouratt, Krassner, and Marshall Bloom, head of the Liberation News Service (LNS), flew to Chicago to discuss the logistics of the upcoming demonstrations with representatives of the local and national antiwar movements. First they attended an early planning session sponsored by the Mobe, interrupting the scheduled speakers to expound upon, among other things, the evils of pay toilets. After the Mobe's meeting, the Yippies met with a number of Chicago-based activists to discuss different ways of publicizing the Festival of Life both locally and nationally. Local activists were anxious about the Yippies' plans, fearing retaliation from the police and Chicago mayor Richard Daley. To assuage these fears, Rubin and Hoffman promised that they would apply for the legal permits required to hold a concert in Lincoln Park.[65]

Nevertheless, while they tried to appease local organizers, the Yippies continued to use the media to antagonize the authorities and the general public. While in Chicago, Hoffman and Rubin scheduled two press conferences in which they discussed "plans" for the Festival of Life. They promised to taint Chicago's water supply with LSD, and to send Yippie women into the convention to flirt with and drug the delegates while "hyperpotent" Yippie men seduced their wives. They told reporters that the Youth International Party would hold its own counterconvention as part of the Festival of Life, during which they would nominate a pig, to be named "Pigasus," for president. At one press conference, Hoffman distributed a written statement declaring, "The present day politicians and their armies of automatons have selfishly robbed us of our birthright. The evilness they stand for will go unchallenged no longer. Political Pigs, your days are numbered. We are the Second American Revolution. We shall win. Yippie!"[66] This statement was paired with a floor plan of the Conrad Hilton Hotel in which Democratic Party delegates and nominees would stay, labeled, "Headquarters for the Opposing Pig and His Forces." Of course, Hoffman quipped, the Yippies would be willing to call the whole thing off if the city would simply pay them $100,000.

As with their call to "rise up and abandon the creeping meatball," and Hoffman's promise to levitate the Pentagon, the absurdity of the Yippies' threats was part of the point. And although the authorities suspected the Yippies' antics to be nothing more than a put-on, they were compelled to play the "straight man." Whether or not they took

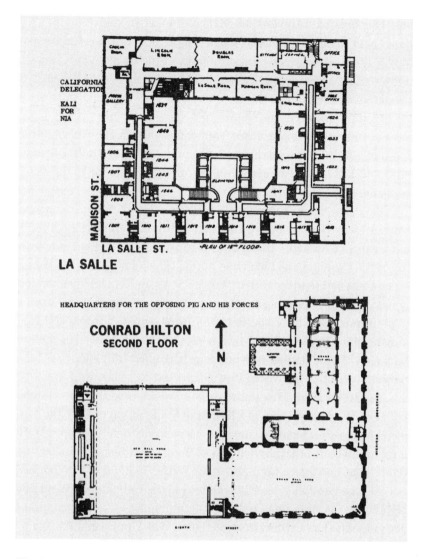

"Headquarters for the Opposing Pig and His Forces."
Image courtesy of the Estate of Abbie Hoffman.

the Yippies' threats seriously, they feared that the rest of America
would. Given the student strike at Columbia University, in which five
University buildings were occupied by students and protestors for a
full week in late April, and the student-led uprisings in Paris shortly
thereafter, a large-scale rebellion led by American youth seemed

entirely plausible. So even though the FBI and CIA knew that the Yippies' "plan" to spike Chicago's water supply with LSD was ludicrous, Mayor Daley was forced to station police officers at each reservoir access point all the same. This official posturing eventually turned proactive when, later in the summer, Daley issued his own threats designed not to force the Yippies to behave in a more orderly fashion but to keep demonstrators from coming to Chicago at all. Most famously, he guaranteed that Chicago police would be authorized to "shoot to kill" any demonstrators they deemed a threat to the city's security.

Indeed, the mayor's threats did frighten many of those who would otherwise have gathered in Chicago for the demonstrations. In "A Letter from Chicago," distributed through LNS, Abe Peck, the editor of the *Chicago Seed* who had at one time identified himself as a Yippie, warned readers with a twist on Scott McKenzie's well known lyrics: "If you're coming to Chicago, be sure to wear some armor in your hair." Similarly, the *Berkeley Barb* stated, "Flower children may be quickly 'radicalized' by having their heads busted by a cop's billy club."[67] The Yippies' provocations had apparently exhausted the patience of those for whom they purported to speak, and to many, it began to seem as if the entire project was doomed. In the months between the Grand Central YIP-In and the Festival of Life, the Yippies' requests for legal permits were repeatedly deferred, until Hoffman and Rubin officially withdrew them. As a result, most of the bands that had agreed to participate in the Festival of Life backed out—in the end folk singer Phil Ochs and the radical rock band The MC5 were the only ones willing to participate—and a number of activists who had earlier declared themselves Yippies quickly turned on Hoffman and Rubin personally. Dissenters argued, in what would become a familiar refrain, that the Yippie "leaders" had become more concerned with their own celebrity than with real social change.

Three years later, New York Newsreel's Norman Fruchter reiterated this sense of frustration with the Yippies in an essay "Games in the Arena: Movement Propaganda and the Culture of the Spectacle." According to Fruchter, the Yippies' ultimate downfall lay in their willingness to engage the media on its own terms. In their attempts to use the media as a revolutionary tool, he argued, Hoffman and Rubin had ultimately betrayed the youth culture for which they claimed to speak. "By using youth-culture's surfaces as values and as challenges," he wrote, they "reduced the entire content of youth-culture for convenient assimilation by the spectacle."[68] The Yippies' celebrity was thus counterproductive, for ultimately their public personae served only to discredit the causes they claimed to advocate. By "defining the mass media as a Yippie tool of communication and politicization of unorganized youth," Fruchter argued, "the Yippie leadership was able to singlemindedly exploit its individual relationship with the mass media—indeed, it defined its assimilation by the spectacle *as its primary political work*."[69] True opposition, on the other hand, could exist only in its enactment. As Fruchter put it, "Individual spokesmen, however sensitive, could never have performed or represented" the values of the American youth culture, "for [those values] were embodied in collective work."[70] When they willingly played the role of the youth culture's "leaders," Hoffman and Rubin effectively sold out their own movement. Whether they intended to or not, the Yippies had reduced the youth culture "on the stage of the spectacle, and therefore in the mass mind of the national audience, to its lowest common denominator surfaces."[71]

For Fruchter, not unlike Brustein, the Yippies were not the only ones to make this fatal mistake. In fact, they were one of many organizations that had been defeated by their own naïve faith in a new technology. According to Fruchter, any attempt to use the mass media to build a revolutionary movement in the United States would be doomed to failure. "The spectacle is not subversive," he wrote, "it is the negation of subversion." Presented as reality tout court, the spectacle "is the most insidious and perfect employer of ideology, because it has achieved a total ideological construct which claims absolute neutrality for itself because it represents reality. *The problem of participation in the spectacle is the problem of finding the terms to struggle against a total ideological construct from within that construct, when that construct represents itself as reality*."[72] The media, in spite of its claims to an exhaustive realism, would never present the truth of political opposition. In representing activists and activism, the media only domesticated them, made them consumable. The mass media stripped protests and demonstrations of any real political import, and offered up their surfaces as truths.

What makes Fruchter's argument particularly interesting is that, when placed next to Brustein's complaints regarding the theatricality of calls for "revolution," the two authors effectively restate the dialectic of "repressive tolerance" outlined in 1966 by a frustrated Herbert Marcuse. As I have already explained, in the mid-1960s, Marcuse argued repeatedly that in the context of American liberal democracy, "tolerance" had become a parody of itself. The mass media, lauded by some for its democratic potential, had only served to negate political dissent. The press no longer acted as a check on state power but instead justified the status quo. In the papers, on the radio, or in television news broadcasts, one could say virtually anything one wanted because nothing was at stake. To use Hoffman's own example, no one would switch from being a Democrat to a Republican after watching *Meet the Press*, nor would they suddenly be convinced of the moral correctness of pacifism after hearing the arguments of an antiwar spokesman such as David Dellinger. Value judgments, as Marcuse explained, had been placed on all positions prior to their articulation. Given this unspoken bias, the apparent objectivity of the media had become an offense "against humanity and truth."[73] It had robbed individual acts and pronouncements of their political significance. One could "speak truth to power," but nothing would come of it, for a "spurious" tolerance had separated the public from its true "political existence." The normative order had colonized any and all opposition so thoroughly that particular grievances had been rendered largely meaningless. As a result, individuals had taken refuge in "the satisfactions of private and personal rebellion."[74] They had adopted the language of self-fulfillment, identifying in the process with an inherently hostile social order. In this context, nonconformity and "letting go," no matter how shocking they appeared to some, nevertheless left "the real engines of repression in the society entirely intact."[75] The apparently limitless tolerance for political disagreement was, in other words, simply another aspect of the more general phenomenon Marcuse described in *One-Dimensional Man* as "repressive desublimation" (a concept, it is worth noting, that essentially reversed the theory of perversion presented in *Eros and Civilization*). Thus, whether in the form of political speech or personal behavior, rebellion had been turned against itself; it had become the ultimate in conformity. And for Fruchter and Brustein, this is precisely what groups like the Yippies had failed to recognize. By treating the youth culture's appearance as a value in itself, Hoffman and Rubin had not rebelled so much as they had embodied a compromised, spectacular image of "rebellion."

To be sure, in arguing that the values of the youth culture were only ever accessible through their enactment, rather than their representation, Fruchter appears far more optimistic than Marcuse. For Fruchter, "real" progress could be made only through "real" personal and political work. Thus, he believed, the true value of the youth culture lay in its commitment to locating a form of personal authenticity without mistaking that authenticity for an end in itself. Similarly, in the case of the student New Left, victories, no matter how small, resulted not from outrageous pronouncements made to the media regarding the size or effectiveness of a given demonstration, but from the difficult work of grassroots political organization. The spectacle did not necessarily preclude these forms of personal and political labor, but in its equation of images and reality it had made them far more difficult. In spite of what Marcuse depicted as a set of virtually ineluctable historical limitations, it was still possible, and necessary, Fruchter believed, to envision and work toward substantive social change. And, like Brustein, Fruchter insisted that the way forward lay in "writing off" calls for "revolution" as little more than theater or spectacle, and rededicating oneself to the "real" task of grassroots organization. For the Yippies, however, the work of "real" organizing was no more immune to its own domestication than any other form of theater or politics: this was one of the points they sought to make with the Festival of Life. To their dismay, however, the Democratic Party seemed to have beaten them to the punch.

First, Lyndon Johnson announced in a televised speech on March 31 that he would not seek reelection. "He dropped out," Hoffman punned. "Remember a guy named Lyndon Johnson? He was so predictable when Yippie! began. And then pow! He really fucked us. He did the one thing no one had counted on. . . . 'My God,' we exclaimed. 'Lyndon is out-flanking us on our hippie side.'"[76] While the Yippies claimed to be bemused by Johnson's withdrawal, those involved with more traditional antiwar organizations were devastated. Certainly, there were those who saw Johnson's abdication as a victory; after all, one of the major factors in his decision had been the domestic unrest fomented largely by antiwar activists. Many more, though, were simply stunned. On one hand, Johnson's resignation had been coupled with an announcement that, in the wake of the Tet Offensive, the United States would soon deploy over 13,000 more troops to Vietnam. His announcement could in no way be interpreted as the beginning of the end of the war. Moreover, by recusing himself, Johnson robbed the antiwar movement of one of its most potent symbols. Activist Sam Brown recalls feeling that, though Johnson's withdrawal may have seemed a success to some, "emotionally, it was like, 'Oh my God. . . . We had this guy that we could point a finger at, and now it's more diffuse, it's impossible to get a handle on it, you can't see it anymore.'"[77]

Of course, the pressure exerted by antiwar activists was only part of the reason for Johnson's withdrawal. More than the activists themselves, Johnson had begun to fear the potential opposition of candidates who might capture the Democratic Party's presidential nomination by running on an antiwar platform. Apparently it was not America's disaffected youths that Johnson feared but the possibility of their incorporation within the Democratic Party. Eugene McCarthy's candidacy offered the first indication of this. McCarthy drew support from a number of peace activists, many of whom were willing to cut their hair, shave, and change their style of dress—to "Go Clean for Gene," as one of his campaign slogans urged—to legitimize his candidacy. McCarthy's advisers feared that the image of an antiwar candidate endorsed by unkempt, untamed "hippies" would make it difficult to be taken seriously, and the activists who supported him, willing to do whatever was necessary to end the war, complied. But no matter how "clean" his supporters were, McCarthy's campaign was never really taken seriously—insofar as a "serious" candidate is believed to be capable of winning—even by McCarthy himself. His hope in running, he explained, was merely to "build up enough pressure to force a change in policy."[78] Winning the Democratic Party nomination simply seemed unrealistic. To his surprise, however, voters responded favorably to the idea of an antiwar candidate, awarding him 42 percent of the votes cast in the New Hampshire Democratic primary. Many began to feel that if a peace candidate could fare so well in New Hampshire, a notoriously hawkish state, a candidate running on an antiwar platform truly could win the Democratic nomination. McCarthy, however, was still not perceived as the "right" candidate.

The antiwar candidacy that presented Johnson, and, oddly enough, the Yippies, with the most serious threat was that of Robert F. Kennedy, who began preparing to oppose Johnson early in 1968. One of Kennedy's first steps in plotting his campaign was to meet with prominent members of the antiwar movement. In January, Kennedy and his staff conferred with SDS leaders Tom Hayden and Carl Oglesby, asking them if they believed that Kennedy could secure the vote of the student antiwar movement. Far more optimistic about Kennedy's chances as a candidate than McCarthy, Oglesby told them that he would do his "damnedest, personally, to bring them in."[79] Virtually everything that McCarthy seemed to lack as a candidate, Kennedy possessed. Good-looking, charismatic, and the brother of one of the most popular presidents of the twentieth century, Kennedy appeared almost unbeatable. And when he officially announced his candidacy on March 16, it was a significant blow not only to Lyndon Johnson but also to the more radical members of the New Left. Battles were waged within movements such as SDS and the Mobe. Members concerned with doctrinal purity squared off against those who believed that the possibility of bringing an end to the war in Vietnam justified their participation in the two-party system of American politics. As Oglesby recalls, "To me there was no cooptation about it. If anyone was getting coopted, it was the Democratic Party. The movement was coopting the Democratic Party."[80]

Much as this would have seemed to prove the Yippies' point about the state of oppositional politics, it also presented a significant challenge to the Festival of Life. McCarthy "wasn't much," Hoffman explained. "One could secretly cheer for him the way you cheer for the Mets. It's easy, knowing he can never win." Kennedy, however, seemed just as adept at using the media and speaking to the youth of America as the Yippies. He was a "direct challenge . . . to the charisma of Yippie! *Come on*, Bobby said, *join the mystery battle against the television machine*. Participation mystique. Theater-in-the-streets. He played it to the hilt. And what was worse, Bobby had the money and power to build the stage. We had to steal ours. It was no contest. . . . When young longhairs told you how they'd heard that Bobby

turned on, you knew Yippie! was really in trouble."[81] The Democrats
had stolen the Yippies' thunder. "We took to drinking and praying
for LBJ to strike back," Hoffman wrote, "but he kept melting. Then
Hubert came along with the 'Politics of Joy' and Yippie! passed into
a state of catatonia which resulted in near permanent brain damage."[82] Though Kennedy's candidacy confirmed the party's ability
to annex the antiwar movement, if the Yippies hoped to pull off the
Festival of Life, what they needed most was not to be proven correct,
but theater.

Hoffman's problem was solved, to put it rather crudely, on June 5,
when Kennedy, just after his victory in the California primary, was
assassinated by Sirhan Sirhan, an event that, like the assassination
of his brother John, was its own sort of media event. Following on
the heels of the murder of Martin Luther King, Jr., for many members
of the student New Left Kennedy's death signified American society's
intransigence toward any version of reformist politics. Within SDS,
Kennedy's assassination set off a chain of events that ultimately
led to the organization's reformulation as the Revolutionary Youth
Movement, and finally, Weatherman.[83] As historian Tom Wells writes,
SDS's annual convention in June became "a time for determining
who had the mettle for battle and who didn't." For example, when
asked if she was a socialist, future Weatherleader Bernardine Dohrn
bristled at the use of such a demure descriptor. "I consider myself,"
she declared, "a revolutionary communist."[84]

In the July 7 issue of the *Realist*, the satirical newspaper edited
by Paul Krassner, Hoffman followed suit, in a sense. Describing Kennedy's assassination, he wrote, "The United States political system
was proving more insane than Yippie! Reality and unreality had in
six months switched sides. . . . How could we pull our pants down?
America was already naked."[85] Nevertheless, he explained, in the
wake of these events the Festival of Life was more important than
ever. Kennedy's assassination had essentially righted the Democrats'
ship. No longer threatened by the challenge of a truly electable antiwar candidate, Johnson's vice president, Hubert Humphrey, who
privately opposed the war but refused to do so in public, had all but
won the official nomination. It would be a mistake for demonstrators and partiers to shy away from Chicago because the Democratic
Party was, in Hoffman's words, "back to power politics, the politics

of big city machines and back-room deals. The Democrats had finally got their thing together by hook or crook and there it was for all to see—fat, ugly, and full of shit."[86]

Seeking to capitalize on the opportunity afforded by Kennedy's death, Hoffman distanced himself from the more outlandish rhetoric of his earlier statements, returning to the language of the Diggers' guerrilla theater. "What we need now," he told readers,

is the direct opposite approach to the one we began with. We must sacrifice suggestion for a greater degree of precision. We need a reality in the face of the American political myth. We have to kill Yippie! and still bring huge numbers to Chicago. . . . We will in Chicago begin the task of building Free America on the ashes of the old and from the inside out. . . . Do not come prepared to sit and watch and be fed and cared for. It just won't happen that way. It is time to become a life-actor. The days of the audience died with the old America. If you don't have a thing to do, stay home, you'll only get in the way.[87]

The "reality" to which Hoffman alludes in this passage certainly sounds like the reality of ticketless theater. The goal, he suggested, was not to expose the truth of the Democratic Party—the Democrats had already done that themselves—but to create a new reality, to present America with a vision of an alternative future. In his biography of Hoffman, Jonah Raskin cites this passage as an indication that the assassination of Robert Kennedy marked a turning point in Hoffman's political strategies and persona. "He didn't feel like 'Dwight Eisenhower on an acid trip' anymore," Raskin writes. Instead, he had become "the Lenin of the Flower Children."[88] According to Raskin, Kennedy's assassination turned Hoffman from mythmaker to revolutionary. Having been out-spectacled by the Democratic Party, Hoffman placed his put-ons and media tactics to the side in a sincere attempt to bridge the gap between the hippie counterculture and the New Left. As Hoffman put it, "The radical will say to the hippie: 'Get together and fight, you are getting the shit kicked out of you.' The hippie will say to the radical: 'Your protest is so narrow, your rhetoric so boring, your ideological power plays so old-fashioned.'" Nevertheless, each one could enlighten the other, "and Chicago—like the Pentagon demonstration before it—might well offer the medium to put forth that message."[89] In the wake of Kennedy's assassination, Raskin argues, the Festival of Life was no longer about imagery but about bringing America's oppositional youth cultures together as a unified movement.

To take this supposed political transformation seriously, however, one must ultimately take Hoffman at his word. This, as it should by now be clear, was always risky. Shortly after "The Yippies Are Going to Chicago" appeared in the *Realist*, Hoffman and Krassner flew to Chicago in a last-ditch effort to obtain the necessary legal permits for the Festival of Life. Having agreed to meet privately with Yippie representatives, deputy mayor David Stahl asked what, precisely, the Festival of Life would involve. "I dunno," Hoffman replied, "but whatever it is, it'll be designed to, uh, bring down the Democratic Party."[90] The Yippies had hardly put aside their hoaxes and put-ons. Hoffman's newfound sincerity, it seems, was itself little more than a ruse. Stahl, though, took Hoffman quite seriously, and for the last time denied the Yippies' request for a permit. Following the meeting, Stahl even composed a memo to city officials, warning that the Yippies would "try to involve their supporters in a revolution along the lines of the Berkeley and Paris incidents."[91] In response to Stahl's rejection, Hoffman held yet another press conference in which he offered a highly detailed schedule for the week of the convention. He promised that protestors would seize Chicago's Lincoln Park—which would, he told them, be officially renamed "Che Guevara National Park"—and camp out there throughout the convention. He then showed reporters a map that divided the park into areas with names like "Future City," "Free City," "Grub Town," and "Biker Park," and set aside space for a Free Store, a Church of the Free Spirit, a Free Theater, a hospital, and, most importantly, a Yippie Pentagon.

As in the earlier Yippie press conferences, none of these claims was actually true. Beyond the most basic elements of the Festival of Life—a stage, music, and an audience—concrete plans for Yippie activities in Chicago were virtually nonexistent. In spite of the increased urgency of his rhetoric in the *Realist*, Hoffman had no intention of organizing the creation of a new reality. This was not because he believed that to organize this new reality would be to hinder others' creativity, but because, much as the Diggers had suspected, that was never his goal. What the Yippies hoped would take

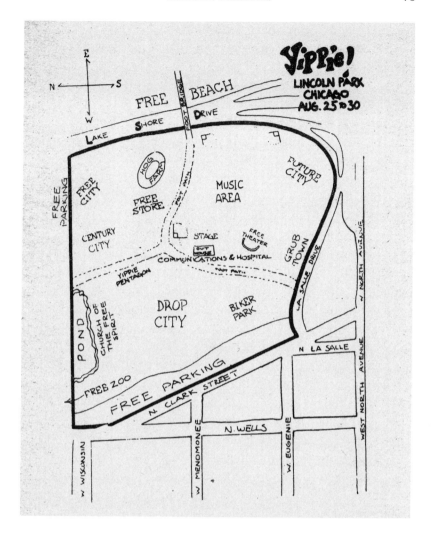

"Yippie! Lincoln Park." Image courtesy of the Estate of Abbie Hoffman.

place in Chicago, both before and after Kennedy's death, was monkey theater. The Festival of Life, much like the Pentagon demonstration, the YIP-in, the action at the New York Stock Exchange, and each of the Yippies' press conferences, was to be an image of "revolution," not the enactment of an authentic personal and political transformation. Rather than attempting to determine when and why Hoffman's political activism shifted from satire to seriousness, therefore, it seems far more important to determine why his version of monkey theater might have seemed a viable alternative for the work of political opposition.

Historian David Farber has argued that, beneath it all, the Yippies saw their misleading statements and outlandish performances as a new form of communication. He contends that the Yippies believed that the power of youth culture as such could render their media manipulations meaningful. They seemed to trust that their chosen audience would see all of the group's shenanigans, from the promised levitation of the Pentagon to the nomination of a pig for president, for what they really were. "At their most hopeful and committed," Farber writes, "the Yips really believed that the turned-on generation they were playing to could use their acid vision and dope dreams, the energy of their rock 'n' roll hearts, and even the jaded sophistication of their TV souls to take the Yippies' mixed fantasies for their structural riches and absurdly correct political message."[92] The Yippies may have sounded ridiculous, that is, but not to fellow members of the youth culture. According to Farber's reading, therefore, critics such as Fruchter, Brustein, and Roszak were ultimately guilty of a regrettable oversimplification. In attempting, rather cynically, to reduce the Yippies' pronouncements to nothing more than a simple case of misguided hyperbole, these authors failed to account for the Yippies' guiding vision of a "Free America"—a vision, Farber writes, fueled largely by the more intense forms of experience and perception available through "drug consciousness."[93] Hoffman and Rubin saw the counterculture not as a simple pathway to fame and personal gain but as a community capable of enacting real, substantive change. The Yippies truly believed, Farber writes, "that they shared a counterculture, a counterepistemology, with a whole generation who were just waiting to turn their truths into workable power."[94] The Yippies' performances were not nonsensical but intentionally misleading. By playing on Americans' fears regarding the counterculture, Hoffman and Rubin stole airtime from the networks and used it to broadcast a message decipherable only by their peers. That message would be one of truth and empowerment, a call urging members of the counterculture to come together and create a new, free society. For Farber, therefore, it would be a mistake to say that Hoffman's mission was somehow fundamentally different following the assassination of Robert Kennedy. To the contrary, "Dwight Eisenhower on an acid trip" was, both before and after Kennedy's death, the ironic caricature that enabled the "Lenin of the Flower Children" to speak. While Farber's attempt to salvage the Yippies' political legacy is admirable, he overlooks one crucial detail. The Yippies' pronouncements and protests were, as Hoffman described them, put-ons. As such, according to Jacob Brackman, they were designed not to conceal deeper truths but to repeatedly frustrate any attempt to speak of an underlying "truth." The put-on, as Brackman put it, "inherently *cannot* be understood."[95] It was not a way of saying one thing to indicate another but a way of uprooting any conversational position that one might have presumed fixed. By embodying stereotypes, the put-on artist sought not a new, technologically savvy form of communication but a means of highlighting the always already circumscribed language of opposition. In this sense, Hoffman's deployment of the put-on as a political tactic may have been rooted not in his faith in a liberated "counterepistemology" but in his relation to the work of Marcuse. Contrary to those who, like Brustein, Roszak, and Fruchter, claimed that Hoffman's antics were counterproductive because they were, in essence, not Marcusean enough, I believe that it is possible to read his put-ons as an attempt to grapple with the difficulties of representing dissent in the face of what seemed a truly "repressive tolerance."

If rational arguments and traditional activism had been rendered effectively toothless by the "normal course of events," if they had indeed become just another facet of that "normal course of events," how could one hope to speak of resistance in anything other than the inherently compromised terms of one-dimensional society? This, as I have already indicated, was the problem that vexed Marcuse throughout the 1960s. Perversion, art, grassroots politics: virtually all forms of opposition seemed to have succumbed to the logic of the technological society. It had become nearly impossible to locate a potential space of critique. But for Hoffman, it was precisely this hope for transcendence that had to be abandoned. Rather than lamenting one's inevitable submission to the constraints of one-dimensional society, it was instead necessary to concentrate on the ways in which one's gestures capitulated to those constraints. "Hippies," as Hoffman wrote in 1967, "are a myth created by the media and as such they are forced to play certain media-oriented roles. They are media-manipulated. . . . We have learned to manipulate the media."[96] What makes this last distinction fascinating is that "media-manipulating" and "media-manipulated" were, for many audiences, indistinguishable. As an elaborate put-on, the Yippies appropriated and re-presented the images of spurious liberation made available through popular culture itself. On one hand, they did so in an effort to appeal to the media. To ensure media coverage for their actions, they adopted the formal qualities of that which had already been deemed newsworthy. On the other hand, the stereotypical notion of hippie culture as nothing more than unchecked hedonism was, in the Yippies' media performances, pushed to the point of sheer absurdity. Seeking to capture the attention of journalists without falling into the traps of media manipulation—without, in other words, simply reinforcing the logic of repressive tolerance—the Yippies performed a campy exaggeration of what many assumed to be the "hippie ethos." As Hoffman wrote, "We cry 'No one understands us,' while at the same time winking out of the corner of our eye, recognizing that if the straight world understood all this . . . it would render us impotent, because understanding is the first step to control and control is the secret to our extinction."[97] Through the self-conscious redeployment of images of countercultural "liberation" and "revolution," Hoffman and the Yippies interrogated the assumptions of dominant culture, and, by extension, the oppositional practices shaped by those assumptions.

Again, my intention is not to contend that Hoffman's antics offered a "pure" or uncompromised counterpoint to the New Left's and counterculture's callow calls for "authentic" forms of politics or liberation. This would only be to reintroduce the notion of critical transcendence that the put-on showed to be historically and politically bankrupt. It may be more accurate to read Hoffman's facetiously "revolutionary" rhetoric as an attempt to give form to what one might call, for lack of a better term, something like a postmodern mode of resistance, one that proclaims its own liberation while demonstrating the absurdity of that very claim. Where Marcuse, Roszak, Brustein, and Fruchter hoped for a form of rebellion that would provide a path of flight, Hoffman's performances of a "rebellious," hypersexualized, drug-addled vision of "revolution" suggested that any traditional notion of escape was no longer valid. Interpreting the Yippies' performance of "cultural revolution" as a put-on, rather than an ill-conceived effort to communicate a "counterepistemology," we can perhaps start to see the appeal of waging "revolution for the hell of it." Hoffman's willingness to embrace his own stardom, in other words, betrayed not the "revolution" of the New Left but its historical preclusion.

2. "WATCH OUT FOR PIGS IN QUEEN'S CLOTHING"

Camp and the Image of
Radical Sexuality

SURELY, THE YIPPIES' APPROACH TO ACTIVISM WAS NOT WITHOUT its critics. As I have already explained, there were many in the antiwar movement who believed that the group's grandstanding stood in the way of the "real" work of grassroots organizing, and advocates of the counterculture who believed that Hoffman and Rubin had simply missed the point of calls for "free love" and personal liberation. But in the summer of 1969, a different critique of these tactics began to gain traction, one leveled, perhaps most surprisingly, by former Yippie Jim Fourratt. Fourratt's feelings about the political utility of a pseudo-organization based solely on a series of put-ons changed dramatically following the Stonewall riots in New York. For Fourratt, the only openly gay Yippie, practices of impersonation and dissimulation had come to seem a political luxury that gay men and lesbians simply could not afford. Having stood up to the New York police in Greenwich Village, he believed, a new generation of radicalized gay and lesbian activists would henceforth reject any form of role-playing. "Homosexuals" had been "camping it up" for far too long; gay liberation would never be achieved through further masquerade. For Fourratt, gay men and lesbians could not impersonate police officers, judges, or soldiers, just as they could no longer impersonate heterosexuals or the opposite gender. It was time, he believed, to be honest with themselves and with the rest of the world. As he told a community meeting that fall, gay men "have got to radicalize, man! . . . No matter what you do in bed, if you're not a man out of it, you're going to get screwed up. Be proud of what you are man! And if it takes riots or even guns to show them what we are, that's the only language the pigs understand!"[1] No longer content to remain closeted, gay liberationists such as Fourratt believed that perhaps the most radical gesture available to lesbians and gay men was to "come out," presenting the world with an adequate vision of what same-sex sexuality really was.

Yet many who fought for gay liberation were less put off by Hoffman's and Rubin's antics. As Pat Maxwell put it in one issue of the Gay Liberation Front's newsletter *Come Out!*, "Jerry Rubin and Abbie Hoffman, hippie and yippie, why did you dress in all those costumes, Indian drag, police drag, Uncle Sam drag, and never once cross the sex role boundary? You came so close to the point, and then you petered out. Just couldn't keep it up, hippie brother."[2] For transsexuals and drag queens, Maxwell suggests, the problem with the Yippies was not their willingness to engage in campy political masquerade but their failure to recognize the most profound implications of those acts. Their put-ons may have highlighted certain fissures present within images of the counterculture, but because they refused to perform any roles other than those clearly marked as masculine, the Yippies' tactics left the foundational myths of gender and sexuality firmly in place. "Men write the script, design the costumes, and direct the play," Maxwell continued; "roles are not clearly understood and we need to fully explore the way that we use roles, and the roles use us."[3] To shed light on the oppressive conventionality of sex roles, the "masquerade" would have to assume a different form. For this reason, Maxwell argued, the figure of the drag queen, who crossed the boundaries of gender and effectively renounced any claim to "masculine privilege," embodied the potential critical power of a radical social and sexual politics.[4] For Maxwell, what Hoffman and Rubin had only begun to understand, namely the potential critical power of masquerade, had been a central theme in queer culture from at least the early twentieth century. From the drag queen to the radical transsexual, he argued, cross-dressing's self-conscious inversion of gender was the most radical form not just of gay liberation, but of *all* contemporary political and cultural opposition.

This debate, between those who see an unflinching sincerity as the key to gay liberation and those who believe that practices of camp, drag, butch/femme, and so on are in the end far more challenging to an oppressive system of gender and sexuality, has been rehearsed repeatedly over the past forty years.[5] In this chapter, therefore, I would like to hold that debate, at least temporarily, in abeyance, and to focus on the aesthetics of gay liberation, asking if the act of "coming out," the authenticity advocated by certain members of this movement, might also be read as a form of drag. What conceptions and conventions governed the disclosure of one's sexual identity in the summer of 1969? How was the radical gay identity called for by Fourratt and others formulated? What did its enactment reveal not only about the gay liberation movement but also about its ideological and aesthetic sources? And finally, could an unapologetic gay or lesbian identity have been turned back upon itself? Might it have been used not to reveal the "truth" of same-sex sexuality but to place the very notion of homosexuality in quotes, as it were, just as the visible forms of this identity were being codified? A careful analysis of different positions represented within the movement for gay liberation in the year following the Stonewall riots, I believe, highlights the ways in which the actions and writings of individuals within that movement often emphasized not the sincerity, authenticity, or adequacy of self-presentation but the political and cultural limitations on that self-presentation. Rather than rejecting "the homosexual role," many proponents of gay liberation seem to have considered that role, precisely because of its purported shortcomings, politically useful.[6] And, perhaps most interestingly, by placing the post-Stonewall gay liberation movement alongside, first, the actions of earlier "homophile" organizations such as the Mattachine Society, and second, the work of contemporary film critic Parker Tyler, one begins to see that in spite of the apparent ideological rift between drag and the enactment of an authentic/radical gay identity, the two were in important ways inseparable. It is important, therefore, to consider the divisions within the gay liberation movement not as a case of radicalism versus reformism, as many have argued, but as another version of the contemporary struggle over the relationship between politics and performance.

To make sense of the battle over personal and political (re)pre-sentation within the gay liberation movement of the late 1960s, it is first necessary to understand the relation of that movement to the "homophile" organizations of the 1950s and early 1960s, particularly the organization known as the Mattachine Society.[7] Although often dismissed by members of the post-Stonewall gay liberation move-ment for its "assimilationist" agenda, Mattachine had not always taken social integration to be its goal. Founded in April 1951 by Harry Hay, the Mattachine Society was conceived as a radical organization working to secure the rights of gay men as a political and cultural minority. Motivated by the State Department's decision to purge suspected homosexuals from the federal workforce in the years 1947–49—a decision that resulted in the dismissal of ninety men and women who were said to be "security risks," as their "deviant" sexuality purportedly made them vulnerable to blackmail—Hay's initial manifesto evoked visions of Nazi Germany. An entire class of men and women had been singled out for virtual eradication; it was tantamount to the rise of an "American fascism."[8] If gay men and les-bians failed to stand up for themselves, Hay argued, the revocation of government security clearances would be only the beginning. If they were refused the security clearances required in working for the federal government, then, given the increasing dependence of private industry on government contracts, those men and women would soon be unable to find gainful employment of any kind. Hay thus urged homosexuals to stand together as a social minority based in a shared cultural tradition. In so doing, they could show that these efforts to purge gay men and lesbians from the federal workforce were nothing less than a form of discrimination. Homosexuals, he contended, should never accept an essentially meaningless "equal-ity"—one that could be guaranteed only if gay men and lesbians were willing to adopt the roles and mannerisms of the dominant culture. Rather, "Society's Androgynous Minority," as he originally called his proposed organization, should work toward freedom and equality for homosexuals *as homosexuals*. The goal was not to be assimilated, or even tolerated, but to be accepted as the true equals of the het-erosexual majority. As the first step in this process, Hay's organiza-tion would need to promote the sense of a homosexual community.

The Mattachine Society, as he eventually came to call it, thus held regular meetings, published and distributed its own newsletter, and constantly sought ways to bring gay men together so that they might recognize themselves as a political force.

Not long after the organization's founding, however, a number of Mattachine's members became uncomfortable with Hay's calls for political intervention. Even with the organization's support they still feared for their jobs and their safety, and preferred to keep their sexual identity a secret. The tension between these two positions boiled over just two years after the society's founding, when member Kenneth Burns used rumors of Hay's past involvement in the Communist Party to affect a coup. Given the ease with which communism and homosexuality had been equated and even conflated during the McCarthy hearings, the awareness of Hay's communist past could hardly have comforted the society's more anxious members.[9] Burns argued that Mattachine could better serve its members by providing them with moral and social support while maintaining a certain level of secrecy—allowing them to feel a sense of community without threatening their livelihoods. A majority of the members agreed, and in November 1953, Hay's involvement with the Mattachine Society came to an end.

Ironically, by going underground the society flourished. New chapters, not to mention a number of smaller, local "homophile" organizations, formed in cities around the country. The members of these organizations chose to be known as homo*philes*, as opposed to homo*sexuals*, in an attempt to emphasize the emotional dimension of same-sex relationships. They hoped that by eliding the sexual aspect of those relationships, they would be more likely to gain the respect of heterosexuals. As Mattachine's new leaders explained, "The Society's aims" were now "primarily directed toward full integration . . . and not the establishment of any special 'culture.'"[10] Rather than seeking to win their rights as a cultural or political minority, these men and women looked first to convince the rest of society that, aside from what they happened to do in the privacy of their own bedrooms, they were in fact no different from anyone else. Looking to avoid the stigma of sexual "inversion," Mattachine's members insisted on the ability of one man to love another—as a man. Gay men, they argued, were not women trapped in men's bodies; with the exception of their sexual choices, they were "normal," "natural" men.[11] Much as with their adoption of the term "homophile," Mattachine's members believed that by insisting that homosexuality left one's "natural" gender undisturbed, they could eventually make heterosexuals realize just how much they had in common. Emphasizing their similarities rather than their differences, they believed, would enable them to assimilate.

The society's official pursuit of integration and invisibility, not surprisingly, began virtually at the same moment that the United States government intensified its own efforts to make gay men and lesbians visible. With the publication of the first volume of Alfred Kinsey's monumental study of human sexuality, *Sexual Behavior in the Human Male*, many Americans had begun to fear that virtually any of their friends, family members, or coworkers could experience erotic feelings toward someone of the same sex. On one hand, as Mary McIntosh argued, Kinsey's findings opened the possibility of radically new solutions to the "problem" of the "homosexual condition." His report offered proof that the "homosexual" was a stereotypical social role rather than an actual identity, and that, contrary to popular belief, a great deal of homosexual behavior occurred independently of any purportedly recognizable "homosexuality." Kinsey's report, McIntosh wrote, suggested that "the polarization between the heterosexual man and the homosexual man is far from complete," and that the stigmatization of homosexuals in society was the result of nothing other than "ethnocentric bias."[12] But the timing of Kinsey's report opened his findings to a second, very different interpretation as well. As Jonathan Dollimore has demonstrated, at times of intense social struggle, conflict is often displaced onto the sexual "deviant." This practice succeeds, he explains, because the essential instability of dominant cultural identities enables particular forms of transgression to be "not only loosely associated with the sexual deviant, but 'condensed' in the very definition of deviance."[13] Much as sodomy was associated with witches, demons, werewolves, and papists in Renaissance England, in late-1940s America, Kinsey's report seemed for many to provide evidence of the invisible menace threatening the stability of the government and the country as a whole: communism.[14] In the interest of "national security," it appeared absolutely essential that these "deviants" be ferreted out, made visible.[15]

But enumerating the visual indices of sexual "deviance" proved quite difficult. After all, what made minority sexualities so threatening in the first place was their reputed ability to go undetected. The attempt to forge an official position on homosexuality was therefore caught between the desire to make this particular form of "deviance" legible and the need to emphasize its theoretical dangers. To balance these two competing goals, as Robert Corber has shown, the Senate Appropriations Committee formulated its definition of homosexuality through a peculiar combination of medical discourses and popular stereotypes. On one hand, the committee's report repeatedly called upon the notion that homosexuality was little more than a "sickness" or "perversion." This reinforced the impression that gay men and lesbians were in every other way "just like everyone else," and thus intensified the hysteria regarding homosexuals as a scarcely detectable menace lurking among, and preying upon, the general population. Yet this also forced the committee to confirm that homosexuals were not entirely indistinguishable from their heterosexual colleagues, that gay men and lesbians could indeed be identified and expunged from the federal workforce. To this end, while the male homosexual was at times said to be capable of appearing just as masculine as his heterosexual counterpart, the committee's report also invoked stereotypical notions of the gay man as, among other things, "effeminate in his mannerisms and appearance."[16]

Worried that gay men may never gain acceptance if they continued to associate themselves with the same stereotypical personae that had been used to vilify them, the Mattachine Society turned all potential transvestite and transsexual members away. Nevertheless, no matter how Mattachine's members presented themselves, making homosexuality appear respectable in the eyes of a culture for which it was, by definition, beyond respectability was a nearly impossible task. The very grimness of their predicament, as John D'Emilio writes, ultimately "created a crippling dependency" on the "expert" opinions that constituted the other half of the government's attack.[17] And, as the organization attempted to deal with this predicament, the politics of assimilation often slipped into a more pernicious form of self-loathing. As Burns put it in his 1956 address to the Mattachine Society's annual convention, "We can never adequately solve the problems which face us without first solving the problems within us. . . . We must blame ourselves for much of our plight. When will the homosexual ever realize that social reform, to be effective, must be preceded by personal reform?"[18] Publications such as the *Mattachine Review* and the Daughters of Bilitis's *Ladder* even began to open their pages to articles and essays that, speaking from a position of scientific "expertise," described same-sex desire as a symptom of individual neurosis or psychosis.[19] For these authors, homophile organizations of the 1950s seemed to offer a convenient forum for group therapy.

Not all of the society's members agreed with these analyses, of course, and certain local chapters became directly involved in the pursuit of political and legal reform.[20] By the end of the decade these internal tensions had brought the national organization to its knees. Although there were still a number of local chapters using the Mattachine name, by 1960 each one operated virtually independently of the others. In 1961, however, Franklin Kameny, a former government astronomer, attempted to resurrect Mattachine's more radical past, beginning with a new chapter in Washington, DC, modeled on the African American Civil Rights movement.[21]

Dismissed by the government in 1957, and unable to find a new position because of his official classification as a "security risk," in 1961 Kameny was virtually penniless, and unwilling to wait for whatever changes might result from the "genteel, debating society approach" of the existing homophile movement.[22] The new Mattachine Society of Washington (MSW), as Kameny's constitution declared, would not "act as a social group, or as an agency for personal introductions"; it would function as a "social action group . . . dedicated to improving the status of the homosexual in our society, in the interest both of that minority group and of the Nation."[23] Under Kameny's leadership, MSW would not accept assimilation as its goal. Following the lead of Hay's manifesto, the organization would fight for the equality of gay men and lesbians as a minority. Never again would the pages of the newsletter be filled with the opinions of medical professionals seeking to "cure" the reader. As Kameny said in a speech to the Mattachine Society of New York (MSNY) in 1964, "Our opponents will do a fully adequate job of presenting their views, and will not return us the favor of presenting ours; we gain nothing in virtue by presenting theirs."[24]

The following year, Kameny, working together with Craig Rodwell and Dick Leitsch of MSNY, and Randy Wicker, founder of the Homosexual League of New York, managed to forge an overarching coalition of East Coast Homophile Organizations (ECHO), comprised of groups from Washington, Philadelphia, and New York. Bringing organizations like the Daughters of Bilitis and MSNY together with more openly political collectives like MSW and the Homosexual League of New York, ECHO enabled the militant faction of the homophile movement both to solidify its own ideology and, eventually, to overwhelm the more cautious leadership of the homophile old guard. Indeed, this had been Kameny's and Wicker's goal all along—not simply to bring together geographically distant homophile groups but also to make ECHO the driving force behind a radical transformation of the movement as a whole. And by the end of 1965, two of the largest moderate organizations had been directly affected by the resulting shift in the movement. Leitsch, once a disaffected radical within MSNY, was elected the organization's president, and a heated internal debate had begun within the New York chapter of the Daughters of Bilitis over the organization's refusal to endorse a proposal to stage official ECHO demonstrations in places like Philadelphia and Washington, DC.

In retrospect, these demonstrations were anything but immoderate. Much like the organizers of the 1963 March on Washington, Kameny formulated specific guidelines explaining how ECHO members should behave when on official picket lines. Picketing was not to be seen as "an occasion for an assertion of personality, individuality, ego, rebellion, generalized non-conformity or anti-conformity."[25] Like the rest of ECHO's leaders, Kameny hoped to distance the organization from stereotypes, and to emphasize that, no matter how militant their stance, homophiles were ultimately "conservative and conventional" human beings.[26] Participants, therefore, were to march in single-file lines; women were to wear dresses, and men suits, regardless of the weather. Outward displays of anger or affection, along with less obviously challenging behaviors such as smoking and talking, were forbidden, and signs were to be approved by ECHO officials, who would determine the order in which they were to be carried. Organization officials would be in place on the day of each protest to remove any demonstrators who dared break Kameny's rules. In

Franklin Kameny, Philadelphia 1965. Photo by Kay Tobin Lahusen.
Image courtesy of the New York Public Library.

1966, for example, at the second "Annual Reminder," a yearly march
staged on July 4 outside of Philadelphia's Independence Hall, Kameny
pulled one man from the picket line for attempting to march in sneak-
ers and shirtsleeves. Three years later, just days after the Stonewall
riots, two women who had been bold enough to march side by side
holding hands were scolded and separated.

Not surprisingly, 1969 was the last year that ECHO held its Annual Reminder. This was not only because activists had grown weary of ECHO's strict code of conduct, but also because in the summer of 1969 another, younger generation of activists, inspired by the political actions of the student New Left and the counterculture's talk of personal and social liberation, had begun to assert its own pressure on the movement for gay and lesbian equality. These activists rejected more than the political tactics of the homophile movement; they rejected the notion of the "homophile" altogether. As Dennis Altman wrote in his classic text, *Homosexual: Oppression and Liberation*, this new, unapologetic movement for "gay liberation" drew on the counterculture's rejection of pretense, its presumed disdain for role-playing. For these activists, he wrote, "to be told not to come out publicly because of social consequences becomes merely a reason to be more blatant." Taking their inspiration from the counterculture's "rejection of euphemisms," gay radicals, like their straight counterparts, hoped ultimately to rid themselves of hypocrisy—though, as Altman acknowledged, there was also "a desire to assault the old consciousness by shock tactics and to find phrases that cannot easily be co-opted by the mass media."[27]

The rejection of secrecy, of the "closet," was one of the central tenets of the redefined movement for gay liberation. But for many of the movement's members, the closet signified more than just the work of concealing one's sexuality. In much of the early literature of the gay liberation movement, to acknowledge one's homosexuality while insisting that one was nevertheless "the same as" heterosexuals was, in effect, to deny one's identity, and hence to remain "in the closet." One had to recognize that to be a gay man or a lesbian was to be somehow fundamentally different. As Brian Chavez wrote in the San Francisco paper *Gay Sunshine*, "It's time to be YOURSELF! Don't blend in with Straight people—that's oppressing yourself. BLATANT IS BEAUTIFUL!"[28] Gay liberationists such as Chavez would no longer hide or apologize for themselves; they would not pretend to be "the same as" anyone else. Secretive organizations, double lives, and "conservative and conventional" calls for equal rights had failed. Any demonstration that required one to wear a suit or a dress, or to carry a sign bearing a "reasonable" slogan, was no longer acceptable. Gay men and lesbians, they believed, had to be honest with "straight society," and, more importantly, with themselves. It was no longer enough simply to "come out." By the summer of 1969, visibility, like its perceived opposite, the closet, meant something more.

Just what visibility should come to mean was one of the organizing themes of Carl Wittman's pamphlet "Refugees from Amerika: A Gay Manifesto." Writing in San Francisco virtually as the Stonewall riots were taking place, Wittman urged all gay men and lesbians to follow the example of the "hip revolution" and end, once and for all, their "mimicry" of the roles of "straight" society. That society, he explained, was maintained through role-playing and dissemblance. The institution of marriage, for example, required strict adherence to a set of conventions that "smother[ed] both people, denie[d] needs, and place[d] impossible demands on both people."[29] Instead of castigating themselves for their failure to conform to these roles, Wittman argued, gay men and lesbians should attempt to recognize the power to be gained by refusing to play them at all: "For too long we mimicked these roles to protect ourselves—a survival mechanism. Now we are becoming free enough to shed the roles which we've picked up from the institutions which have imprisoned us."[30] Only by refusing to carry on the "burlesque" of heteronormative society, by rejecting the dissimulation and isolation of "closet queenery" in favor of an authentic, visible community, could gay men and lesbians ever be free. "If we are liberated," Wittman wrote, "we are open with our sexuality."[31]

Many took this call to root out all forms of role-playing and mimicry quite literally. In an early issue of *Come Out!*, Perry Brass wrote that it was the duty of every gay man to "reject what straight society has straight-jacketed us with and form our own life as *real* people, not merely imitating the old male chauvinist roles left over from a dodo society."[32] It was important to recognize, according to Brass, that identifying oneself as a gay man did not make one innocent. One could be gay and still perpetuate the oppressive "games" of heterosexual society. The "cruelest" of those games, he argued, was that of "cruising," seeking sexual partners in bars, bathhouses, and so on, while playing a predetermined role to gain the upper hand in any resulting relationship. No matter the venue, "there are always the same roles," from the "aggressive animal," always seeking his "type," to the "put-up artist who has to first off embarrass you with how you're the most beautiful thing he's ever seen."[33] Whether dominant or submissive, assertive or coy, these roles were "designed by fear. Just as we act in straight society out of fear that they will discover us, we react with each other out of fear that we will discover ourselves also."[34] For Brass, only by refusing to play these "male chauvinist roles"—by facing up to "the reality of our situation: that we are all outcasts"—could gay men ever achieve true liberation.[35]

But the forms of role-playing most frequently denounced in these polemics were those of camp and drag. As Craig Alfred Hanson put it, the movement for gay liberation was "an escape from the old fairyland, and Judy Garland, and from the traditional gay subculture."[36] These behaviors, according to Hanson, were perhaps the most insidious forms of self-deception. They were the refuge of "gay traditionalists" who mistook the ruling classes' fascination for acceptance. Five years after Susan Sontag had written that "homosexuals [had] pinned their integration into society on promoting the aesthetic sense," Hanson, and many others, asserted that any integration achieved in this fashion was merely illusory.[37] Historically, he wrote, this "fairyland . . . was reserved just for us as our very special place to live our very special way of life. . . . Despised as we were, we were still their pampered pets in gilded cages."[38] Gay men, that is, as "fairy princesses," were allowed to exist only because they were perceived as wholly innocuous. They were limited to providing luxuries to the wealthy that merely reinforced and romanticized dominant fictions of class, gender, and sexuality. It was absolutely essential, therefore, that "we . . . make our gay brothers realize that the princess trip is a rotten one, a self-deluding flight into a past that never was, an artificiality, and an escape from reality."[39] The "aesthetic sense" would have to be abandoned in favor of true expressions of what Gary Alinder called "gay soul."[40]

In the more recent essay "Making the Homophile Manifest," Mark Jordan writes that this disdain for the mimicry of "straight" society was rooted in a desire to distinguish the post-Stonewall gay liberation movement from the integrationist politics of pre-Stonewall homophile organizations like the Mattachine Society. In the months following the riots, the question of what would ultimately "count as a truly homosexual identity—which is to say, as appropriate homosexual visibility" was central to the "quarrel" between homophiles and gay liberationists.[41] According to Jordan, what distinguished gay liberationists from the older generation of homophiles was the former's commitment to a particular notion of literal self-display—not literal self-display as a gay man or lesbian but, more specifically, as a gay liberationist. True as this may have been in a number of cases, however, the purported literalism of gay liberation foundered on the place of practices like camp and drag within the movement. While there were those who, like Hanson, saw the "fairy princess" as a regressive, delusional mode of role-playing, there were others who, like Wittman, believed that it was instead the vilification of the "princess" that was regressive. As he put it, "There is a tendency . . . to deplore gays who play visible roles—the queens and the nellies. As liberated gays, we must take a clear stand. (1) Gays who stand out have become our first martyrs. They came out and withstood disapproval before the rest of us did. (2) If they have suffered from being open, it is straight society whom we must indict, not the queen."[42] While the "queens and nellies" may have been guilty of playing roles, those roles nevertheless seemed to Wittman a clear affirmation of an alternative sexual identity. If members of the gay liberation movement sought to distinguish themselves from the earlier generation of homophiles by embracing their visibility, it would be unwise to dismiss these "queens and the nellies" out of hand.

This ambivalence over the acceptability of camp and drag is evident in Altman's analysis as well. Although he argued that the gay liberation movement was founded on a "rejection of euphemisms," he nonetheless failed to resolve the relationship between self-disclosure and the exaggerated role-playing of camp and drag. On one hand, he argued that these practices were inherently tied to the stereotypes of effeminacy and gender inversion that had long plagued gay men. For this reason, "there is something vulgar or pathetic in a group of middle-aged homosexuals, freed momentarily from the need for concealment, 'shrieking' together. . . . Because there is, as yet, no genuine homosexual community, homosexuals take their cues from the straight world, and, as is often true of out-groups . . . end up *plus royaliste que le roi*."[43] Like Hanson and Brass, Altman would have liked to dismiss camp and sexual role-playing as nothing but the last vestiges of an oppressive sexual and social hierarchy. On the other hand, he explained that part "of coming out is the adoption of the characteristics seen as belonging to homosexuals, so that men will sometimes seem effeminate or women over-aggressive."[44] Much as Altman disliked them, that is, clichés of sexual "inversion" were undeniably useful. In spite of its apparently regressive nature, role-playing was an integral part of personal liberation. Although it perpetuated the damaging stereotypes of a hostile social order, it also served as the essential first step toward combating that order.

In practice, this inability to come to terms with camp, drag, and so on, meant that drag queens, transvestites, and even lesbians who appeared too butch were often either patronized or shunned. Whatever one might say about their visibility or their personal political commitment, for many, practices of cross-dressing or gender "impersonation" still seemed to be the effects of a corrupt political and sexual system. As one cartoon on the cover of an early *Gay Flames* pamphlet warned, those interested in gay liberation should "Watch out for pigs in queen's clothing." Historian Martin Duberman notes that in the Gay Liberation Front some members did attempt to defend drag queens' right to attend meetings, pointing out that the riots at the Stonewall Inn or at San Francisco's Compton's Cafeteria three years earlier would not have happened without them. These explanations, however, "would usually be greeted by more boos than applause."[45] As the aforementioned cartoon suggests through its depiction of a pig posing as an odalisque in a rigid, cone-shaped bra—one that might be used, one supposes, to give the appearance of breasts where none exist—no matter how seductive these queens might have appeared, beneath the surface lurked an oppressive, chauvinistic swine. When street queens such as Sylvia Rivera began attending GLF meetings in 1969, they encountered a great deal of personal resistance. Although some of the men and women in the group eventually befriended Rivera, they were nevertheless uncomfortable with what they saw as the inherently regressive politics of drag. No matter how they felt about her as an individual, the "jewelry, makeup, and tight clothes" she wore ultimately signified "exactly what women were trying to get rid of."[46] Karla Jay attempted to explain to her more than once that drag queens "are *not* really women, you are biological men and can reclaim that privilege at any time. *We* are females forever."[47]

In response to their exclusion from organizations such as the GLF, a small number of transvestites and transsexuals argued that they

"Renoir," Watch Out for Pigs in Queen's Clothing, *Gay Flames* 4, 1970.

too deserved to be acknowledged as a social minority. In an early issue of *Come Out!*, Laura McAlister wrote, "Transvestism, unfortunately, is a practice frequently misunderstood by nearly everyone, including gay people, and this misunderstanding has bred much intolerance. The time has now come to change this."[48] Transvestites were not "imitation women," she insisted, nor were they the manifestation of sexual inversion. To the contrary, they were a "diversified" group of heterosexuals and homosexuals "who receive a psychic and physical thrill from wearing the clothes of the opposite sex."[49] Although transvestites constituted, in McAlister's view, a subculture quite distinct from that of gay men and lesbians, almost no one seemed to recognize the difference.[50] Few publications catered to transsexuals or transvestites (Times Square, she wrote, "that remarkable repository of exotic books, has only one bookstore that regularly carries books and magazines on the subject"[51]) and very little effort had been made to understand them. Even the "scientific" community, with the exception of Harry Benjamin, had largely ignored transvestism and transsexualism.[52] The result, as McAlister put it, was a generalized ignorance, "which in turn has produced enormous anxieties, guilt feelings, and a terrible sense of isolation in many transvestites, and has also given rise to oppressive laws and attitudes in our society."[53] The time had come to recognize that transvestites and transsexuals were a distinct minority, oppressed in the very same ways that African Americans, women, gay men, and lesbians were, and that it was just as important to fight for their liberation.

While McAlister chose to argue for the rights of transvestites and transsexuals as a distinct minority identity, in the following issue of *Come Out!*, Pat Maxwell contended that transsexuals and drag queens should be viewed not as a minority identity but as a symbol of the gay liberation movement's true potential. Drag queens were not remnants of an oppressive masculinity, s/he explained, but perhaps the most radical of all cultural revolutionaries. "When a man in our society grows his hair long, puts on a dress, and walks among us she is in effect giving up her male privilege." As a result, "she is not oppressing women, she is threatening men! The queen is the lavender menace to the male chauvinist. When every man is able to cross the sex role boundary, then and only then will women cease to be sex objects. The Gay Liberation movement should affirm and not deny the transsexual in us all. Queens are in the vanguard of the sexual revolution."[54] For Maxwell, drag queens, butches, and transsexuals were neither a regressive, insulting "imitation" of gender roles nor a painful reminder of the stereotypical conception of gay men and lesbians as sexual "inverts." Rather, these figures, which in a single gesture called attention to and problematized the assumption that the bipartite division of genders was somehow "natural," presented another, more powerful critique of sexual norms. As Marjorie Garber would argue roughly twenty years later, the figure of the cross-dresser offered a challenge to easy suppositions of a male/female binary, casting doubt on those very categories, whatever their assumed origin.[55]

Maxwell was certainly not the only one to recognize the challenge contained in the figure of the transvestite. As Parker Tyler put it in his book *Screening the Sexes*, "If the female impersonator has one serious moral function, it is to inform the world that sex is a sense of style, a predilection of the mind and senses, and is not answerable to nature's dully blunt decision about gender."[56] Given his interest in "sex as a thing naturally, perennially taking offbeat forms—truly free forms," however, Tyler was unwilling to extend his praise for the transvestite to the transsexual.[57] For while "deception is not essential to male or female impersonation," transsexualism, according to Tyler, was an act of dissimulation.[58] The transsexual "wishes to come true . . . the fantasy of female impersonation"; s/he "knows the price of every penis, but the value of none."[59] Drag queens, on the other hand, in their willingness to highlight the artifice of their performance, brought "the basic sexes into a stream of full, constant, and fluid variations that develop new forms quite aside from surgical transsexualism."[60] For Tyler, where transsexualism's essentialist approach to gender placed a blind faith in the "dully blunt" classifications of male and female, transvestism suggested the protean potential of human sexuality.

Much as Tyler may have been guilty of "essentializing essentialism," to borrow a phrase from Diana Fuss, his argument is particularly interesting in the context of this discussion, as he eventually extends this fundamental critique of transsexualism to the gay liberation movement's calls for literal self-display. For Tyler, so long as one adhered to a rigidly defined gender or sexual identity—whether male or female, heterosexual or homosexual—one placed arbitrary limits on sexual experience. As oppressive as the system of compulsory heterosexuality may have been, to conceive of oneself as "gay" was in the end no less constricting: in either case, the assumption of a fixed sexual identity negated the potential for erotic experience outside of or beyond that category. Even if one could accept the notion of homosexuality as an end in itself, the movement's adherence to notions of personal authenticity and its ostensible rejection of role-playing, camp, drag, and so on were nevertheless logically flawed. When witnessing the street demonstrations and "happenings" of gay power and gay liberation collectives, Tyler wrote, it was necessary to ask oneself, "What does all this actually mean as public spectacle? It means a rudimentary theatricalization of some hypothetic set of performances . . . which will take place (one hopes) somewhere else in more satisfying and palpable, more definitive forms." Demonstrations, picket lines, and protest marches were therefore "a lot like a circus parade, whose only purpose is to titillate appetite and advertise the joys to come at the *real* performance."[61] Regardless of what those who implored fellow gay men and lesbians to "come out" might have believed, their sexuality would never be on display in any literal fashion. For Tyler, no matter how vehemently these individuals denied playing a role, their unapologetic, "literal" self-presentation was merely a series of suggestions and innuendos, figurative performances that had almost no choice but to draw on common stereotypes. In their attempts to confront straight society with its purported opposite, those who were so vocal in their pursuit of "liberation" had succeeded only in reciting a caricature of difference. Try as they might to overturn the rigid sex roles of "straight" society by embodying some "authentic," "nonoppressive" gay or lesbian identity, that identity would remain just as compromised as the heterosexuality, camp, and drag it opposed.

More damningly, Tyler then questioned just how "oppositional" this movement for gay and lesbian liberation, or calls for any liberation, for that matter, really was. Organizations fighting for gay liberation, black liberation, and women's liberation appeared to speak for the interests of the collective, he wrote, but only insofar "as group interests seem to favor the maximum freedom of the individual to assert not merely his right to make his own moral decisions (within sane and reasonable limits) but moreover his right to reasonable privacy in his pursuit of total integrity." In that sense it was no surprise to see these causes gaining traction. After all, "during the last few decades in the United States, the emphasis placed on the legal issue of 'invasion of privacy' is but one sign of the principle of moral license that especially benefits homosexuals at a moment when public opinion leans so much weight on all aspects of individual freedom."[62] Thus, rather than presenting a powerful alternative to a heteronormative social order, the gay liberation movement may only have demonstrated, even more powerfully, the ability of neoliberal society to assimilate virtually any "revolution" waged in the name of personal freedom. Much as the advocates of gay liberation might have protested, American culture was marked by a "democratically inflected let-live for minorities, all of which have reached the conclusion—with disconcerting simultaneity—that a show of aggression will make the point for them and perhaps win the day."[63] For Tyler, in other words, contemporary critiques of American racism and (hetero)sexism were, in a very important way, a product of the very system they claimed to oppose.

For this reason, perhaps, although Tyler frequently offered drag as a counterpoint to what he saw as the flawed identity politics of gay liberation, he never contended that the transvestite was truly liberated. To the contrary, drag queens and kings served only as an allegory of the nearly limitless potential of human sexuality. They could offer no more than a glimpse of that potential because, like nearly all forms of personal "liberation," drag had proven ultimately reconcilable to the demands of consumer capitalism. As Tyler put it, although the "sheer fun-image of the male's addiction to imitating the manners and outward appearance of the female" still persisted, "the modern era, with its new, ultrapermissiveness toward the exhibition of all sexes and sex acts, has compromised the traditional dignity of the theatrical drag act."[64] In this sense, neither drag nor gay liberation could be said to offer a true alternative to contemporary sexual and social norms. Both had been defanged by the general climate of "ultrapermissiveness" and the insistence on individual "freedoms."

Tyler's frustration is in some sense understandable. After all, in the late 1960s, homosexuality was no longer a taboo subject. As he points out, by 1971, themes of homosexuality, transvestism, and transsexualism had become almost commonplace in popular film. *Myra Breckenridge*, *The Boys in the Band*, *Midnight Cowboy*, *The Caretaker*, *Advise and Consent*, *The Detective*, and *The Christine Jorgensen Story*—by the end of the 1960s, the representation of non-normative sexualities in popular culture was hardly proscribed.[65] Offensive as they may have seemed, even films such as *M*A*S*H*, in which homosexuality appeared only as a joke, could not be excluded from discussions of contemporary "permissiveness." Ironically, Tyler wrote, "the sexual joke tends to be propaganda for whatever 'vice' or idiosyncrasy it may utilize, barring none. Making a formal joke of homosexuality is what unites even heterosexuals with homosexuals. Ten or twenty years ago, I daresay some damaging ridicule was attached to the vulgar 'fairy joke,' depending on the company to which it was told. Can the same be said today?"[66] Whatever the advocates of "gay power" might have argued, popular attitudes toward same-sex sexuality could scarcely be described as "repressive" in any traditional sense. Instead of describing the gay liberation movement as "oppositional," therefore, it may have been more accurate to describe their "show of aggression" as further proof of Marcuse's theory of "repressive desublimation."

Quite interestingly, though, while Marcuse believed repressive desublimation to be nearly total, there was, in Tyler's account, one group that managed largely to escape the stifling effects of contemporary society's "ultrapermissiveness": the hippie counterculture. Tyler believed that the hippies truly embodied the sexual and social ideal of "unisexuality." Seemingly capable of "*un*conditioned reflex[es] in any one sex toward any other—any time, any place, in any manner," the hippies had given themselves over to sexuality in its "truly free forms."[67] With their "ambiguously sexed" faces, bodies, hairstyles, and clothing, their hallucinogenic drugs, and their truly liberated eroticism, he argued, hippies had succeeded in blurring the boundary between sex and aesthetics, and, as a result, between male and female as well.

> For chic hippies, the sex experience and the aesthetic experience are automatically one: there is no dialectic of interaction between moments, levels, moods . . . the hippie-rock-drug idea allows no moral testing, no intellectualizing, not even any poetizing above the pop level, no exposure whatever to disturbance or challenge. It is a closed, a static, proposition, and the chief closure is a ritual blur tending to homogenize the senses and their discrimination—their connoisseurship, as it were—so that even the basic sexual choice of hetero or homo object is smudged, becoming the value we have started calling unisex.[68]

The hippie subculture, in Tyler's view, had discovered a passive, fluid form of sexuality. These young men and women had cultivated a form of eroticism freed from "conscious . . . moral practice."[69] In the fabled "public love-ins," he explained, "no gender distinctions are present except mechanical ones; there are no regulations regarding correspondence; every sex fits another sex."[70] In the counterculture, the "orthodox sexes" were capable of veering "toward their homosexual coefficients, without necessarily or typically arriving at homosexuality."[71] Where drag queens could offer only an imperfect image of an idealized sexuality, the hippie counterculture was a sexual utopia achieved, a polymorphous perversity that stymied the processes and progressions of consumer capitalism.

It is fascinating to note, therefore, that the "ambiguously sexed" faces, bodies, and clothing that marked the hippie counterculture as the embodiment of Tyler's unisexual ideal were, in Altman's account of the gay liberation movement, subject to appropriation by gay men and lesbians as a way of signifying their rejection of dominant values. Drawing on and embellishing the sexual ambiguity of the counterculture, Altman argued, the proponents of gay liberation would ultimately demonstrate that true liberation could deliver not only "freedom from sexual restraint, but also freedom for the fulfillment of human potential."[72] Collapsing the arguments of the gay liberation movement with the theory of polymorphous perversity found in Marcuse's *Eros and Civilization*, Altman suggested that the ultimate goal of gay liberation was not simply to live in freedom as a gay man or lesbian but to live in a society in which sexuality would be replaced with eroticism, one in which individuals would be free "from the surplus repression that prevents us recognizing our essential androgynous and erotic natures."[73] For Altman, same-sex sexuality should function not as an end in itself but as a constant reminder of both the repressive nature of procreative heterosexuality and the unexplored spectrum of potential erotic experience. Thus the "rejection of euphemisms" in the name of an authentic gay identity should remain provisional. A reified homosexuality, after all, would be no different than a reified heterosexuality. "Homosexuals who like to point out that everyone is queer," he wrote, "rarely concede that everyone is equally straight, and that to repress one is as damaging as to repress the other."[74] While Altman emphasized the potential of the gay liberation movement, therefore, his attachment to the notion of polymorphous perversity led to a conclusion not entirely at odds with Tyler's. The gay liberation movement offered a means to an end, but its greatest promise lay in its style, not its ideology.

Again, the GLF's members saw these "stylistic" choices not as a reminder of human potential but as the expression of an "authentic," radical homosexuality. Jim Fourratt saw his decision to wear long hair as a challenge both to prevailing social and sexual mores, and to the homophiles who wanted, perhaps above all else, to deny their difference from "straight" society. In an article for *Esquire* magazine, Tom Burke made this contrast in generational styles clear. Describing a confrontation between Fourratt and representatives of the homophile movement, Burke wrote that Dick Leitsch, of MSNY, "in a staid brown suit, strides to the front. . . . With professional aplomb, he reopens the meeting." Stressing the importance of protesting police brutality, Leitsch nonetheless insisted that "the gay world must retain the favor of the Establishment, especially those who make and change laws." In response, Burke reported, a "tense boy with leonine hair" arose and shouted, "We don't want acceptance goddam it! We want respect! Demand it! We're through hiding in dark bars behind Mafia doormen. We're going to go where straights go and do anything with each other they do and if they don't like it, well, fuck them!" When another Mattachine representative, attempting to ignore the interruption, suggested a candlelight "gay vigil," saying they should be "firm, but . . . amicable and sweet," Fourratt, "the radical who burned money on the floor of the New York Stock Exchange," leapt to his feet. "Sweet! Bullshit! There's the stereotype homo again, man! . . . Bullshit! That's the role society has been forcing these queens to play, and they just sit and accept it."[75] Fourratt, and others like him, did not want to be perceived as the "stereotype homo"—whether that meant the "queens and nellies" of the bar scene or the "conservative and conventional" homophile. Those in the Gay Liberation Front wanted neither tokenism nor acceptance. Their aim was not to find a place within contemporary society but to transform society. Gay liberation, they believed, would be achieved not through the simple abolition of dominant sexual hierarchies but through a radical reformulation of *all* social structures. Echoing the hippie subculture, therefore, members of the GLF would do their "own thing," seeking, not unlike the Diggers, to bring about an alternative future by enacting it in the present. For activists such as Fourratt, in spite of their often openly masculinist rhetoric, "hippie" style was not sexually ambiguous but an expression of the extent to which liberated gay men were necessarily closer to and more accepting of the "feminine" aspects of their personality.[76] The literal self-presentation of the GLF's members was to offer a response to those "experts" who attempted to "cure" gay men and lesbians by reconciling them with "natural" forms of sexual expression. Through their unapologetic adoption of purportedly "feminine" styles, GLF members asserted that *their* sexuality, not that of "straight" society, was natural, that they, not heterosexuals, were superior.[77]

In spite of their stated desire to "express themselves" through personal style, however, the fashions and mannerisms adopted by those in the GLF were also intended to signify the deep ideological affinities between gay liberationists and the larger constellation of social, cultural, and political organizations known at the time as "the Movement." As Allan Warshawsky and Ellen Bedoz explained in the second issue of *Come Out!*, it had become clear that homosexual liberation could not "develop in a vacuum."

> We are one of many oppressed groups, the roots of whose oppression lies within a diseased capitalist system. . . . It is a mistake to think that we are oppressed only as homosexuals. We are oppressed as people employed at meaningless, alienating, unnecessary jobs to support a work ethic we no longer believe in. We are oppressed by our own guilt at watching helplessly as our government, in the name of the people, slaughters Vietnamese, ignores the rights of tens of millions of black, brown, and red skinned Americans, and exploits all the colored peoples of the world. We are oppressed by a social system that defines sex roles in such a limiting manner as to violate the rights and potentialities of women and severely curtail the emotional development of men. It is for reasons like these that we must now join forces with our sisters and brothers in the Movement so that we can begin to struggle for *total* human liberation.[78]

Discrimination against gay men and lesbians, in other words, was symptomatic. To attempt to address "Gay Liberation" as a singular issue was thus foolish. And, like Fourratt, Bedoz and Warshawsky believed that, given its interest in radical social transformation, the GLF would eventually be accepted as an integral part of the larger New Left. Their ideological harmony with groups such as Students for a Democratic Society, the Black Panther Party, and others, their common belief in "total human liberation," would, once understood, seem virtually self-evident.

Yet, no matter how GLF members dressed or how sincere they were in their quest for personal liberation, the work of carving out a space for gay liberation within "the Movement" proved exceedingly difficult. Although members chose to use the name Gay Liberation Front, believing that the reference to Vietnam's National Liberation Front would emphasize their place within the global spectrum of

grassroots politics, few straight radicals took their concerns seriously. As far as many of those involved in the New Left were concerned, calls for gay liberation seemed at best misguided. The task of
true social transformation, they believed, required putting aside such
"personal" concerns and working toward a singular, collective political goal. Once that goal had been achieved, it was said, all forms of
oppression would fall away. For others, however, the idea of aligning
themselves with a movement for gay liberation was simply ludicrous.
Given the way in which gay-baiting was so frequently used to dismiss
oppositional politics as a whole—Chicago district attorney Thomas
Foran's comment that America's children were being corrupted by
the "freaking fag revolution" is only the most famous example of
this—to offer support for gay liberation would be political suicide.
Obviously, the logic of this argument was seriously flawed. Why,
after all, should organizations committed to opposing the status quo
have been so concerned with what government spokespersons said
about them? These arguments against offering official support for
gay liberation thus made it clear to members of the GLF that before
society could be changed, "the Movement" to change it would have
to be altered.[79]

The GLF therefore began its public political career with a series of
actions designed to raise awareness of the ways in which the underground press was complicit in the propagation of antigay bias. Unlike
major commercial media outlets, which were dismissed out of hand
for having a "stake in perpetuating mores that buttressed capitalistic
profit-making," the underground press claimed to speak directly to
and for those with an interest in overturning those mores.[80] When
New York's *Village Voice* deleted the "obscene" word "gay" from an
advertisement for a GLF dance, it seemed the perfect opportunity for
the organization to make a statement to the paper's readers. So they
picketed the offices of *Voice* editors and publishers, demanding not
only that future advertisements for GLF events be printed without
alteration, but also that the paper stop printing insulting, homophobic articles by authors such as Norman Mailer. How could a paper
like the *Voice*, they asked, which considered itself truly progressive,
run offensive pieces by straight authors while refusing to print the
word "gay" in advertisements for GLF-sponsored events? At the end
of the day, the *Voice*'s publisher agreed to allow the words "gay" and

"homosexual" to appear in future classified ads, but refused to censor authors who made disparaging remarks about homosexuality in their articles. Despite what would appear a tepid compromise, GLF leaders were nevertheless encouraged. "'Gay' is no longer a four-letter word, even at the *Village Voice*," they proclaimed on a flier posted throughout the West Village. "Friday . . . members of the homosexual community demonstrated the reality of gay power. . . . GLF hopes that all members of the community will take note of this, and that they will take appropriate action to bring about the day when the *Voice* may become truly representative of the people of the Village."[81]

In some cases, however, GLF members' eagerness to be included within the larger New Left caused them to compromise in more surprising ways. For example, more than one member of the GLF attempted to force others within the movement to take them seriously by showing that gay politicos could be just as "manly" as their straight counterparts. This, it seems, may have been the reason for Fourratt's claim that "if it takes riots and guns to show them what we are, well, that's the only language the pigs understand."[82] More shocking, though, was Fourratt's later statement that members of the GLF would have to toughen up, as it were, and stop allowing the antigay language of straight radicals to bother them so much. In an article for *Come Out!*, Fourratt cautioned those who were critical of the use of terms such as "faggot" by members of groups like the Black Panther Party. For those in "the Movement," he explained, the word was "used to describe any castrated male made impotent by society." Black males, for example, had "traditionally been castrated by white society by its refusal to allow [them] the dignity of meaningful work. It has been the black woman who has had to play the black male role in white society; she who can get the jobs; she who can collect welfare; she who holds the family together; rendering the male useless—hence, castrated; hence faggot."[83] While it was necessary to confront those who continued to use this word with "our community," he argued, it was also necessary for those offended by its use to remember that these individuals were "actively working for an alternative to this society," one in which, Fourratt seems to have assumed, no one would be "useless—hence, castrated; hence faggot."[84]

But no matter how far the GLF's members were willing to bend to gain acceptance within "the Movement," their attempts to build a multi-issue radical coalition repeatedly ended in frustration. Just days after the organization's official founding in August 1969, members joined in a large demonstration commemorating the end of Hiroshima/Nagasaki Week, marching under a large GLF banner. When, at the concluding rally in Central Park, members of the crowd came to tear down the banner, the GLF was blamed for creating the disturbance—their mere presence, it seems, had provoked the assailants. Three months later, a GLF contingent marched in the antiwar Moratorium in Washington, DC. Upon the group's arrival in the capital, as Dan Smith recounted for *Come Out!*, it quickly became apparent that "there was something wrong in Washington."[85] "Personally, I'm fed up with all the shit we take from the right and left," Earl Galvin kvetched. "Saturday morning, during the march up Pennsylvania Ave., I felt inclined to discount the reactions we got as we explained what our 28th of June GLF banner was about. . . . Most of the young men smiled slightly, tightened their sphincters, grabbed mom's hand, and gravitated discretely to another area of the street."[86] The GLF's belief that gay liberation should function in concert with black liberation, women's liberation, socialist revolution, or the movement to end the war in Vietnam had met with resistance from all angles. Even when GLF representatives were invited back to Washington, DC, to take part in the Revolutionary People's Constitutional Convention, organized by the Black Panther Party in the summer of 1970, they found themselves and their concerns quickly dismissed. Panther representatives, Lois Hart reported, "insulted us with words of democratic proceedure [*sic*] while bulldozing through their agenda. I felt intimidated, angry and defensive. 'I have come here to find out why and if gay people should relate to this convention. Is there receptivity to Women's and Gay Liberation?'" Hart was understandably distraught when a few of the Panthers responded, "We'll tolerate that crazy talk about 30 seconds and you'll be asked to leave!"[87]

The faith GLF members had placed in the political perceptiveness of the New Left and the counterculture was apparently ill advised. The organization's androgynous styles; its rhetoric of authentic personal liberation; its official support for the antiwar movement, Black Power, and the women's movement; and its attempts to formulate the oppression of gay men and lesbians as but an extension of the individual's enslavement under modern capitalism had all failed to foster any satisfactory political coalition.[88] No matter how much members of the GLF made themselves look and sound like their "straight" counterparts, who, in an ironic double entendre, often spoke out against the constraints of "heterosexual" society, the majority of those within the broader "movement" refused to see the value or usefulness of gay liberation as an issue. As Jim Owles, one of a handful of members who in November of 1969 split with the GLF to form the Gay Activists Alliance (GAA), told the *New York Times Magazine* the following summer, "To me they were begging for that same kind of acceptance they had accused some of the older homosexuals of wanting."[89] In their attempts to fit in with the counterculture and the New Left, "they were . . . saying 'Look, see my hair's the same way as yours. I'm out in the picket line. Please accept me.' *And they were still getting spit at*. The word faggot was still being used at them."[90] Despite the counterculture's sexually ambiguous fashions and its rhetoric of personal liberation, the idea of "free love" did not apply to same-sex sexuality. Thus, while Tyler was critical of the gay liberation movement for failing to recognize the extent to which its purportedly "radical" form was ultimately the performance of an historical style, he failed to notice that the hippies' mode of self-representation was hardly the incarnation of a "unisexual" ideal.

Much like that of the gay liberationists he criticized, of course, Tyler's analysis faltered on his rather simplistic—even in relation to his own arguments—attempt to equate a historical style with a truly oppositional, utopian sexuality. After all, if the gay liberation movement was, in Tyler's account, hampered by a belief in its own literalism, how could his faith in the "sexually ambiguous" fashions of the hippie counterculture have avoided the same pitfalls? Not unlike Theodor Roszak, who believed that the men of the counterculture embodied a certain "feminine softness," Tyler seems to have conflated accusations of a compromised or insufficient "masculinity" with an enlightened openness to an essential "femininity."[91] In many cases, however, as I have already argued, and as GLF members quickly discovered, the men of the counterculture were not cultivating any sort of "feminine softness" so much as they were enacting a regressive form of masculinity.[92] Long hair was often not a signifier of sexual ambiguity but a sign of one's refusal to subscribe to what seemed a debased Cold War masculine ideal, that is, the "organiza-

tion man."[93] For many members of the counterculture, the thought of
gay men—sexual "inverts"—claiming that the androgyny of "hippie"
fashions allowed for the expression of an underlying male femininity
would have produced severe anxiety in a way that Abbie Hoffman's
put-ons never could.

And for some members of the GLF, this was precisely the point. As
Martha Shelley wrote in her 1970 essay "Gay Is Good," "the function
of a homosexual is to make [heterosexuals] uneasy."[94] Gay men and
lesbians should have wanted heterosexuals to be uncomfortable.
How better to make them aware of the roles they imposed upon themselves and others, and to force them to understand "how much sex-
role differentiation is pure artifice . . . nothing but a game"?[95] They
should have been willing to "behave outrageously," to make individuals recognize their own ignorance and prejudice.[96] All heterosexuals
should be confronted in this fashion, she argued, especially those
who went to such great lengths to denounce what they labeled
"straight" society. Surely, "straight" society needed to be made aware
that gay men and lesbians would no longer apologize for or regret
their "condition." But for members of the counterculture, with so
much at stake in their commitment to "free love," the discomfort
produced by an encounter with "the flaming faggot or the diesel dyke"
could be particularly intense and, as a result, instructive.[97] These
confrontations did more than simply strip the masks from normative
gender roles; they exposed the hollowness of the counterculture's
claims to personal "liberation." In practice, "free love" was little more
than a myth, a farcical performance of "straight" society's notion of
the "way out." One could never shed the privileges associated with
heterosexuality simply by adopting purportedly "androgynous" fashions. Indeed, the belief that a style of clothing could render a man
"sexually ambiguous" by allowing him to embrace his "femininity"
simply enshrined the very notions of gender he claimed to flout.

Of course, much as the GLF's vision of liberation haunted the
counterculture and the New Left, a different image of gay liberation haunted the GLF. The organization was consistently nettled by
the image of gender presented by transvestites, transsexuals, drag
queens and "bulldykes." At this point, it is not difficult to understand
why members of the GLF were uncomfortable with the implications
of what they saw as "gender impersonation." Given their desire to

challenge what they believed to be prejudicial gender roles, individuals who appeared to conform to, or even revere, those roles while claiming to support the cause of gay liberation would have seemed naïve. Nevertheless, if, as Tyler pointed out, cross-dressing had nothing to do with illusion as such, if drag queens were uninterested in being mistaken for "real girls," then perhaps the gay liberationists' discomfort in relation to these practices was rooted in a more basic disagreement, one concerned not with "regressive" forms of behavior but with questions of authenticity and doubts about the soundness of "gay liberation" as a political goal.[98] Where the early advocates of gay liberation repeatedly stressed the tactical importance of the literal presentation of oneself as a gay radical, the practices like cross-dressing and camp that made them so uneasy invited one to recognize the theatrical or aesthetic dimension of all self-presentation. In the words of Jonathan Dollimore, camp translates conceptions of gender—and, in this case, gender politics—into "a question of aesthetics;"; it reveals the extent to which "what seemed like mimetic realism is actually an effect of convention, genre, form, or some other kind of artifice."[99]

Ironically, a similar challenge to the GLF's notion of personal authenticity can be found in what most historians have described as the organization's more "conservative" spin-off, the GAA.[100] That organization formed when Jim Owles, Marty Robinson, Arthur Evans, and Arthur Bell split with the GLF over concerns that the latter organization's commitment to being included within the larger "Movement" was ultimately counterproductive. To avoid the traps that seemed to have ensnared the GLF, the GAA's founders declared that their organization would devote itself only to what they deemed "gay" issues. Instead of seeking to effect a broad transformation of consciousness, the GAA, as an organization, would devote itself to fighting the various forms of legal and social discrimination that plagued sexual minorities in their daily lives, things such as police harassment and discrimination in housing and employment. While members were free to participate in antiwar demonstrations or rallies for women's and black liberation, they were to do so only as individuals, not as official representatives of the GAA. And although these restrictions have often led the organization to be described as the "reformist" arm of the gay liberation movement, the GAA's political tactics suggest that there may have been something more to the group's approach than mere caution.

In a form of public shaming that has since become a staple of media-based activism, the GAA's "media zaps" sought to use sensationalist news coverage to gay liberationists' advantage. In the words of historian and filmmaker David Carter, zaps were a combination of "militancy, guerrilla theater, and . . . camp."[101] They were a form of confrontation designed to shame and embarrass unsympathetic public figures in front of reporters and cameramen. As Arthur Evans put it, "The noise, abuse and general camping-up demoralize the oppressors. Sometimes even top pigs are not too proud of the work they do. Activists can capitalize on this weakness and degrade high-ranking bureaucrats in front of their employees. [They] are usually taken off-guard and come out looking either ridiculous or violent. When the scene is replayed on TV . . . they look foolish and vulnerable."[102] The GAA looked not to shun the mass media, as the GLF had done, but to capitalize on its appetite for outrageous imagery, to use that imagery against those in power. In many zaps, the organization would send individuals to pose as audience members or bystanders during political rallies and fundraisers only to surprise the guest of honor with pointed questions regarding his or her official stance on discrimination against gay men and lesbians. When New York mayor John Lindsay and his wife attended an event at the Metropolitan Opera House, for example, one GAA member stepped in front of the mayor and asked in a loud voice, hoping to be clearly understood in any resulting television coverage, "What are you going to do about ending police harassment of homosexuals?" As security guards escorted the man from the building, twenty-nine other GAA members began to chant "End police harassment!" and "Gay Power!" At the next meeting, Jim Owles, who served as GAA's first president, told members, "The confrontation was very fast, but not without effect: *The New York Times*, *Women's Wear Daily*, and WCBS News gave it coverage."[103]

Building on the attention the organization had received for this zap at the Opera House, the GAA held its first official, large-scale demonstration outside of New York's City Hall on March 5, hoping to grab the attention of major local news outlets with an even more outrageous display of "gay power." Arthur Bell, head of GAA's publicity committee, alerted the press on the eve of the demonstration, and, as he later recalled, when demonstrators emerged from the subway, "photographers and reporters were there to greet us. They followed us from the subway to City Hall, taking outrageous shots, asking outrageous questions. . . . 'How do the sodomy laws suppress homosexuals?' 'Do your parents know?' 'How would it feel if your parents knew?' 'Are you proud of what you're doing?' 'Ashamed?' And, ever so timidly, 'What do you guys do in bed?'"[104] However absurd or insulting the reporters' questions, though, the action was doing exactly what the GAA had hoped: providing them with airtime. "Cameras ground as men kissed men. . . . Here, for all Wall Street, City Hall, and the press of America, were honest-to-God flesh-and-blood gorgeous, gorgeous gays."[105] Concerned neither with appearing "conservative and conventional" nor with the danger of being perceived as "stereotype homos," to use Fourratt's phrase, GAA members camped it up in front of City Hall, rendering themselves and their cause literally spectacular. Long hair, in other contexts a symbol of rebellious masculinity or unflinching political commitment, was in this case placed front and center for the cameras, serving as a signifier of stereotypical gay male femininity. And, as Bell recalled, "That evening we watched ourselves on ABC-TV news, gloating at the sight of our own happy faces, proud that our march on City Hall was successful, and ready and eager for another full-scale attack on the forces that oppressed us."[106]

Of course, where Bell and his fellow GAA leaders were pleased with ABC's coverage of the demonstration, other gay liberationists were simply offended. The newsletter *GAY* called the coverage "an insult to the homosexual community." *GAY*'s editor commented, "Such remarks as 'limp wrists stiffened today' and 'pickets marched under a slightly effeminate statue' exposed the network's bias."[107] In light of this irritation at the network's prejudice, Bell's enthusiasm is perhaps even more striking. Although coverage may have been predictably biased, and although no GAA member managed to speak to the mayor—which was, after all, the stated purpose of the action— Bell nevertheless described the demonstration as "successful." The goal, it seems, was less to enlighten the mayor or ABC's newscasters than simply to engage in a bit of political theater, to "steal" airwaves, as Hoffman might have put it. What Mayor Lindsay may not have

Marty Robinson with police officers outside the Metropolitan Museum,
April 13, 1970. Photo by Kay Tobin Lahusen. Image courtesy of the New York
Public Library.

realized, therefore, was that in refusing to speak to GAA representatives, he had, in fact, played right into the organization's hands. He
had stepped directly into the role of the villain.

On April 13, the organization zapped Mayor Lindsay yet again,
this time at a scheduled appearance to dedicate the newly finished
fountain in front of the Metropolitan Museum of Art. Distracted by
the events of the day, Bell explained, no one at the museum seemed
to notice the zap unfolding before their eyes. "By paying too much
mind to the celebrities and the band and the high school kids and
the museum patrons and the milling throng of out-of-towners," Bell

wrote, "the police paid no mind at all to the young man who was slowly ascending the museum steps to the podium where Lindsay was perched."[108] Amid the fanfare and photographs, Marty Robinson had bypassed police and museum security, climbed the Met's front steps, and sidled up next to the mayor for all of the cameramen, reporters, and onlookers to see. Once there, he shouted, "When are you going to speak out on homosexual rights, Mr. Mayor?" Police quickly escorted Robinson away, holding him aside to ensure that he would not make another attempt to embarrass the mayor. But security and the mayor's staff had failed to notice that GAA members were also scattered throughout the audience. As Lindsay made his way through the crowd, they stepped forward to shake his hand, smiling like the rest of his supporters, but holding on long enough to offer a leaflet and ask questions such as "Now when the hell are you going to speak to homosexuals?"[109] Even when personally confronted, the mayor never broke character. He still refused to offer anything other than passing pleasantries to GAA representatives. Six days later, therefore, having procured tickets to a taping of the mayor's weekly television talk show for WNEW-TV, *With Mayor Lindsay*, GAA members scattered themselves throughout the studio audience, hoping for yet another televised confrontation.

On the day of the taping, GAA members gathered at Bell's apartment, dressed in a number of different styles so that they might blend in among the studio audience, and received instructions on precisely how to applaud, chant, and stamp their feet during the show for maximum televisual effect. Upon arriving at the studio, GAA members distributed themselves in small groups evenly throughout the audience, but before the show could begin, Lindsay's council, Michael Dontzin, recognized Bell and approached him about a meeting the following week, hoping that formally acknowledging the organization might put an end to any plan to disrupt the taping. Given the suspicious timing of Dontzin's request, Bell agreed to the meeting, but pretended to know nothing of any plans to zap the mayor that afternoon. In spite of Bell's professed ignorance, however, Lindsay and his staff were "visibly nervous" all the same.[110] The GAA's zaps had already made the mayor look and feel "foolish and vulnerable" at public gatherings; the thought that he could be ambushed during his own talk show was obviously unnerving. As the show began taping, and Lindsay and his guest, environmentalist Arthur Godfrey, took their seats, Evans moved toward the stage shouting, "Mr. Mayor, what are you doing to end job discrimination against homosexuals?" On the heels of Evans's outburst, Bell writes, "a loud eruption takes place in the audience. A stampede of stamping feet. Voices everywhere: 'Answer the question, answer the question.' Someone yells, 'Are you in favor of repeal of the sodomy laws?' The TV cameras stop rolling."[111] After the zap at the Metropolitan, Lindsay and his staff had been wary of any unidentified persons approaching the mayor, and security guards were at the ready to keep anyone from getting to the stage. The mayor and his staff were truly foxed, however, to find that once Evans had been escorted from the set the remaining GAA members were far more difficult to head off. Anticipating the mayor's heightened security, Evans and Bell had instructed others in their group not to approach the stage but instead to heckle the mayor and his guest. When Godfrey mentioned the problem of abandoned cars in New York City, one GAA member asked wryly from his seat, "What about abandoned homosexuals?" And when the mayor, discussing various forms of noise pollution, remarked that it was illegal to blow one's horn when stuck in traffic, another GAA member simply called out, "It's illegal in New York to blow anything," and walked out of the studio as others in the group applauded and stamped their feet.[112]

Given GAA members' willingness to play the role of the "stereotype homo" for the mass media, not to mention the organization's decision to concentrate solely on "gay" issues, members of the GLF were highly critical of the newer organization, arguing that its approach to gay and lesbian rights was in the end too short-sighted. For those committed to the GLF's vision of liberation, "gay rights" legislation was insufficient. What good was the right to spend one's evenings in a gay bar, they asked, if one remained oppressed by the systems of capitalism and imperialism? As Bedoz and Warshawsky so succinctly put it, gay liberation could not "develop in a vacuum." So long as one viewed the oppression of gay men and lesbians as a singular issue, distinct from the oppression of women and African Americans, the war in Vietnam, the Cuban Revolution, and so on, any "progress" one made, and any mass media coverage one received, would only perpetuate the myth of tolerance that secured the contemporary social order. In the estimation of many members of the

GLF, the GAA could only ever succeed in establishing "homosexu-als" as a niche market, thereby robbing gay men and lesbians of their potential to present meaningful opposition to "straight" society. The GAA's practical, media-based approach to political activism would prevent the organization from making any real contribution to the greater social, cultural, and political revolution that would liberate *all* victims of oppression.

In an important sense, this critique of the GAA's methods echoes Tyler's account of drag and gay liberation. That is to say, much as Tyler was critical of the ways in which cross-dressing and the gay liberation movement were ultimately reconcilable to the systems they claimed to mock or detest, for the GLF, the real problem with the GAA was that the organization was unable to resist being assimi-lated by the social order in which its members' problems were rooted. True opposition, for both Tyler and the GLF, was only to be found in those individuals and movements that enacted a utopian vision in the present, one that marked quite clearly their difference from the dominant culture, and made them irreconcilable with the demands of consumer capitalism and the mass media. Authentic dissent needed to assume an adequate, authentic form. But what Tyler's analysis also makes clear is that this emphasis on personal and political authenticity coincided historically with the popularization of camp. For Tyler, at least in this case, the politics of irony and the politics of authenticity were effectively inseparable: both were symptoms of the "ultrapermissiveness" of contemporary society, and were thus rendered impotent by what Marcuse labeled the system of "repres-sive tolerance." Both, that is, could be evaluated and understood in terms of their thorough, and ultimately neutralizing, conventionality. Each one suffered from its inability to separate images from "true" opposition.

But what Tyler, not to mention the GLF, failed to recognize was the way that practices such as drag and camp attempted to maintain a self-conscious distance from the images upon which they drew. The GAA in its "zaps," like drag queens and "bulldykes" in their anti-illusionist cross-dressing, sought not to forge some wholly new, entirely unassimilable model of gender or sexuality. Rather, they performed an exaggerated, and thus critically compromised, ver-sion of normative *and* alternative sex and gender roles, "actualizing the stereotype" of their own presumed position in the process. In these instances, camp and drag were not merely foolhardy attempts to escape the restrictions of the dominant social order, but a mode of self-representation deployed by those who perceived nearly all potential forms of expression and opposition to be always already rooted in and constrained by the dominant culture. Images and opposition were conflated at these moments not out of a mistaken belief in some supposedly correct political tactic but in recognition of their historical fusion. Like the political put-ons of the Yippies, these practices made clear that critique without convention, without aesthetic form, was inconceivable. The ideological tension within the post-Stonewall gay liberation movement surrounding camp, drag, and butch/femme—practices that, as Maxwell correctly pointed out, had been central to the struggle for gay liberation since at least the early twentieth century—illustrates the extent to which questions of visual representation had become absolutely central to the discourse of radical politics in America.[113] For the GAA, like the Yippies, the perceived inability to elude the grasp of dominant culture led to a form of activism that offered what Jonathan Dollimore has described as "a simultaneous avoidance and acting out of the ambivalence which constitutes subordination, and a pushing of that ambivalence to the point of transgressive insight and possibly reinscribed escape."[114] For groups such as the GAA, it was not visibility per se that was the trap, as Peggy Phelan has so famously asserted, but faith in the oppositional power and authenticity of any single visual form.[115]

3. "ERECT ... STRONG ... RESILIENT AND FIRM"

Eldridge Cleaver and the
Performance of "Black" Liberation

A S THE PREVIOUS TWO CHAPTERS SHOW, FOR MANY IN THE LATE 1960s the visual form of political resistance was the focus of a great deal of thought and experimentation. Yet one might say that, in the cases of the counterculture and the gay liberation movement, this is understandable. Each group, after all, was faced from the beginning with the task of determining just how to present itself to the world in terms of a collective identity. In this final chapter, therefore, I would like to offer one last case study examining the political persona of one of the more consistently vilified characters of the late 1960s, Eldridge Cleaver. As Herbert Marcuse's admiration for the civil rights and Black Power movements made clear, for many in the 1960s, questions of visual form in relation to racial politics seemed pointless, if not wholly inappropriate. Racial difference, they thought, was simply self-evident. This makes Cleaver, and in many ways the Black Power movement more generally, a particularly interesting subject of investigation.

Due to his willingness to equate the struggle for black liberation with the effort to reclaim a full black masculinity, Cleaver has been dismissed repeatedly as an example of the most misguided, even regressive, form of identity politics. For authors such as Michelle Wallace, Robin Morgan, Kobena Mercer, Isaac Julien, Leerom Medovoi, and others, more people were hurt than helped by Cleaver's brand of racial antagonism. In spite of his critics' easily understandable frustration, however, it seems only logical at this point to ask if there could have been something more to Cleaver's "adoration of his genitals," as Wallace has put it, than the mere internalization of a stereotypical masculinity. Is it possible to read in his performance of this persona not a naïve or wrongheaded version of identity politics but a critical and self-conscious engagement with the forms of masculinity that Wallace and others have found so detestable? To reassess the potential value of Cleaver's political career, I want to look closely at his enactment of a violent, "supermasculine" version of black liberation, from his attack on novelist James Baldwin in the essay "Notes on a Native Son" to his threat to kick California State superintendent of public instruction Max Rafferty's ass. In the process, I will place Cleaver's outrageous pronouncements alongside both the activities and ideologies of the Black Panther Party, paying particular attention to the actions and writings of party founder Huey P. Newton, who, in spite of his eagerness to enlist Cleaver as a Panther in the late 1960s, repeatedly denounced him just a few years later. I will also revisit the work of more recent authors such as Wallace, Mercer, Julien, and others. By placing these writings next to the acts they describe and/or deride, it is possible to interrogate not only the "masculinist" version of black liberation that Cleaver propagated but also the assumed historical necessity of dismissing it.

In their essay "True Confessions: A Discourse on Images of Black Male Sexuality," cultural theorist Kobena Mercer and filmmaker Isaac Julien describe Cleaver as the proponent of a short-sighted vision of black liberation that could only have come about at the expense of women, gay men, and lesbians. They contend that Cleaver, like a number of spokesmen for Black Power, promoted a "heterosexist version of black militancy which not only authorized sexism . . . but a hidden agenda of homophobia."[1] Cleaver's emphasis on a militant, confrontational version of racial politics "not only ignore[d] the more subtle and enduring forms of cultural resistance which have been forged in diaspora formations" but also depoliticized "'internal' conflicts and antagonisms, especially around gender and sexuality within black communities."[2] In contrast to Cleaver's vision of a fully realized black masculinity, Mercer and Julien point to a series of musicians who, throughout the 1960s, '70s, and '80s, enacted an alternative to the heterosexist model of black power, and used their celebrity to "undercut the braggadocio to make critiques of conventional models of masculinity."[3] In future attempts to comprehend the complicated sexual politics of "blackness," they write, it will be necessary to look not to the example of preposterously macho "freedom fighters" like Cleaver but to "artists like Luther Vandross, Teddy Pendergrass and the much-maligned Michael Jackson," and to come to terms with the "camp and crazy 'carnivalesque' qualities of Little Richard—the original Queen of Rock 'n' Roll himself." These men, Mercer and Julien explain, "disclose the 'soft side' of black masculinity (and this is the side we like!)."[4]

Valorizing the "soft side" of black masculinity in this fashion, Mercer and Julien distance their version of "black sexual politics" from one of Cleaver's essays in particular, "Notes on a Native Son." In that essay, cited by so many critics of Black Power's chauvinist tendencies, Cleaver wrote that novelist James Baldwin, as a gay black intellectual, had devoted himself and his literary career to the justification of the "racial death-wish" that plagued far too many black Americans.[5] "From the widespread use of cosmetics to bleach the black out of one's skin," Cleaver wrote, "to the extreme, resorted to by more Negroes than one might wish to believe, of undergoing nose-thinning and lip-clipping operations, the racial death-wish of American Negroes" could be observed taking "its terrible toll."[6] For Cleaver, these procedures, through which black men and women imprinted upon their bodies the visual signifiers of "whiteness," were indicative of a larger racial "power struggle" waged throughout American history. It was not any inherent quality of white skin that gave birth to this overriding disdain for nearly all things black, that is, but the historical inseparability of dark skin and servitude. Nevertheless, according to Cleaver, it would be a mistake to reduce this racial self-hatred to a matter of habituation. To the contrary, he argued, through the cunning of the "white man," black men and women had been not simply accustomed but *bred* to despise the physical manifestations of their African heritage. European standards of physical beauty had been imposed and reinforced not only culturally but hereditarily: "What has been happening for the past four hundred years is that the white man, through his access to black women, has been pumping his blood and genes into the blacks, has been diluting the blood and genes of the blacks . . . and accelerating the Negroes' racial death-wish."[7] As a result, for many blacks the thought of "two very dark Negroes mating" was anathema, for in such a case, "the children are sure to be black, and this is not desirable."[8]

Carrying this logic further, Cleaver went on to assert that the historical desirability of "whiteness" colored more than just "traditional" heterosexual relationships. For anyone attracted to men, the myth that treated the social advantages attached to white masculinity as inherent virtues precluded the possibility that a nonwhite man might be found desirable. Thus, Cleaver explained, when the gay black man "takes the white man for his lover . . . he focuses on 'whiteness' all the love in his pent up soul and turns the razor edge of hatred against 'blackness'—upon himself, what he is, and all those who look like him, remind him of himself."[9] Moreover, he argued, this neurosis was compounded by the inability of same-sex relationships to produce offspring. Unlike black women, who, according to this model, were mollified by the possibility of bearing their potential white lovers' children, gay black men, Cleaver wrote, were only further maddened. "It seems that many Negro homosexuals, acquiescing in this racial death-wish, are outraged and frustrated because in their sickness they are unable to have a baby by a white man," he wrote. "The cross they have to bear is that, already bending over and touching their toes for the white man, the fruit of their miscegenation is not the little half-white offspring of their dreams but an increase in the unwinding of their nerves."[10] That Baldwin suffered from this particular form of "racial death-wish" could be seen, Cleaver wrote, in his critique of the work of author Richard Wright. Reflecting on Wright's work following his death in 1960, Baldwin had claimed that, in retrospect, Wright's own belief in his social and political acumen was foolish. "In my own relations with him," Baldwin wrote, "I was always exasperated by his notions of society, politics, and history, for they seemed to me utterly fanciful."[11] Any social or historical insights Wright's work may have contained were mitigated by a stubborn refusal to look beyond the surfaces of his own experiences. In Wright's novels, as in "most of the novels written by Negroes until today . . . there is a great space where sex ought to be." What filled this space, according to Baldwin, was a "gratuitous and compulsive" violence.[12] And because Wright never really examined the root of this violence, it remained untransformed, "a terrible attempt to break out of the cage in which the American imagination has imprisoned him for so long."[13]

To Cleaver, who believed that of "all black American novelists" Wright displayed perhaps the most profound social and political insight, Baldwin's critique was nothing other than "audacious madness."[14] If violence had replaced sex in Wright's novels, it was "only because in the North American reality hate holds sway in love's true province."[15] To offer visions of sex in a time of hatred, he wrote, would have required Wright to forsake his "rebellion" for a "lamblike submission." Wright was never "ghost enough" (his books, as Cleaver explained in another passage, were "strongly heterosexual") "to achieve this cruel distortion."[16] Baldwin's essay, therefore, although ostensibly concerned with the ways in which an unexamined rage seemed to dominate Wright's work, was in fact a moral struggle over the proper forms of black masculinity. Where Wright, not unlike Malcolm X, offered an uncompromising image of "our living black manhood," Baldwin seemed to embody "the self-flagellating policy of Martin Luther King . . . giving out falsely the news that the Day of the Ghost has arrived."[17] Baldwin could not "confront the stud in others—except that he must either submit to it or destroy it. And he was not about to bow to a *black* man."[18] According to Cleaver, this was because Baldwin, like most black men and women, and particularly gay black men, had "succumbed psychologically" to the power of the white male. The only way Baldwin could free himself from this oppression, therefore, was "to embrace Africa, the land of his fathers."[19]

Yet, in relation to the rest of Cleaver's essay, as well as the rest of *Soul on Ice*, this call for Baldwin to "cure" himself by seeking out his African racial and psychological origins comes as something of a surprise. Just a few paragraphs before his angry dismissal of Baldwin's life and work, Cleaver explicitly rejected the argument that a cultural nationalism could undo the neuroses that plagued black men and women. Calls from "Black Muslims, and back to Africa advocates" for strict segregation in the name of a renewed sense of racial identity were merely the inversion of this racial death-wish—an attempt to deny the potential social value of integration.[20] For Cleaver, the "cure" for black Americans' racial death-wish lay not in separatism but in a more thoroughgoing miscegenation. Society would only overcome the innumerable effects of its protracted racial power struggle through a process of physical, mental, racial, and sexual "convalescence," in which the "black," "white," "male," and "female" moments of human existence and experience would be "grafted onto" one another. Before one could hope to enter into this process, however, one would need to understand more fully the intricate and intimate relations of sexual and racial power that structured American history.

Every social order, Cleaver wrote, reproduced itself through the projection of a corresponding "sexual image," an ideal to which all individuals and sexual relations in a given society aspired.[21] A utopian society, he claimed, taking a page from Plato's *Symposium*, would approximate the "Unitary Sexual Image," a glimpse of a prelapsarian past in which the male and female "halves" of the human race were fused into one being, "a unity in which the male and female realize[d] their true nature."[22] When, in the course of history, the "Primeval Sphere" represented in this Unitary Sexual Image divided itself (an event described only as an "evolutionary choice made long ago in some misty past") the male and female hemispheres of the human being were separated from one another.[23] From that moment, these hemispheres felt an "eternal and unwavering motivation . . . to transcend the Primeval Mitosis and achieve supreme identity in the Apocalyptic Fusion."[24] Until the late 1950s, Cleaver argued, this fusion had been impossible largely because historical impediments had thwarted all attempts to achieve it. Primary among those impediments had been class antagonism.

Class-based societies were sustained by the individual's alienation or fragmentation—two terms Cleaver used virtually interchangeably. These societies were able to reproduce themselves only through the projection of multiple images of "fragmented sexuality." Rather than viewing themselves in terms of their alienation from the Unitary Sexual Image, individuals in class-based societies evaluated themselves in terms of their difference from members of other social classes. The upper and lower classes thus both saw themselves as somehow deficient, but, according to Cleaver, their deficiencies were conceived, incorrectly, through comparisons to flawed models. Just when it appears that Cleaver would like to reduce all class conflict to a function of this sexual alienation, however, he argues precisely the opposite. Foregoing any attempt to measure the distance between the individual and the Unitary Sexual Image, he instead offers a description of the psychological, social, and, of course, sexual distance separating men of the elite classes from those of the lower classes. It was in this distance, the "fragmentation" of society and the individual, that the historical roots of racial antagonism lay.

This fragmentation had been cemented, he explained, through the functional separation of "Man as thinker" from "Man as doer." As he put it, "When the self is fragmented by the operation of the laws and forces of Class Society, men in the elite classes usurp the controlling and Administrative Function of the society as a whole—i.e., they usurp the administrative component in the nature and biology of the men in the classes below them."[25] Men of the upper classes, in an attempt to insulate themselves from all reminders of bodily existence, expropriated the minds of lower-class men, forcing those men to labor in their service. Men of the lower classes were thus reduced to mere physicality, as the "administrative component in their own personalities" was "denied expression."[26] As in the Hegelian model of lordship and bondage, these men are forced to be the body that the administrators require yet renounce. In a racially homogeneous society this distinction between laborers and administrators would at least appear to be fluid: with no visible difference between the elite and the lower classes, individuals could more easily imagine occupying a social position different from their own. A field hand could dream of becoming a landowner, for example, and a landowner could perhaps even envision himself working the soil. In the United States, however, the alienation of mind from body appeared absolute, as the class antagonisms upon which this alienation rested were ultimately figured as the putatively biological and, more importantly, visible difference between black and white.

Nevertheless, in spite of the social and historical power consolidated in the figure of the Omnipotent Administrator, the title Cleaver uses to refer to (white) men of the upper classes, these men were inevitably filled with anxiety. To deny his physicality, the Omnipotent Administrator had been forced to renounce his own masculinity. This figure was "markedly effeminate and delicate by reason of his explicit abdication of his body."[27] As a result, Cleaver wrote, women of the elite classes, compelled to maintain heterosexual relationships with these Omnipotent Administrators, had been forced to affect a kind of "ultrafemininity." To assuage the fears of the Omnipotent Administrators, they had gone to every extreme to deny their own corporeality. Like the Omnipotent Administrator, therefore, the "Ultrafeminine" eschewed all manual labor, and projected the "domestic component" of her character onto the women of the lower classes. In doing so, she expropriated the femininity of these "Subfeminines," or "Amazons" as Cleaver calls them, redoubling her own so that the Omnipotent Administrator might appear masculine by contrast.

Men of the lower classes were forced to occupy an equally precarious and contradictory position. On one hand, relegated to a purely physical existence, these men appeared somehow "Supermasculine." As Cleaver puts it, "The men most alienated from the mind, least diluted by admixture of the Mind, will be perceived as the most masculine manifestations of the body."[28] But these "Supermasculine Menials," as he labeled them, signified through the very bodiliness that had been used to oppress them the instability of the Omnipotent Administrator's position. They served as a constant reminder to the men of the upper classes that any social or political power they might hold was ultimately founded in a ruse. In spite of his position, therefore, the Omnipotent Administrator secretly resented the lower classes. He was "launched on a perpetual search for his alienated body," becoming, in the process, either "a worshiper of physical prowess" or disgusted by "the body and everything associated with it." Left to fear his own impotence, the Omnipotent Administrator's "profoundest need is for evidence of his virility. His opposite, the Body, the Supermasculine Menial, is a threat to his self-concept.. . . . Yet, because of the infirmity in his image and being which moves him to worship masculinity and physical prowess, the Omnipotent Administrator cannot help but covertly, and perhaps in an extremely sublimated guise, envy the bodies and strength of the most alienated men beneath him."[29] In a cruel twist, the Supermasculine Menial, forced to enact an exaggerated version of his own physicality, is mythologized. In the mind of the Omnipotent Administrator, he becomes a hypersexual being. For this he is both despised and admired. He serves as both the ground against which the Omnipotent

Administrator defines himself, and the "psychic bridegroom" of the Ultrafeminine, who, Cleaver argues, receives only frustration from her relations with the Omnipotent Administrator.

The historical myth of the "Primeval Mitosis" aside, Cleaver's theory of the relations between race, class, gender, and sexual identities was hardly unique. In 1966 sociologist Calvin C. Hernton echoed these arguments regarding the interconnectedness of white and black male sexuality when he wrote that the self-esteem of white males "is in a constant state of sexual anxiety in all matters dealing with race relations. So is the Negro's, because his life, too, is enmeshed in the absurd system of racial hatred in America. . . . [He] cannot help but see himself as at once sexually affirmed and negated. While the Negro is portrayed as a great 'walking phallus' with satyr-like potency, he is denied the execution of that potency."[30] As Frantz Fanon so succinctly formulated this impasse in *Black Skin, White Masks*, which, it is worth noting, first appeared in English in 1967, "The Negro is fixated at the genital; or at any rate he has been fix-ated there."[31] According to Fanon, when confronted with the black male, the white male feels compelled "to personify The Other," and thus convinces himself that "the Negro is a beast."[32] Yet alongside his intense fear of the black male's physicality there is an equally strong attraction: "If it is not the length of the penis, then it is the sexual potency that impresses him. . . . The Other will become the mainstay of his preoccupations and desires."[33]

What is most interesting about this fixation, at least for my own purposes, is the prominent role it played in the formulation of Black Power politics. As literary theorist Robyn Wiegman has argued, many proponents of black liberation looked merely to invert the racial and sexual relations of white and black men, and thus turned the mythical potency of the black male into one of the animating concepts of that movement. In her essay "The Anatomy of Lynching," Wiegman demonstrates the ways in which much of the rhetoric of Black Power, from Cleaver's call for the reassertion of a fully realized black "manhood" to LeRoi Jones's assertion that "Most American white men are trained to be fags," simply turned these racial and sexual stereotypes on their heads.[34] "The threat that this inversion pose[d] to the cultural framework of white masculine power cannot be underestimated," she writes, "as Black Power quite rightly read lynching and castration as disciplinary mechanisms saturated by the hierarchical logic of sexual difference."[35] Regardless of its liabilities, Wiegman argues, the "intense masculinization" attributed to the black male following the abolition of slavery as a justification for the highly ritualized and sexualized practice of lynching provided these young men with a ready-made form for the performance of social antagonism. In writing that "most American white men are trained to be fags," then, Jones looked not to interrogate the myth of the black male as hypersexualized beast, but to draw attention to the striking homoeroticism of practices such as lynching, and, by extension, racial oppression as such, in an effort to invert the power relations of black and white males in America.

For Cleaver, though, the key to abolishing the contradictory sexual and social roles of the "Omnipotent Administrator" and the "Supermasculine Menial" was not the reclamation of any "satyr-like potency." Rather, the solution lay in the reunification of body and mind, the fusion, within white and black men and women, of both menial and administrative faculties. And to the dismay of the Omnipotent Administrators, he explained, American society was already in the midst of its own "convalescence." "If the separation of the black and white people in America along the color line had the effect, in terms of social imagery, of separating the Mind from the Body," he writes, the Supreme Court's 1954 ruling in *Brown v. Board of Education* was "a major surgical operation performed by nine men in black robes on the racial Maginot Line which is imbedded as deep as sex or the lust for lucre in the schismatic American psyche. This piece of social surgery, if successful . . . is more marvelous than a successful heart transplant would be, for it was meant to graft the nation's Mind back onto its Body and vice versa."[36] In declaring the doctrine of "separate but equal" to be unconstitutional, the Supreme Court had laid the groundwork for racial equality in America. Thus, in what were potentially the final moments of an American culture headed for "chaos and disaster," a "lascivious ghost" appeared and guided the nation "down a smooth highway that leads to the future and life."[37] And in the years since the Supreme Court's decision, the record was "clear and unequivocal . . . the whites have had to turn to the Blacks for a clue on how to swing with the Body, while the blacks have had to turn to the whites for the secret of the Mind."[38] As blacks attended previously white schools and boycotted buses, Elvis Presley appeared on television "sowing seeds of a new rhythm and style in the white souls of the white youth of America."[39] Once these initial "bridges" were erected between the Body and Mind, Cleaver wrote, the mutual attraction of society's figurative halves could never again be denied. As much as those who opposed this personal and collective reunification "would strike out in the dark against the manifestations of turning, showing the protocol of Southern Hospitality reserved for Niggers and Nigger Lovers—*SCHWERNER—CHANEY—GOODMAN*—it was still too late." The culture of racial convalescence had already been established. "For not only had Luci Baines Johnson danced the Watusi in public with Killer Joe, but the Beatles were on the scene, injecting Negritude by the ton into the whites, in this post–Elvis Presley–beatnik era of ferment."[40]

In some sense it is thus surprising to think that at the very moment that the "future and life" of America were said to lie in an individual and social fusion of Body and Mind, masculinity and femininity, Cleaver was about to embark on a political career that emblematized not a utopian androgyny or racial hybridity but the image of the black male as "the bestial excess of an overly phallic primitivity."

Upon his release from prison in 1966, Cleaver moved to San Francisco, where he wrote frequently for *Ramparts* magazine and helped found a cultural center known as the Black House. According to historian Kathleen Rout, "Cleaver's dream in 1966 had been to cut off all contact with the criminal world and to work to benefit himself, his race, and his country."[41] Much as he began with hopes of participating in a cultural revolution, however, early in 1967 Cleaver's political career appeared to undergo a dramatic transformation. In February of that year, a San Francisco–based organization known as the Black Panther Party of Northern California had planned a memorial rally in honor of slain civil rights leader Malcolm X, at which Betty Shabazz, Malcolm's widow, was to be the guest of honor.[42] As this organization, with whom Cleaver was loosely affiliated through his work at the Black House, was concerned primarily with issues of cultural nationalism rather than armed revolution, members were reticent to carry loaded weapons for fear of running afoul of the law. They were therefore in search of bodyguards capable of escorting Ms. Shabazz safely to and from the event. For this they had contacted another,

unrelated group from Oakland calling itself the Black Panther Party
for Self-Defense, which had recently attracted a great deal of attention with a practice known as "Panther Patrols."

In these patrols, carloads of armed party members would follow
and "observe" the actions of officers from the Oakland Police Department. When the officers either made a traffic stop or simply questioned someone on foot who looked "suspicious," the Panthers, each
carrying either a pistol or a shotgun, would climb out of their own car
and observe the interaction from a "safe" distance. The patrols were
entirely legal—laws concerning the possession of firearms and inter-
ference with police procedures were studied scrupulously in their
planning—but for the officers they were wholly unnerving. In Oakland, a city in which accusations of police brutality were common,
a group of armed black men (and eventually women) roaming the
streets citing laws and legal codes regarding arrest procedures and
encouraging members of the community to join them, engendered
a profound reversal of long-standing power relations. And although
these patrols gave rise, in turn, to a focused campaign of harassment by the Oakland Police Department, they nonetheless earned
the Panthers a local reputation as something like the vanguard in
the struggle for black liberation. It should thus come as no surprise
that the San Francisco Panthers would have asked Huey Newton and
Bobby Seale, the Oakland Panthers' founders, to provide protection
for Ms. Shabazz. Nor is it surprising that Newton and Seale, who saw
themselves and the Black Panther Party for Self-Defense as Malcolm
X's true legatees, leapt at the offer. To them, it seemed the perfect
opportunity to generate greater publicity for their party, and to show
the people of the Bay Area just which Black Panther Party was truly
serious in its revolutionary aspirations.

On the day of the rally, Newton and a cadre of Oakland Panthers
arrived, fully armed, to meet Shabazz at the airport. The police,
watching anxiously, were effectively helpless to stop the Panthers,
for as always their carrying of firearms conformed precisely to the
letter of the law. The party members made their way through the
airport fully armed, and escorted Shabazz to the San Francisco
offices of *Ramparts* magazine, where she sat for an interview with
Cleaver. When she emerged from the building surrounded by Newton
and the Panthers, a local television cameraman stepped closer for a

clearer view. As Shabazz had asked not to be photographed, Newton placed a magazine in front of the camera's lens. When the cameraman grabbed the magazine and tried to push Newton out of the way, Newton sensed a golden opportunity. He dropped the magazine, punched the cameraman, and demanded that his adversary be arrested for assault. The police, of course, refused, telling Newton that he, if anyone, should be arrested for assault. The Panthers responded by surrounding the police with their shotguns and rifles drawn. The few officers that were there, each carrying only a revolver, were outnumbered and overpowered. In broad daylight, on camera, the Black Panther Party for Self-Defense had once again rendered the police visibly vulnerable.

In contrast to Wiegman's contention, rather than simply inverting the standard lynching narrative, a standoff like this one, not to mention those that often resulted from the Panther Patrols, seemed to invoke the black folk character known as the "badman," an outlaw hero who, as John W. Roberts explains, defied legal authorities and thus came to be seen as something like a champion of the people. Having begun, in the wake of emancipation, to see the forms of structural racism as the greatest obstacle to their freedom and equality, the black community embraced the figure of the badman. From Stackolee to John Hardy, the badman, associated "with a kind of secular anarchy peculiar to the experience of free black people," breaks the law not for purely selfish reasons but to "restore a natural balance . . . in the social world."[43] Often starting as a participant "in a lifestyle in which illegal activities are pervasive," the badman inevitably undergoes a personal, political transformation.[44] With an act of spectacular violence, he embarks on a journey in which his deeds begin to serve ends beyond mere self-preservation; they begin, as Roberts puts it, to serve "as an emulative model of heroic action."[45] African American readers saw these deeds, which, to others, might appear simply illegal, as being based in a higher morality. They interpreted the badman's violent confrontations with authority as "a reflection of values guiding action traditionally accepted as advantageous in maintaining the harmony and integrity of black communal life."[46] For this reason, according to Roberts, the badman was the opposite of the "bad nigger," whose violent behavior was never directed at any goal beyond immediate, personal gratification, and so inspired fear in blacks as much as whites.[47] Unlike the badman, who helped to define and demarcate the black community in opposition to the "law," the "bad nigger" provided police with an excuse to enter and intervene in that community, thereby threatening its solidarity. As Jon Michael Spencer has written more recently, whereas the badman practices "self-determinative politico-moral leadership," the "bad nigger" is caught in a cycle of "narcissism and hedonism"; simply put, his acts are "genocidal."[48] Where Civil Rights leaders such as Martin Luther King, Jr., looked to avoid both of these characterizations, attempting instead to speak to white America in its own terms, Newton and the Panthers seemed to feel that the black folk tradition could in fact be a useful tool in organizing within the black community.

Appropriately, in recounting the standoff between the Panthers and the police, Cleaver wrote, almost literally, as if he were retelling a folk tale. When *Ramparts* staff members asked Cleaver who that was challenging an officer to draw his gun, he told them only that it was "the baddest motherfucker I've ever seen. I was thinking, staring at Huey surrounded by all those cops and daring one of them to draw, 'Goddamn that nigger is c-r-a-z-y!' Then the cop facing Huey gave it up. He heaved a heavy sigh and lowered his head. Huey literally laughed in his face and then went off up the street at a jaunty pace, disappearing in a blaze of dazzling sunlight."[49] Cleaver's account was undoubtedly embellished, but all the same, or perhaps for that very reason, it points to something quite important. Although surprising to the officers, the particular way in which Newton and the Panthers presented themselves as real-life badmen was all too conventional. Cleaver's retelling allows one to see that, drawing on more than just the black folk tradition, Newton's "revolutionary" tactics also drew heavily on the standard forms of mass culture. The "vanguard" of the struggle for black liberation, in other words, had begun to look very much like they had been lifted straight from a Saturday matinee. As virtually any fan of midcentury cinema can attest, armed outlaws fighting for "the people," standing up to lawmen acting on behalf of a cruel, oppressive system were all too common in films of the period. Thus, one reporter for the *San Francisco Chronicle* quipped, "If a Hollywood director were to choose [the Panthers] as stars of a movie melodrama of revolution, he would be accused of typecasting."[50] The Panthers, for all of their apparent revolutionary zeal, seemed almost *too* perfect for the role of urban American guerrilla warriors. Their popularity with local media therefore seemed both shocking and, at the same time, entirely predictable.[51]

Rather than dismissing the Panthers' revolutionary tactics as being inherently compromised for this reason, Cleaver joined the party shortly after the scene in front of *Ramparts*, taking a position as the party's Minister of Information. Accepting nearly full responsibility for the party's public relations, Cleaver began working with Newton and Seale to design actions that would capture the imagination not only of the people but of reporters and photographers as well.

A rare opportunity soon presented itself when Newton and Seale spoke as guests on a local radio talk show in Oakland. During the show, conservative assemblyman Donald Mulford phoned the station to announce that he planned to introduce a bill that would "get" the Panthers by outlawing the carrying of firearms in California.[52] The legislation was obviously designed to bring an end to the Panther Patrols, and, likewise, Mulford's public announcement was an attempt to counter the growing embarrassment that authorities across the state were suffering at the hands of various local party chapters. In response, therefore, Cleaver, Newton, and Seale orchestrated what became perhaps the most famous of the Panthers' actions: their descent upon the state capitol in Sacramento.

On May 2, thirty Panthers, twenty of whom were visibly armed, entered the capitol building in Sacramento seeking to take the floor for a public address during a meeting of the California state legislature. Once inside the building, after a series of wrong turns, the group found its way to the floor, but was quickly ushered into a separate conference room. There Seale read the Panthers' prepared statement, "Executive Mandate Number One," for a group of photographers and journalists. The text, prepared by Seale, Newton, and Cleaver, referenced the recent police slaying of a black teenager named Denzil Dowell in Richmond, California, and decried the Mulford bill for its attempt to remove guns from the hands of the lower classes. Although the event's climax proved relatively sapless—the Panthers, effectively declawed, delivered their statement from a peripheral conference room while the bill passed in the legislature—the party had achieved its goal nonetheless. Cleaver, Newton, and Seale had

Bobby Hutton and Bobby Seale, California State House, May 2, 1967.
Photo by Wade Sharrer.

conceived of the event as the historical counterpoint to the 1963
March on Washington. Where earlier demonstrators avoided even
the suggestion of anger or violence, lest Congress and television
viewers get the impression that they were attempting to force the
passage of civil rights legislation, the Panthers deliberately courted
that perception. Their plan was not to bully legislators into rejecting
Mulford's bill but to force reporters to pay attention. "That we would
not change any laws was irrelevant, and all of us . . . realized that
from the start," Newton later explained. "Since we were resigned to
a runaround in Sacramento, we decided to raise the encounter to a
higher level."[53] Their goal was to use the media to deliver the party's
message to every potential ally and enemy in the state: "Dozens of
reporters and photographers haunt the capitol waiting for a story.

This made it the perfect forum for our proclamation."[54] In 1967 a sit-in was no longer newsworthy. To appeal to the media, activists would have to offer reporters something truly spectacular.

Nevertheless, while Newton admitted that the Panthers had carried their guns into the building to capture the reporters' attention, he insisted that the degree to which members of the press were fascinated by this was truly bemusing. Seeing the breaking news on television that afternoon, he wrote, he could not help but be surprised. By carrying guns into a meeting of the legislature the Panthers had ensured themselves a spot on the news but had obscured their "revolutionary" message. "Executive Mandate Number One" was "definitely going out," Newton recalled. "Bobby read it twice, but the press and the people assembled were so amazed at the Black Panthers' presence, and particularly the weapons, that few appeared to hear the important thing."[55] To correct the mass media's distorted coverage Newton and Seale planned a special edition of the party's newspaper, the *Black Panther*, that would tell "the truth about Sacramento." As Seale later wrote, it was important for the Panthers to provide their side of the story, for "there were so many lies about the Black Panther Party. . . . Lies by the regular mass media—television and radio and the newspapers—those who thought the Panthers were just a bunch of jive, just a bunch of crazy people with guns."[56] The *Black Panther* would present the party's official account of the events that took place in Sacramento, counteracting the media's sensationalism with the truth.

Upon Cleaver's urging, however, the "truth" about Sacramento ran alongside what would ultimately become the most reproduced of all Panther images: a photograph of Newton seated in a wicker throne, holding a spear in one hand and a rifle in the other. Far from telling the "truth" about party activities and ideologies, the photograph further embellished the mythology of Newton and the Panthers. By presenting Newton in his full Panther uniform—white shirt, black pants, black shoes, black leather jacket, and a black beret—and surrounding him with a collection of objects connoting what one might call, taking a cue from Roland Barthes, a stereotypical "Africanicity," the photograph drew a hackneyed parallel between the struggles for black liberation being waged almost concurrently on the two continents. Although the African liberation struggles were certainly fought with guns, this juxtaposition of rifle and spear, Black Panther wardrobe and tribal shields, Huey Newton and what looked to be a selection of props left over from *Sanders of the River* (the film famously disowned by star Paul Robeson because of its blatant racism) served to encode the Panthers' political project in not only racial but also in mass cultural terms. Ironically, Newton claimed to dislike the image for this very reason. On one hand, from the time of the party's founding, he and Seale had taken great care to emphasize the Panthers' opposition to the rhetoric of cultural nationalism and racial separatism. On the other hand, the image appeared to place undue emphasis on Newton as an individual, thereby betraying the party's efforts to forge a collective, community-based political movement. To present any single Panther as a celebrity, the new messiah of black liberation, risked sending conflicting messages to the *Black Panther*'s readers. The image, one might say, came uncomfortably close to suggesting something like a rapprochement of the vanguard and kitsch.

Poster of Huey Newton in Black Panther Headquarters window. Photo by Pirkle Jones. Image courtesy of the Pirkle Jones Foundation.

Sanders of the River, 1935. © Douris UK, Ltd.

To Newton's dismay, this seemed to be exactly what Cleaver wanted from the image. Cleaver, along with Beverly Axelrod (the attorney who had helped negotiate his release from prison in 1966 and at whose house the Panthers had worked on the newspaper), assembled these props, and arranged for a "white Mother Country radical" to take the photograph. Upon seeing the final prints, Cleaver insisted that the image be featured in each subsequent issue of the *Black Panther*, that local offices display it prominently, and that copies be made available for sale in the form of a sixteen-by-twenty poster. Few seemed to understand his attachment to the photograph. As his longtime friend, and eventual Yippie, Stew Albert recalls, a number of the party's supporters had reservations as well. "Cleaver showed up at my pad and wanted to put up a large personality poster of Huey," he later wrote. "Because Eldridge was so happy with his new friends, I agreed. But when he gave me a bunch of posters for my 'associates,' I felt unspoken reservations about their corniness.

Besides, personality posters were relatively new. Even our San Francisco rock stars hadn't as yet made use of them. They seemed narcissistic and quasi-cultic, not really ideal food for egalitarian revolutionaries."[57] Not unlike Newton, Albert was, at least at the time, uncomfortable with the photograph because it presented the Black Panther Party less as the vanguard of a "people's revolution" than as an unwitting mirror of the society its members claimed to despise. The poster thus seemed as if it might alienate the party from all potential allies, both black and white.

For many involved in Black Power politics, it was all just too much. Radio interviews, media stunts, publicity posters: were the Panthers truly focused on revolution, or were their tactics just an attempt to gain fame and notoriety? In the summer of 1967 Newton responded to questions like this in an essay explaining "the correct handling of a revolution," arguing that it would be a mistake for radicals to shy away from publicity, as the "sleeping masses must be bombarded with the correct approach to struggle and the party must use all means available to get this information across to the masses." The party's critics seemed to "want the people to say what they themselves are afraid to do. That kind of revolutionary is a coward and a hypocrite."[58] A "real" revolutionary had to be willing to risk his/her life, and to stand in the face of the "dog power structure" not to ask for equal rights but to show that s/he would take them by any means necessary. To inspire the masses to make a revolution themselves, the vanguard party would have to show them how. True revolutionaries, that is, would make themselves visible. For this reason, Newton continued, the Watts Riots, much as the violence may have caused many young blacks to fear the repercussions of openly defying authority, were nevertheless a powerful revolutionary catalyst. They did not bring about real, qualitative change—the immediate effect of the riots, after all, was the death of large numbers of young blacks—but for Newton that was not the point. The riots in Watts, Philadelphia, Chicago, Jersey City, and Detroit, to name only a few, provided an expression of the very real frustration and hostility felt by the inner-city poor. They were, as Fanon called the anticolonial uprisings in 1950s Africa "the sign of the irrevocable decay, the gangrene ever present at the heart of colonial domination."[59] At the same time, though, Newton was equally interested in the way in which

Rioters in Watts pose with "captured" police cruiser, August 1965. Photo by AP.

these actions seemed to appeal to the media. While any riot was destined to end disastrously for its participants, those in Watts had been "transmitted across the country to all the ghettoes of the Black nation. The identity of the first man who threw a Molotov cocktail is not known by the masses, yet they respect and imitate his action."[60]

For all of the very real damage they had caused, the Watts riots provided a stunning image, one as inspiring for many young blacks as it was dreadful for whites.[61] For this reason, as important as it might be to organize in individual neighborhoods, if the vanguard hoped to foment revolution on a national (or international) level, local interventions would never be sufficient. They would need to distribute images of their activities to a mass audience; they would need, like the rioters in Watts, to get the country's attention. "Millions and millions of oppressed people may not know members of the vanguard party personally, but they will learn of its activities and its proper strategy for liberation through an indirect acquaintance provided by the mass media."[62] To "capture the imagination" of the people, revolutionaries would have to engage the press.

To be sure, disagreements over whether, or how, civil rights or Black Power advocates should seek to use the media as a tool were nothing new. Questions about the media's role in depicting and defining racial politics, an integral part of the civil rights movement, from the March on Washington to the Selma-to-Montgomery voting marches of 1965, were quite familiar by the time the Panthers arrived on the scene. Speaking of the March on Washington, for example, Malcolm X, who had himself appeared on television numerous times in the late 1950s and early 1960s, denounced the event's organizers for having played so obviously to the cameras. The problem was not, as one might expect, that the media distorted the demonstrators' message. In fact, he said, the media had no need to misrepresent what had happened, for the entire event had been created just for them: "The marchers had been . . . told *how* to arrive, *when*, *where* to arrive, *where* to assemble, when to *start* marching, the *route* to march . . . even where to *faint*. . . . Hollywood couldn't have topped it."[63] As historian David Carter has shown, internal tensions over media coverage of civil rights/Black Power politics can be seen quite clearly in the 1966 "Meredith March Against Fear." As he set out to complete James Meredith's march from Memphis to Jackson, Mississippi (Meredith had been ambushed and sent to the hospital with multiple gunshot wounds) Martin Luther King, Jr., claimed to have heard words that "fell on my ears like strange music from a foreign land."[64] Angry young blacks had begun to shout that they would no longer suffer beatings at the hands of white racists; they refused to follow King in singing "We Shall Overcome," instead switching the hymn's lyrics to "We Shall Overrun." And in what was—at least for the collection of journalists following the march—the most shocking inversion, when they heard the familiar call "What do you want?" marchers responded not with the standard cry of "Freedom!" but with the much more confrontational cry of "Black Power!" This very vocal disagreement had been orchestrated by one of the other organizers behind the march, Stokely Carmichael, the new leader of the Student Nonviolent Coordinating Committee (SNCC). Carmichael and other SNCC officers had requested King's attendance because they understood that his presence would guarantee the interest of journalists and photographers. When King arrived, however, SNCC essentially used his image against him. King, in other words, was invited to march so that SNCC might dramatize the tactical and ideological shift taking place in American racial politics.

What struck people as new, or discomfiting, in the Panthers' actions was not so much their opportunistic staging, therefore, but the forms they chose to appropriate. These concerns regarding the Panthers' "revolutionary" images and tactics only intensified in the months that followed the Party's appearance in Sacramento. In October of 1967 Newton was imprisoned, charged with the murder of Oakland police officer John Frey, and Seale was involved in a series of trials, including the original conspiracy trial of the Chicago 8, and the New York trial of the Panther 21, accused of murdering undercover police officer Alex Rackley. In their absence, Cleaver surprised many Panthers by assuming the role of the party's leader and spokesman, ushering in what David Hilliard has called the "second life of the Party."[65] Prior to Newton's arrest, Cleaver had refused even to sign his name to the pieces he wrote for the *Black Panther*, preferring instead to use the byline "Minister of Information, Underground." In Newton's absence, however, Cleaver seemed to make a concerted effort to become the public face of the party. He exploited the interest aroused by actions like the one in Sacramento, playing upon and embellishing mass-media coverage of the party's actions. By the time *Soul on Ice* appeared in February 1968, Cleaver was already a national celebrity. He traveled cross-country, making appearances on television talk shows, giving speeches to large audiences on college campuses, securing endorsements for the Panthers from celebrities such as Marlon Brando, and running for president on the Peace and Freedom Party ticket with Yippie Jerry Rubin as his running mate.[66]

Of course, like Newton and Seale before him, Cleaver's role as the party's spokesman made him the target of an organized campaign of official harassment. On April 6, in the midst of riots set off by the assassination of Martin Luther King, Jr., Cleaver and a group of Panthers were pulled over by the Oakland police, and what the officers claimed was a routine traffic stop quickly turned into a shootout.[67] After fleeing the scene, only to be trapped in the basement of a nearby home and inundated with teargas, Cleaver and fellow Panther Bobby Hutton surrendered. Hutton emerged from the home disarmed, only to be shot in the back and killed by the officers, and Cleaver, having been shot in the leg while inside the house, was arrested and imprisoned. His parole was revoked immediately, forcing him to spend the next two months fighting to regain his freedom, a legal battle that ultimately enabled him to intensify the Panthers' media campaign.[68] Upon his release from prison he began to bombard the masses not with Newton's "correct approach to struggle" but with a series of images presenting the Panthers as defiant "Negroes with guns." Calling upon the distinction made famous by Malcolm X, he told reporters that with the death of Martin Luther King, Jr., the "field nigger" takeover of the black liberation movement had been completed. Later he wrote in a statement for *Ramparts* magazine, "The assassin's bullet not only killed Dr. King, it killed a period of history. It killed a hope, and it killed a dream . . . the war has begun. The violent phase of the black liberation struggle is here, and it will spread. From that shot, from that blood, America will be painted red."[69] Cleaver was not the only one to call upon this kind of rhetoric in the wake of King's death. As SNCC chairman H. Rap Brown wrote in his 1969 political autobiography, *Die Nigger Die!*, although nonviolence "might have been tactically correct at one time in order to get some sympathy for the Movement," in 1969 "the stark reality remains that the power necessary to end racism, colonialism, capitalism and imperialism will only come through long, protracted, bloody, brutal and violent wars with our oppressors."[70] The "respectable Negroes" of the 1950s and early 1960s, Cleaver and Brown suggested, had been superceded. The violence that was purportedly inherent in every black male was on the verge of boiling over.

More than Brown, however, or any other Black Power spokesman for that matter, Cleaver seemed to capitalize on the perceived threat of a stereotypical black masculinity. In 1968, for example, he was invited to participate in teaching an experimental sociology course on race relations at the University of California at Berkeley. Upon hearing that Cleaver would be placed on the state's payroll, then governor Ronald Reagan demanded that the state board of regents block the course. Asking Cleaver to speak on the causes of social unrest, Reagan said, would be like "asking Bluebeard of Paris, the

Eldridge Cleaver at the University of California, Berkeley, October 3, 1968. Photo by Pirkle Jones. Image courtesy of the Pirkle Jones Foundation.

wife murderer, to be a marriage counselor."[71] Reagan's reaction, of course, only helped publicize the lecture, which, when finally held, drew such a crowd that it had to be moved out of the lecture hall and into the public square. Later that year, Robert Scheer of *Ramparts* magazine wrote, "As the U.C. issue splattered across California newspapers Cleaver moved . . . from Humboldt to Orange County, 'roasting Reagan's tail' in a series of public addresses . . . and the TV and newspaper coverage of the duel between the Sanctimonious Reagan and the Freewheeling Cleaver was fantastic."[72] At each stop on his statewide tour, Cleaver delivered the kind of absurdly fiery rhetoric audiences had come to expect. That fall he spoke at Stanford University, opening his lecture with a pointed verbal attack on Reagan. "Fuck Ronald Reagan," he said. "Fuck Stanford University, if that's necessary, dig it? That may or may not be the limit of my vocabulary, I don't know."[73] He repeated the sentence "Fuck Ronald Reagan" throughout his address, almost as if it were a kind of mantra, and at one point declared,

> Someone said that [state superintendent of public instruction] Max Rafferty has a Ph.D. in physical education, in football and baseball and basketball and ball-head, I don't know. I don't know what his credentials are. I know that he has a yackety-yak mouth and I can only relate to one adversary at a time. I want to challenge Max Rafferty to a duel, but he's too old to whip me, I could kick his ass. But I challenged Ronald Reagan to a duel, and I reiterate that challenge here tonight. I say that Ronald Reagan is a punk, a sissy, and a coward, and I challenge him to a duel, I challenge him. I challenge him to a duel to the death or until he says Uncle Eldridge. And I give him his choice of weapons. He can use a gun, a knife, a baseball bat or a marshmallow. And I'll beat him to death with a marshmallow.[74]

While audiences seemed to hang on Cleaver's every word, some were becoming increasingly uncomfortable with these performances. In 1970 journalist Don Schanche wrote of a conversation with a press photographer who was concerned that the Panthers, and Cleaver in particular, had not yet learned "to adjust their speech and actions to the audiences they face. . . . They want support from middle-class people, but they're turning them off with that kind of talk."[75] For others, however, the issue was not a lack of middle-class support but the *wrong kind* of middle- (and upper-) class support. The caricature of Black Power that Cleaver performed seemed to resonate less with "street brothers" than with those who had no personal experience of racial discrimination. In other words, the more Reagan and Rafferty sought to silence Cleaver, the more white supporters flocked to the party. And because Cleaver's tactics appeared almost to embrace stereotypical notions of black masculinity, the new cross-racial alliances he was cultivating seemed thoroughly problematic. As Tom Wolfe quipped, white liberals and "radicals" had been attracted to Cleaver and the Panthers not because of the party's ideological purity but because the Panthers appealed to a kind of *"nostalgie de la boue,* or romanticizing of primitive souls."[76] That is to say, the white audiences that filled lecture halls and penthouse parlors to hear Cleaver speak saw the Panthers' combination of violence and vulgarity as proof less of their revolutionary fervor than of their racial authenticity. For white audiences, whether they supported or despised the Panthers, Cleaver and other party members seemed to speak with the voice of an essential "blackness"—a violent rage that could no longer be suppressed.

Even after eventually fleeing the United States to avoid returning to prison, Cleaver, still officially a member of the party's executive committee, continued to issue statements urging blacks to engage in armed conflict throughout America, and calling for a full-scale guerrilla war in the country, to begin on Long Island in 1969. That year, exiled in Algiers, Cleaver told journalist John McGrath that if a plan could be devised allowing him passage back into the United States, he would lead the country's oppressed in a real uprising, one that would reveal America to be a "skeleton in armor."[77] For Newton, still in jail awaiting trial, regardless of the moral and monetary support Cleaver had secured for the party, statements like this were a serious concern. He worried that Cleaver's rhetoric threatened not only to provoke official retaliation but also to alienate the black community. Following his release from prison in 1970, therefore, Newton began to distance the party from Cleaver's increasingly outrageous pronouncements. References to guerrilla warfare were eschewed; the Panthers stopped patrolling; the Black Panther Party for Self-Defense became, simply, the Black Panther Party; Bobby Seale campaigned for local office; and social initiatives like the Breakfast for Children program, in which the Panthers provided poor inner-city children with free breakfast each day before school, became official talking points. Newton even renamed his position. No longer wanting to be called the "Minister of Defense," he asked first to be known as the party's "Supreme Commander," and later, finding that title too self-important, settled on "Supreme Servant."

Ignoring these obvious changes, Cleaver continued to speak of revolution. The increasing tension within the party came to a head in February 1971, when Newton was asked to appear on a local television talk show in Oakland. During the show, host Jim Dunbar phoned Cleaver in Algiers so that the three might participate in a roundtable discussion on what appeared to be the Panthers' new direction. As the cameras rolled, rather than praising the party's social programs as Newton had hoped, Cleaver accused Newton and the rest of the party's leaders of cowardice.[78] The Black Panther Party, he said, had lost its nerve. Not surprisingly, when the program finished, Cleaver was immediately excommunicated. Not long after, Newton wrote an essay for the *Black Panther* in which he claimed that Cleaver's expulsion had been inevitable.

According to Newton, the party's leaders had learned from their mistakes. They had begun to discourage "actions like Sacramento and police observations because we recognized that these were not the things to do in every situation or on every occasion." The party had come to see actions such as the Panther patrols and the confrontation in front of *Ramparts* magazine as failures, he wrote, for "the only time an action is revolutionary is when the people relate to it in a revolutionary way."[79] Although these performances had at one time provided a model for the Black Panther Party, in the end they had proven more costly than Newton had imagined. The community had simply been unprepared to interpret the Panthers' imagery correctly. As a result, the party had never connected with the black community in the way that he had hoped. And Cleaver, who had joined the Panthers only after seeing actions like these, emblematized this failure of understanding: "Without my knowledge, he took [the standoff in front of *Ramparts*] as *the* Revolution and *the* Party."[80] The initial efforts to present the Panthers as an organization of "badmen," in other words, had backfired; viewers both black and white had mistaken the Panthers for nothing more than a group of "bad niggers." And Cleaver, serving as the party's de facto leader, merely perpetuated this misunderstanding. "Under the influence of Eldridge Cleaver," Newton wrote, "the Party gave the community no alternative for dealing with us except by picking up the gun."[81] In spite of the party's apparent growth, Cleaver's emphasis on the image of the gun in Panther publicity had left the organization hamstrung. The people—Cleaver included—had not been ready to understand the true significance of that image. Rather than comprehending the party's profoundly revolutionary message, many young black males felt that the Panthers' "uniforms, the guns, the street action all added up to an image of strength," and, like Cleaver, they came to the party seeking a "strong manhood symbol."[82] "This was a common misconception at the time—that the party was searching for badges of masculinity," Newton wrote. But "the reverse [was] true: the Party acted as it did because we *were* men."[83] For Newton, those who really got it knew that manhood could never grow from the barrel of a gun.

The following year, he composed an even more damning version of this argument in an unpublished manuscript entitled "Hidden Traitor Renegade Scab: Eldridge Cleaver." Drawing quite heavily on the essays collected in *Soul on Ice*, Newton argued that one could never understand Cleaver's obsession with the image of the gun without first understanding the depth of his sexual neurosis. Cleaver, Newton argued, suffered from "paranoid dysfunctions" and "nihilistic confusion."[84] Having begun his career in the isolation of a prison cell, Cleaver had regressed upon his release to a vicious cycle of solipsism and narcissism. As a free man, Cleaver found himself unable to distinguish "between stage blood and real blood"; as a result, any discernible political ideology necessarily gave way to "wild monologues of masculine protest, and word salads of sadistic profanity directed at authority figures."[85] His confrontational style and "obsession of the gun" ultimately served to replicate the personal, psychological isolation he experienced in prison. Through violent imagery and language, Cleaver was able to avoid any and all communion, whether sexual, social, or political. His violently sexist and homophobic rants were therefore "never so political as they were rather pitiful counterphobic tactics designed to ward off . . . the political intimacy that the masses demand of their leaders."[86]

As much as he claimed to have been distressed by Cleaver's personal and political isolation, however, it was Cleaver's "repressed homosexuality" to which Newton devoted the lion's share of his analysis.[87] According to Newton, this particular "sickness" was central to Cleaver's persona. And, not surprisingly, the key to understanding this "sickness" lay in his famous critique of James Baldwin. In "Notes on a Native Son," Newton explained, Cleaver may have appeared concerned with Baldwin's political failures, but "in several places the frenzy of his denial breaks down and we catch a glimpse of a very different Eldridge Cleaver."[88] The vitriol Cleaver directed toward Baldwin, though framed as an analysis of Baldwin's reactionary racial/sexual politics, was really a clear indication that Cleaver suffered from a form of "homophiliac phobia, or fear of the 'female' principle."[89] This fear had led not only to Cleaver's repeated condemnations of same-sex desire, Newton argued, but to his personal history as a convicted rapist. Throughout his life, Cleaver had "vacillated between these mechanics of denial of homosexual panic and a pseudo-sexuality directed not at women so much as the *idea* of women."[90] Caught up in the convulsions and compensations of his own denial, his social, political, and literary analyses had, like his behavior, become disjointed. Baldwin *had* to be attacked; "masculinity" *had* to be equated with true liberation—Cleaver's "sickness" allowed for nothing else.

While Baldwin had escaped "the problems of the repressed homosexual" by openly embracing his sexuality, Newton argued, Cleaver remained ensnared in his own self-hatred, a self-hatred Newton illustrated with the story of a 1967 dinner party for James Baldwin. "Cleaver had been invited," Newton explained, and, rather surprisingly, "he in turn invited me." More shocking still, Newton then said, "when we arrived Cleaver and Baldwin walked head onto each other and the giant 6'3" Cleaver bent down and engaged in a long, passionate french [*sic*] kiss with the tiny (barely 5 feet) Baldwin. I was astounded at Cleaver's behavior because it so graphically contradicted his scathing attack on Baldwin's homosexuality."[91] As stunning as this revelation might have seemed, for Newton it was, in retrospect, only too predictable. This was because virtually all of Cleaver's behavior—his history as a rapist, his strident homophobia, his "obsession of the gun," and so on—could be explained in terms of a deeply conflicted sexuality. Likewise, Cleaver's "political" tactics, his absurd braggadocio and apparent need to constantly manufacture conflict, marked him as a man thoroughly terrified of his "'female' principle." "If only this failed revolutionist had realized and accepted the fact that there is some masculinity in every female and some femininity in every male," Newton lamented, "perhaps his energies could have been put to better use than convincing himself that he is everyone's super stud."[92]

But for Newton, the kiss between Cleaver and Baldwin, like Cleaver's purportedly conflicted sexuality, signified more than anything else a lack of authenticity. It was the fatal slip that unraveled Cleaver's entire persona, revealing him to be nothing more than a fraud. In Newton's account, the inability to distinguish reality from play-acting was Cleaver's fundamental failing as a revolutionary: he believed that stage blood was real blood, that guns and erect penises amounted to "true" masculinity, and that, in turn, the reclamation of this "true" masculinity was the equivalent of "real" liberation. According to Newton, the ability to discern truth from fiction was the key to making revolution. The Black Panther Party was, in his words, "out to create non-fiction."[93] The irony of Newton's attempt to discredit Cleaver through what was, in effect, a form of gossip-mongering/gaybaiting is therefore difficult to overlook, particularly as it came on the heels of Newton's public profession of support for the gay liberation movement.[94] But it is the ease with which Newton transformed Cleaver's overwrought masculinity into the signifier of a profound sexual anxiety that I find so fascinating—not only because of the historical persistence of this critical operation but also because it stands in surprising contrast to the theory of racial self-presentation offered in another essay Newton penned simultaneously. As he worked on "Hidden Traitor Renegade Scab," Newton was also composing a "Revolutionary Analysis" of *Sweet Sweetback's Baadasssss Song*, praising the film for its clever deployment of stereotypes.

The film's narrative revolves around the character known only as Sweetback, played by the director, Melvin Van Peebles. One night Sweetback, a young man raised in a Watts brothel, agrees to accompany two police officers to the local precinct to appear in a lineup of murder suspects. On their way to the station, the officers arrest a young black revolutionary named Moo-Moo. Before arriving at the station they stop once more, and the officers begin to beat Moo-Moo savagely. Sweetback, taking pity on the young man, comes to his defense, and in the ensuing struggle nearly kills the officers. The remainder of the film consists of an extended manhunt in which Sweetback, with the help of the "Black Community"—whom Van Peebles credits as the film's true stars—evades the police and escapes to Mexico. On his journey, Sweetback relies on the assistance of pimps, prostitutes, preachers, and gamblers, and more than once exchanges sex for his safety—most famously, perhaps, during a scene in which he literally fucks the leader of a hostile motorcycle gang into submission. As Newton put it, "The corporate capitalist[s]" had made *Sweetback* available to the general public only because they had "fail[ed] to recognize the many ideas in the film."[95] Those in charge of distributing the picture saw it not as a revolutionary call to arms but as a tale of picaresque heroism revolving around the stereotype of the hypersexual black buck. By playing this role, appropriating and resignifying images that had been used to oppress black men for more than a century, Van Peebles secured national distribution for his film (not without some effort, of course), allowing his encoded "revolutionary" messages to reach millions. What made *Sweetback* "revolutionary," in other words, was not, as David Joselit has argued, Van Peebles's insistence on operating outside the studio system.[96] Rather, it was his ability to make radical politics appear utterly conventional. "Van Peebles," Newton writes, "is showing one thing on the screen but saying something more to the audience."[97] Sweetback's sexual escapades, for example, are "always an act of survival and a step toward his liberation. That is why it is important not to view the movie as a sex film or the sexual scenes as actual sex acts. . . . The real meaning is far away from anything sexual, and so deep that you have to call it religious."[98] For Newton, when Van Peebles showed himself (and his son) having sex in the film, he did so not to titillate the audience but to re-present the stereotypes of black masculinity, to manipulate them as symbols, to "signify" as Newton puts it. Where Cleaver seemed to use stereotypical images only to propagate misunderstandings, Van Peebles had devoted his work to correcting them. By providing young black men and women with this "Revolutionary Analysis" and urging them to see the film again, Newton hoped to awaken them to the deeper, "religious" truths of its imagery.

As Henry Louis Gates, Jr., has explained, however, the political potential of the practice known as signifying (or "Signifyin(g)," as Gates writes it, noting the way the final "g" is most often silent in black vernacular speech) is not so simple. Signifyin(g) is not one operation per se but a kind of umbrella term, encapsulating the various modes of figurative language used in African American writing and speech. It is tempting to think of these practices—as Newton apparently did—as a type of direction through indirection, a way of drawing on a pre-existing language while inserting critical connotative differences. But as Gates makes clear, while Signifyin(g) may imply the speaker's disdain for those with whom that pre-existing language is associated, the practice nevertheless underscores the hegemonic power of that language. While it suggests in some sense a "protracted argument over the nature of the sign," it does so only by emphasizing "the chaos of ambiguity that repetition and difference . . . yield in either an aural or a visual pun."[99] Gates, therefore, describes Signifyin(g) not as a traditionally oppositional or revolutionary tactic but as a process akin to the Freudian dreamwork. The real importance of the Signifyin(g) gesture, that is, lies neither in the signifier nor in the signified (the manifest or the latent content), but in the ways in which the speaker somehow exceeds the limitations of the sign itself, exerting pressure on the signifier's form to indicate a desire that is constitutively repressed because its articulation in existing language is impossible. What is at stake in the practice of Signifyin(g) is not revolution, therefore, but the ability to read individual African American subjectivities out of their stereotypical formulations.

Placing Gates's theory of signification next to Newton's "revolutionary analysis" of *Sweet Sweetback* raises two interrelated questions. First, if Signifyin(g) is never a pure expression of opposition, if it cannot avoid reinscribing a pre-existing language or cultural form, why was Newton so willing to offer his unqualified praise for *Sweetback*? And second, if re/citing a stereotypical vision of black masculinity could indeed hold revolutionary implications, what separated Van Peebles's successful performance from Cleaver's apparent failure? One could make quick work of the first question, of course, by suggesting that Newton simply failed to recognize that the act of Signifyin(g) would always be divided against itself. Perhaps, that is, his faith in the film's political potential was simply naïve. Yet, while this may explain Newton's enthusiasm regarding *Sweet Sweetback*'s wide release, it fails to address the far more important distinction that Newton hoped to maintain between Van Peebles and Cleaver, a distinction based, I believe, in the opposition between the "badman" and the "bad nigger."

Once again, according to Roberts, the badman appears to break the law in a way that restores a "natural balance" to the black community. His "transgressions" are only seen as such by those charged with maintaining an official "law and order." For those who are, in effect, the victims of that official system, the badman's acts enable the community to define itself, to police its own borders and behav-

iors. And, although Van Peebles, at the end of the film, referred to
Sweetback as a "baad asssss nigger," the character very clearly
draws upon the "badman" tradition. From his upbringing in a brothel
to his near-murder of two police officers and his subsequent flight,
the often-silent Sweetback clearly develops from one who appears
merely inarticulate to one who forgoes speech in favor of action. His
act of brutal violence functions as a political awakening. If anything,
Sweet Sweetback's Baadasssss Song takes up the figure of the badman only to make the significance of his actions more explicit: rather
than killing a dishonest criminal who violates the community's standards of conduct, Van Peebles's hero confronts the police directly.
Where Gordon Parks's *Shaft* (1971) was based in more conservative,
middle-class ideals, *Sweetback* presented the "black community" as
something like an American underclass exploited by both church
and state. By taking the figure of the badman and turning him into
the hero of a contemporary action film, Van Peebles hoped to reach
young men and women who, though not politically active, may very
well have found themselves the victims of an unjust legal system.
Like the Newton of 1967, Van Peebles believed that in the late twentieth century, mass media imagery, if assembled in such a way that
it "not only instructs but entertains," was perhaps the quickest way
to radicalize the "street brothers [and sisters]."[100]

While Van Peebles used the character of Sweetback to call upon
young black men and women to enforce the borders of their community, and to combat the unjust and inappropriate intrusion of the
state, Cleaver, at least in Newton's portrait, seemed incapable of
moving beyond mere publicity stunts. Much as he may have believed
that his rhetoric could inspire bold, revolutionary action by the
same young men and women who flocked to see *Sweetback*, Cleaver
had failed to recognize the difference between a leading man and
a revolutionary, between "stage blood and real blood." As Newton
makes clear, the Panthers eventually came to see that any attempt
to bring the badman character to life would face a series of nearly
insurmountable obstacles. From official harassment to popular
misunderstandings, the Panthers' early tactics had painted the party
into a corner: Understood less as inspired, radical visionaries than
as egotistical bullies and criminals, the Panthers failed to affect real,
meaningful social change. Instead of fortifying the boundaries of the

"black community," when the badman stepped out of the folktale and into the world, he seemed only to give the state another reason to intervene. Where, in folk tales, the badman might help to define and rally the community, on the streets, face to face with the police, his actions served only to provoke the law, and thus to threaten the community's stability. In the eyes of the authorities, in other words, the badman and the bad nigger were indistinguishable. Faced with the apparent failure of his attempts to embody the myth of the badman, therefore, Newton felt compelled to reassert the distinction between reality and fantasy, fact and fiction, revolution and theater. Fiction was the realm in which the characters of the badman and bad nigger could remain neatly separated, where the badman, as the defender of the community, could serve as an exemplary, self-conscious, moral being. In the realm of "real" political action, on the other hand, the project of building and defending a community would require a different type of action based not in intimidation and neutralization but in communication and education. For the true purpose of the "revolutionary," in Newton's view, was to make the people aware of their collective identity, to draw them together as a community so that they might realize a form of historical, political agency. This, in Newton's most generous passages, is what Cleaver had never grasped. He had never, in Newton's formulation, come to recognize the distinction between fake blood and real blood. It was not that Cleaver was unable to see the pain and suffering inflicted upon the community as a result of the Panthers' violent images and rhetoric but that he never lost faith in the inspirational power of those performances. Cleaver the activist was ultimately incapable of separating himself from Cleaver the neurotic, whose attraction to violent imagery was rooted in deep psychic conflict.

In the years since Newton penned his analyses, of course, Cleaver the actor/activist has been largely erased from the historical record in favor of Cleaver the paranoid misogynist and homophobe. In what is perhaps the most famous example of this, Michelle Wallace described Cleaver as an extreme example of what she called "black macho." Pursuing personal and racial emancipation, he, like many others who fought for the rights of black men in the late 1960s, unwittingly enacted an oppressive, stereotypical vision of African American masculinity, one that, unfortunately, too many individuals were willing to take seriously. *Soul on Ice*, she wrote, was "a book that appealed to the senses. Cleaver was violent and advocated violence. Cleaver was macho and the sixties were years in which macho heroism was highly exalted and taken seriously by many people of all sorts of political and intellectual persuasions. . . . People yearned for the smell of blood on a page and Cleaver provided it."[101] For Wallace, Cleaver embodied the most harmful aspects of the Black Power movement. As much as he appeared to understand the ways in which "sexually, black women and white women were victims of America's history and that the white man was the victim of his own Frankenstein monster," the methods he seemed to believe would undo these historical inequities served only to perpetuate the structures of sexual, racial, and political oppression that he decried.[102] When he envisioned the restoration of a mythical black masculinity, Cleaver foolishly placed the entire task of liberation on his own shoulders, overlooking the real and potential contributions of women and gay men to the struggle for equality, and thus dooming his "revolution" to failure. "When the black man went as far as the adoration of his genitals could carry him, his revolution stopped. A big Afro, a rifle, and a penis in good working order were not enough to lick the white man's world after all."[103] More recently, E. Patrick Johnson has taken up Newton's psychoanalytic reading of Cleaver, seizing on the story of Cleaver's and Baldwin's "passionate french kiss" to say that, aside from "being an explosive bit of gossip, Newton's recollection of the events at this party become rich fodder for discussion of Eldridge Cleaver's anxiety regarding his relationship to James Baldwin, race, and sexuality. . . . Cleaver's disavowal of Baldwin's homosexuality in 'Notes of a Native Son,' [*sic*] then, is actually symptomatic of Cleaver's guilt about his ungrieved homosexuality."[104]

I would never want to suggest that there is no merit in these arguments. After all, it would be difficult to maintain that a convicted rapist who later looked to market men's pants with a built-in codpiece—the "Cleaver Sleeve"—always operated with the most nuanced gender politics in mind. Nevertheless, in their haste to dismiss Cleaver as misogynistic, heterosexist, homophobic, and/or simply neurotic, Wallace and Johnson—along with authors such as Kobena Mercer, Isaac Julien, and Leerom Medovoi—overlook a crucial aspect of Cleaver's political persona, namely that it was, quite literally, a performance. How else could a man so painfully aware of the stereotypes concerning black masculinity—so painfully aware that "what white America demands of . . . black [men] is a brilliant, powerful body and a dull, bestial mind"—have so willingly embodied those very same stereotypes?[105] As Don Schanche explained to the photographer who questioned the appropriateness of Cleaver's rhetoric, "After listening to Cleaver . . . I'd guess it's a tactic. He doesn't talk the same way privately as he does publicly. He's a soft-spoken, obviously literate man. He doesn't even say the same words. . . . It's almost as if he has to remind himself of the tactical rhetoric when he does use it in conversation."[106] Instead of looking to explain this apparent disconnect between Cleaver's private and public personae with speculations about individual neuroses, therefore, I would prefer to return to "Notes on a Native Son," and to reinterpret that essay, along with Cleaver's embodiment of a stereotypical black masculinity, as a potentially critical engagement with the historical limitations of the struggle for black liberation. Before returning to "Notes on a Native Son," however, it is necessary to discuss, however briefly, Norman Mailer's 1957 essay "The White Negro." For, according to Cleaver, his disgust with Baldwin stemmed less from the latter's criticisms of Richard Wright than from Baldwin's critique of "The White Negro" in his essay "The Black Boy Looks at the White Boy."

In "The White Negro," Mailer sought to understand the interest of postwar authors such as Jack Kerouac in nearly all aspects of black culture. Their enthusiasm fascinated Mailer, as, in the wake of World War II, the majority of white society seemed to be suffering from "a collective failure of nerve." It seemed, therefore, that the figure of the "hipster," a true American existentialist, had arisen in response to this. The hipster was, according to Mailer, "the man who knows that . . . if the fate of twentieth century man is to live with death from adolescence to premature senescence, why then the only life-giving answer is to accept death, to live with death as immediate danger."[107] He (in Mailer's account the hipster is always male) is marked by a strong disbelief "in the words of men who . . . controlled too many things" or in the "socially monolithic ideas of the single mate, the solid family and the respectable love life."[108] In opposition to the social system created and controlled by these men and ideas, the hipster cultivated the "antithetical psychopath" within, hoping to "create a new nervous system" that would allow him to engage life wholly in the present, without being burdened by considerations of past or future. Physical pleasure would be the sole justification of his existence. "He seeks love," Mailer wrote. "Not love as the search for a mate, but love as the search for an orgasm more apocalyptic than the one which preceded it."[109] The hipster's valorization of the corporeal and search for the "apocalyptic orgasm" provided him with the courage to perform "unconventional" acts in the face of a "partially totalitarian" society.

At the same time, though, because their immersion in the present also involved a refusal to pass moral judgment on acts of violence, many hipsters would inevitably be susceptible to the influences of "the first truly magnetic leader whose view of mass murder is phrased in a language which reaches their emotions."[110] To prevent this, Mailer argued, the hipster had no choice but to take the "American Negro" as his example, "for he has been living on the margin between totalitarianism and democracy for two centuries."[111] The experiences of black males, filtered through jazz, would inspire this postwar avant-garde in its search not so much for a social or political alternative, but for a sexual utopia. Jazz embodied the black experience, Mailer believed, because "jazz is orgasm." It expressed the rage, the joy, the "constant humility" and "ever-threatening danger" of the black male's life, communicating all of these emotions by way of swinging rhythms that catered to the "obligatory pleasures of the body."[112] The success of hip as a lifestyle, therefore, would depend on whether or not the black male could become "a dominating force in American life. Since the Negro knows more about the ugliness and danger of life than the White, it is probable that if the Negro can win his equality, he will possess a potential superiority, a superiority so feared that the fear itself has become the underground drama of domestic politics." Racial equality would thus "tear a profound shift into the psychology, the sexuality, and the moral imagination of every White alive."[113]

As much as Mailer felt he was promoting the social and cultural value of the black male, Baldwin lamented his seemingly naïve reinscription of the myth of the black male as "a kind of walking phallic symbol."[114] For Baldwin, who claimed to have profound respect for Mailer as a writer, Mailer's willingness to indulge what appeared a blatant exercise in stereotypy was distressing. The hipsters and beatniks Mailer praised as the harbingers of a new, racially ambiguous individual were merely suffering, Baldwin wrote, from a "grim system of delusions."[115] Citing a passage from *On the Road*, in which Kerouac tells of a walk "in the Denver colored section, wishing I were a Negro, feeling that the best the white world offered was not enough ecstasy for me," Baldwin wrote that he was simply confounded by Mailer's professed formal and ideological reverence for such "offensive nonsense."[116] "What in the world . . . was he doing," Baldwin asked, "slumming so outrageously, in such a dreary crowd?" Why had Mailer felt compelled to follow these authors' lead in further demeaning, however unintentionally, the "sorely menaced sexuality of Negroes in order to justify the white man's own sexual panic?"[117]

According to Cleaver, this "flippant schoolmarmish dismissal" could not have been more misguided. Although Baldwin claimed that, had he so desired, he could have "pulled rank" on Mailer "precisely because I was black and knew more about that periphery he so helplessly maligns . . . than he could ever hope to know," for Cleaver there was a "decisive quirk in Baldwin's vision" regarding the very essence of blackness.[118] And, as Cleaver put it in this instance, the root of this "decisive quirk" was Baldwin's sexuality. Baldwin could never have appreciated Mailer's insights, Cleaver argued, because he lacked a true understanding of masculinity as such. He was offended by Mailer's argument only because he had failed to recognize the image of black masculinity put forth in "The White Negro." Much like his critique of the work of Richard Wright, in other words, it was Baldwin's alienation from his own masculinity that rendered him incapable of recognizing the most progressive forms of political, sexual, and racial identity. Thus, a "rereading of *Nobody Knows My Name* cannot help but convince even the most avid of Baldwin's admirers of the hatred for blacks permeating his writings."[119] This passionate defense of Mailer's work should come as no surprise. Cleaver's notion of "convalescence" was clearly rooted in the "profound shift" Mailer claimed would be witnessed in the "psychology . . . sexuality . . . and moral imagination of every White alive" if the black male were to assume a dominant social position—Cleaver even cited this passage in his own essay. Nevertheless, how can one possibly take Cleaver's theory of convalescence seriously, as his attack on

Baldwin and his enactment of the "supermasculine menial" persona contradicted nearly all of that theory's principle arguments? All, that is, except one.

The supermasculine menial was the assumed starting point, in both "The White Negro" and "Convalescence," for the reconciliation of white and black in America. For both Mailer and Cleaver, it was the excessively masculine, excessively physical—fixated at the genital—black male who would eventually teach progressive white youths to "swing with the Body."[120] And, for both authors, the stark opposition of a hypersexualized blackness and an emasculated whiteness leads to the logical conclusion of something like a bisexual utopia. As Mailer wrote, the hipster must "find his courage at the moment of violence, or equally make it in the act of love . . . create a little more between his woman and himself, or indeed between his partner and himself (since many hipsters are bisexual)."[121] For Cleaver, the reunification of the male and female "hemispheres" was the true goal of racial convalescence. But as much as this may have seemed to be little more than a call for an exclusively heterosexual society, Cleaver's alternate description of this utopia as a rejoining of the "male and female principles" of the individual, "Body" and "Mind," throws the assumed heterosexuality of this Unitary Social Image into question. After all, in the scenario he describes, "grafting the nation's Mind back onto its Body and vice versa" amounts to nothing less than the fulfillment of the white male's desire for the black male's body, and, conversely, the willful feminization of the black male. Could this have been what Cleaver was getting at when he wrote that the "driverless vehicle" that was America's soul would be saved at the last possible moment by a "stealthy ghost"? If so, what should one make of his seemingly strident homophobia?

The answer to this question may lie in the concluding paragraphs of "Notes on a Native Son." There, Cleaver, in what appears his most focused attack on Baldwin, invoked a comment by Mailer regarding "homosexual defiance." Mailer, he explains, once wrote that, "carried far enough it is a viewpoint which is as . . . anti-human as the heterosexual's prejudice."[122] Cleaver immediately stated his agreement with Mailer—or at least with a portion of what Mailer's statement suggests—but in doing so, carried the argument literally to the point of absurdity: "I, for one, do not think that homosexuality is the latest advance over heterosexuality on the scale of human evolution," he wrote. "Homosexuality is a sickness, just as are baby-rape or wanting to become the head of General Motors."[123] As offensive and ignorant as this statement may seem, however, in the following paragraph one finds not just this comment but the entire essay placed under erasure. After dismissing both Baldwin and Martin Luther King, Jr., as insufficiently masculine, and thus insufficiently "black," Cleaver writes that the predicament of black masculinity "is reflected in this remark by Murray Kempton, quoted in *The Realist*: 'When I was a boy Stepin Fetchit was the only Negro actor who worked regularly in the movies. . . . The fashion changes, but I sometimes think that Malcolm X and, to a degree[,] even James Baldwin, are our Stepin Fetchits.'"[124] It seems odd, to say the least, that Cleaver would allow Kempton to have the last word in this fashion. Of course, on one hand, Kempton's quote does suggest that Baldwin somehow performed his blackness for a white audience, and thus reinforces Cleaver's argument concerning gay black men. But the real force of the remark was directed not at Baldwin but Malcolm X, whom Cleaver, along with Ossie Davis, praised repeatedly as the embodiment of "our living, black manhood."[125] By suggesting that that "manhood," together with the form of manhood Cleaver looked ostensibly to deny, may have been little more than a form of minstrelsy, Kempton points to the ways in which the pairing of Baldwin and Malcolm X effectively encapsulated the contradictory stereotypes of black masculinity: the docile, conciliatory "boy," and the reckless, confrontational "bad nigger."

While it might be tempting to dismiss this passage as nothing more than an oversight, it is far from the only moment at which Cleaver the rhetorician, the performer, appears to be at odds with Cleaver the theorist of opposition. In his essay on the social and cultural "Convalescence" taking place in the United States, as I remarked earlier, Cleaver wrote that the runaway bus that was American society had been boarded and would be guided to safety by a "stealthy" and "lascivious ghost"—the slang term Cleaver often used to refer to gay men. Later in the same essay, Cleaver spoke of "toss[ing] the Beatles a homosexual kiss" to thank them for demonstrating what was perhaps the most effective means of social and cultural opposition at one's disposal: racial affectation. "Let us marvel," he wrote, at the genius of their image, which comforts the owls and ostriches in the one spot where Elvis Presley bummed their kick: Elvis, with his *un*funky (yet mechanical, alienated) bumpgrinding, was still too much Body (too soon) for the strained collapsing psyches of the Omnipotent Administrators and Ultrafeminines; whereas the Beatles, affecting the caucasoid crown of femininity and ignoring the Body on the visual plane (while their music on the contrary being full of Body), assuaged the doubts of the owls and ostriches by presenting an incorporeal, cerebral image.[126]

It was their savvy use of stereotypical imagery that had allowed the Beatles to inject "Negritude by the ton into the whites."[127] Cleaver felt that he owed the Beatles a kiss, therefore, for showing him that in this historical context the ability to pose, to adopt self-consciously the trappings of one's assumed racial identity, may have been the most effective form of action available. For while it may have seemed to some that the key to overturning the systemic racism plaguing American society was the full reclamation of the black male's "satyr-like potency," that potency, as Kempton's remarks on Baldwin and Malcolm X and Cleaver's telling vacillations indicate, could only ever be meaningful within the very same system of signification. To believe that one could successfully break free of American racism by becoming a real life badman was thus patently absurd. That this stereotype—as popular with the mass media as it was with "the people"—had become the dominant form for the politics of black liberation was less a testament to its power than to its repressive desublimation. This, I believe, is the point of Cleaver's citations: not that liberation will be achieved through a reclamation of black "manhood," or that the bus of American culture will, at the last moment, be redirected and saved by a "lascivious ghost," but that any attempt to reclaim that black "manhood," whether through "the law of [one's] rod" or an affected politeness, will inevitably remain trapped within the system it looks to overturn.

One might say, of course, that this raises even more insistently the question of whether, for Cleaver, the politics of black masculinity were coterminous with black liberation. If, that is, Cleaver's persona was an effort to make viewers recognize that the politics of black masculinity would always be stereotypical, was it also, by extension, an attempt to indicate the futility of the struggle for Black Power? If so, then even if Cleaver's performance was an elaborate put-on, he would still have been guilty of the omissions and simplifications described by so many of his critics. Rather than once again simply casting Cleaver aside, however, portraying his career as a ham-fisted critique of identity politics instead of an imprudent version of the same, it is important to recognize that no matter how stereotypical or contradictory his public statements may have seemed, they still made one thing quite clear: anger. What his statements lacked in coherent revolutionary ideology and subtle historical analysis they replaced with an unambiguous affect. For this reason it would be a mistake to read what I have described as Cleaver's critical engagement with the performance of black masculinity as a gesture of total resignation, or even one of thorough co-optation. The latter, of course, was the real point of Newton's psychopolitical analysis: in attempting to become a real life badman Cleaver had played directly into the hands of authorities, giving them an excuse to intervene in the black community, and to squash the struggle for black liberation in the process. Cleaver's mixture of anger and a stereotypical masculinity, in other words, had only served further to conflate in the eyes of the public the freedom fighter and the bad nigger. But what if this combination of image and affect, so troubling not only to Newton but to many historians of Black Power, could tell us something else about both Cleaver and the potential for an identity-based politics in contemporary culture? What if the performance Newton so feared approached the status not of the "bad nigger" of black folk tales but of the more recent "hardcore nigga" of gangster rap records? While to many this distinction may seem virtually meaningless, recognizing the difference between these two figures is crucial to understanding not only the contemporary state of what would once have been described as an African American cultural form but also the general predicament of all individuals, and thus all forms of political resistance, in the late twentieth century.

In the late 1980s and early 1990s, when "gangster rap" first gained widespread popularity, critics and theorists of African American culture attempted to define it in two opposing fashions. On one hand, there were those who argued that it was necessary to understand rap music as a logical extension of the traditions of black folk culture.[128] The same vernacular practices that Gates described in his analysis of Signifyin(g)—naming, capping, shit-talking, playing the dozens, and so on—laid the formal groundwork, these commentators maintained, for the types of lyrical play one finds in virtually any rap record. By extension, hardcore rap, when done properly, serves to uphold the tradition of authentic black cultural resistance to an oppressive, dehumanizing culture. Thus, instead of lamenting the younger generation's brazenness or lack of respect, we should approach rap music as yet another variation on the forms of culture that emerged, and will unfortunately continue to emerge, from the harsh experience of being black in America. These writers acknowledged, obviously, that hardcore rap was not always properly done—for every "conscious" MC like Chuck D one could find any number of profligate rappers essentially bastardizing the form for their own personal gain—but maintained that these corruptions or deviations were more the exception than the rule. On the other hand, for a second group of critics, gangster rap's supposed deviations effectively rendered the entire genre suspect. Hardcore rap, according to this position, marked a significant break with the traditions of African American culture.[129] Whatever formal similarities one might find between gangster rap lyrics and the rhyming insults and boasts of earlier vernacular forms, to describe these rappers as having somehow upheld tradition was to ignore the obvious change in attitude and tenor. One need not listen long to hear things that would never have been acceptable in earlier eras. Thus, these critics argued, hardcore rap signified not the continued vigor of African American culture but its historical predicament. It was crucial therefore to see this music for what it was: yet another indication of the general moral malaise that had haunted the African American community since the waning of the Black Power movement.

As R. A. T. Judy explains, however, both of these positions were guilty of the same crucial error. Each group was eager to determine the significance of rap music *for* African American society. Both sides of the debate were dedicated to maintaining "the difference between having experience and knowing it," that is, between merely enduring events and maintaining a critical distance from them, a distinction Judy sees as rooted in the foundational, historical opposition "between being a slave and knowing oneself in slavery." Structuring both arguments, then, was a common conception of political agency. For whether simply dismissing hardcore rap as the symptom of a general quandary, or attempting to distinguish between moral and amoral forms of rap, both sides were in fact fully committed to classical liberal conceptions of knowledge and subjectivity. On some level, this commitment is understandable; that conception of subjectivity, after all, has been integral to any number of historical victories and steps toward equality. At the heart of the abolitionist movement, for example, lay a notion of the slave as one who "knows him- or her-self to be other than the experience of slavery, knows him- or herself to be in that knowing," s/he "knows him- or herself as being heterogeneous from the it that is used up in slave labor."[130] This is why, in the debates over rap music, no matter which side one took, it seemed that any mention of the hardcore "nigga" conjured images of "angry, self-destructive violence" and "the armed and insatiable beast of capitalism that knows only exchange-value and the endless pursuit of greater pleasure."[131] That is to say, whether one claimed to appreciate the value of a select few "righteous" rappers, or lamented the way hip-hop music seemed to revel in the demise of African American culture, the hardcore nigga appeared as the latest variation on that most undesirable figure, the bad nigger. And this, according to Judy, foiled—and, one might argue, continues to foil— any effort to understand the real import not just of hardcore rap but of hip-hop more generally.

Like Newton's efforts to distinguish between the negative effects of Cleaver's public persona and the political potential of *Sweet Sweetback's Baadasssss Song*, this dispute over hardcore rap hinged on the question of whether it was in fact possible to draw a clear distinction between the selfish, hedonistic bad nigger and his self-consciously ethical opposite, the badman. For Newton, as for those who distinguished between a morally correct hardcore and its many vulgar imitations, this separation was absolutely necessary, for it enabled one to recognize the persistence of an alternative, authentic form of African American culture and opposition. For those who abhorred hardcore rap, of course, both of these distinctions had become increasingly difficult to maintain. As the traditional family had dissolved and the overall social fabric had unraveled, they argued, the possibility of an authentic African American culture, one removed from—not exhausted by—the domain of economy, had quickly faded. The badman had vanished as a historically meaningful character, leaving in its place a series of mere gangsters who willingly offered themselves as products, commodities to be bought and sold.

As Judy suggests, though, it may be necessary to reconsider the history of this ostensibly straightforward distinction between bad-men and bad niggers, as the apparently stark contrast it presents has not always been so clear. In fact, in its earliest formulations, the figure of the bad nigger was presented not so much as the scourge of a self-policing black community but as a hero. Its complement was not the self-conscious badman but the "nigger-as-thing," the human reduced to an exchangeable instrument of labor, a form of personal property. The bad nigger refused to submit to the laws of the planta-tion, refused to be a "nigger-thing." In this sense, Judy argues, the badman was not the bad nigger's opposite but his/her logical exten-sion. And this is precisely what makes the bad nigger such a conten-tious figure in more recent discussions of African American culture. For as much as it may suggest a form of individual sovereignty, it is an individual sovereignty that comes into being not through a moral act but through an absolute lawlessness: the bad nigger asserts a form of individuality through his/her willingness to put personal appetites ahead of any consideration of disciplinary consequences. Thus, Judy suggests, echoing Hegel's dialectic of lordship and bond-age, the bad nigger steps beyond thingness only by embracing his/ her thingness, accepting the possibility of his/her own death. This, he argues, is what makes it so important for contemporary historians such as Roberts and Spencer to distinguish between the badman and the bad nigger. For the "real threat of the bad nigger is in exhibiting the groundlessness of the sovereign individual . . . the bad nigger indi-cates the identification of human with thing, that the human can be only among things, cannot be beyond or abstracted from things."[132] For anyone with a real investment in maintaining the notion of an African American community composed of moral subjects, then, the inability to distinguish clearly between the bad nigger and the badman, between self-interest and self-consciousness, presents an obvious problem.

The hardcore nigga posed a similar, though not identical, dilemma. In equating the nigga and the bad nigger, those who argued over the cultural significance of hardcore rap suggested that the real danger facing contemporary African Americans may have been the inability to separate an authentic culture or community from the realm of economics, a self-conscious morality from commodification. And in this way, both sides of the argument stumbled over the very same obstacle. Each one, in spite of its stated concern with the maintenance or severance of a tradition, failed to come to terms with the historical reality it faced. Of course, both sides were, in some sense, correct: the hardcore "nigga" of gangster rap was inseparable from the problem of the individual, and of culture more generally, in the age of neoliberalism. For, as Judy writes, this is "the age of hypercommodification, in which experience has not become commodified, it *is* commodification, and *nigga* designates the scene, par excellence, of commodification, where one is among commodities."[133] The key to moving beyond this apparent stalemate, according to Judy, is to think "at the crux," to think "with the commodified nigga," who never failed to assure the listener that his/her rhymes were based in real experience, while at the same time calling the very idea of "real" experience into question by asserting that "virtually everyone involved in the commodified affect of his experience is a nigga."[134] This apparent contradiction, according to Judy, is part and parcel of what it means to "think hardcore." For the "hardcore nigga" comes into being by recognizing that experience "cannot be sold as is but must be abstracted and processed."[135] It must be exchanged for an easily communicable affect. Thus the "realness" to which hardcore rap so frequently refers is not some authentic experience completely removed from the processes of commodification but a "hypercommodified affect," "the value everybody wants." For this reason, while those committed to the notion of an authentic, self-policing African American community portrayed the hardcore nigga as simply the latest form of the bad nigger, the two characters could never fully coincide. Simply put, the bad nigger constituted him/herself through a commitment to unmediated experience, but for the hardcore nigga this notion of unmediated experience is nothing more than a myth. Thus, to adopt the persona of the nigga is not to claim an essential identity but to suggest that there is no subjectivity, no identity prior to its commodification.

Looking back on Cleaver's political career from this side of the "gangster rap" era, we would do well to consider the ways that, like the "militant Negro" in Jacob Brackman's account of the put-on, Cleaver, throughout his career, continued to recite the very terms he denounced, the stereotypes he repeatedly dismissed. Might it be more productive to read Cleaver's "passionate french kiss" with Baldwin, his "word salads of profanity," his challenges to Max Rafferty and Ronald Reagan, his seeming love affair with firearms, and his calls for a guerrilla war to be waged on the United States not as symptoms of a deep, personal neurosis but as put-ons, critical repetitions of a political persona that was, in itself, little more than a recitation of normative conceptions of black masculinity? Rather than attempting to determine what it might have meant for Cleaver to kiss Baldwin, then, or condemning him for extolling the "law of [his] rod," it may be more fruitful to ask if Cleaver and Baldwin both might have been somehow similarly amused by Cleaver's assertion that Baldwin was engaged in a "despicable underground guerrilla war, waged on paper, against black masculinity."[136] After all, how could Baldwin have sabotaged a masculinity that was, according to the logic of Cleaver's own arguments, always already circumscribed, a commodity not unlike the hardcore nigga of gangster rap?

Thus, while Cleaver's pronouncements have for so many years been taken at face value, interpreted as little more than a regrettable form of racial politics, perhaps there was something more, or different, at stake in his actions. From his citation of Murray Kempton to his admiration for the Beatles' racial posing—not to mention his kissing of Baldwin, or his absurd threat to beat Reagan to death with a marshmallow—the way in which Cleaver appears to palter and/or mock his own positions in such curious ways, at such key moments, suggests that he was far from the one-dimensional character condemned in the analyses of Newton, Wallace, Johnson, Mercer, and others. As I have attempted to demonstrate, however, the work of reclaiming Cleaver's political legacy depends not on excavating the "correct" interpretation of his work but on recognizing that in its self-contradictory thorniness his political career may in its own way have offered a critical commentary on the historical viability of utopian identity politics. Although some called in earnest upon an authentic blackness as the key to maintaining one's critical distance from the workings of American culture and society, Cleaver's "supermasculine" posing pushed the viewer to recognize that that distance was in itself nothing more than an illusion, that any purportedly "authentic" blackness was inherently compromised, constrained by the very system it opposed. In this sense, by reading Cleaver's persona as a performance rather than a revolutionary zeal rooted primarily in neurosis, we can begin to understand the critical edge of his "black macho." As with the Yippies and the Gay Activists Alliance, we may start to see in Cleaver's theatrics not the beginning of the end of "real opposition" but the historical emergence of new, more self-conscious and aesthetically complex forms of political resistance.

AFTERWORD

I MAGINE THIS: YOU STAND BEFORE AN ADVERSARY PERFORMING AN absolutely damning caricature of his or her behavior. You pull no punches, carrying each of this person's flaws and failings to their comic extreme. Your performance makes him/her appear incompetent, deceitful, despicable. When you conclude, however, the response is not one of anger, embarrassment, or shame. Instead, the target of your criticism simply looks at you, impressed, and says, "Wow! You have such great ideas! I wish I had come up with those myself!"

On more than one occasion, the contemporary artist/activist collective known as the Yes Men have found themselves in this very situation. Posing, for example, as representatives of corporations such as ExxonMobil promoting products like candles rendered from the flesh of the victims of climate change, "Andy Bichlbaum" and "Mike Bonanno" have infiltrated meetings on free trade and global industry to perform operations of what they call "identity correction," attempting to expose the twisted, inhumane logic of contemporary global capitalism.[1] But to Bonanno's and Bichlbaum's surprise, audiences have often welcomed their contributions—not because they are proud of their own ability to take a joke but because they are sincerely interested in the ideas and products the Yes Men have presented.

Oddly enough, critical discussions of the Yes Men rarely acknowledge these audiences' enthusiasm, a reaction the group's members say leaves them feeling "like inept puppeteers."[2] Those who have addressed the group's work have instead, almost without exception, treated their performances as an example of contemporary art's true activist potential.[3] In bringing this book to a close, therefore, it seems appropriate to look more closely at the apparent failure of signification these works evince, to ask why the Yes Men's efforts to "correct the identity" of various organizations and corporations are greeted more often with enthusiasm than contempt. In a decade that saw ironic performance become something like the standard form of "grassroots" opposition—one can think, here, of groups such as Billionaires for Bush or, on the other end of the (admittedly narrow) American political spectrum, the conservative student groups that staged events such as "affirmative action bake sales" in 2004—why did certain critical positions remain so difficult to recognize? Had the tactics described in the preceding chapters reached the inevitable moment of their exhaustion? Were the insights embodied in the performances of the Yippies, the GAA, and the Panthers simply assimilated like those of so many other artists and activists? Does the emergence of an action or movement like "Occupy Wall Street"/"Occupy" signal definitively, as so many have suggested, that we no longer believe in the potential of, or even the need for, an aestheticized radicalism? These, it seems, are some of the most pressing questions we confront not only in beginning to reevaluate the legacy of the activists I have discussed but also in attempting to forge a radical politics for the twenty-first century.

At the 2006 Lexis-Nexis "Catastrophic Loss" Conference, which brought together representatives of the insurance industry only months after Hurricane Katrina devastated the Gulf Coast, Bichlbaum and Bonanno appeared under the aliases "Fred Wolf" and "Dr. Northrop Goody," claiming to be a pair of spokesmen from the Halliburton Corporation. Taking the podium, "Wolf" announced that, because the reduction in carbon emissions necessary to halt the effects of climate change would be detrimental to the profits of so many corporations, Halliburton had devised what its executives saw as a more practical solution. Rather than pressing for systemic changes that might head off the inevitable climatological disasters, they had instead looked to develop a personal, technological solution designed to sustain those who really mattered. "Those of us in positions of responsibility," he explained, "can't be satisfied with mere survival, but must guarantee, at every instant, the capacity and

Yes Men, Survivaball demonstration, May 2006.

resources to keep our thumbs firmly on the triggers of progress. . . . And the only way to do this is to maintain a highly sophisticated boots-on-the-ground strategy."[4] With this, he ceded the podium to "Dr. Goody," and, with the help of volunteers from the audience, began pulling on a large, inflatable, spherical suit.

As Wolf, along with two volunteers, zipped themselves into these "Survivaballs," Goody began to tell the audience about the many technological wonders it contained. In anticipation of future food shortages, for instance, the suit had been equipped with "Maniple Pods" capable of extracting nourishment from the carcasses of animals, and "Nutrition Refunction Centers" and "Food Reprocessors" to render valuable nutrients from the occupant's waste. Most importantly, these Survivaballs would allow wearers to come together, like amoebas, to form organisms/organizations capable of reasserting their power in the wake of a disaster. This last point was illustrated with a digital animation showing Survivaballs, assembled into the form of a giant woman, dancing through the empty streets of a deserted metropolis. As absurd as this all sounds, however, when Goody concluded his remarks and opened the floor to questions, the audience responded in a way that seemed all too familiar to the Yes Men. One man asked about the Survivaball's applicability in the case of a terrorist attack; another asked if there would eventually be a protective mask to shield the wearer's face; a third inquired about the suit's cost, but quickly withdrew his question upon realizing that, for its intended audience, cost would most likely be no issue. Like so many times before, Bichlbaum and Bonanno had not been caught, but this was only because the audience had failed to see "Wolf" and "Dr. Goody" as anything other than the Halliburton representatives they claimed to be.

Again, this earnest fascination has been one of the most common responses to the Yes Men's actions. For this reason, if one chooses to think of their performances only as hoaxes or pranks, they have been an unqualified success. Presenting the supporters of globalization with an outrageous caricature of their own behavior, the Yes Men manage to capture the wealthy and powerful on camera apparently expressing their greed and callousness openly and honestly. If the goal were merely to make their audiences the butt of an elaborate joke, as in the work of contemporary comedian Sacha Baron Cohen, this would be sufficient. But the Yes Men maintain that their performances are to function as a form of political intervention. These "identity corrections" are intended, they insist, as an enactment of Augusto Boal's "invisible theater," which strove to make the workings of power evident.[5] The goal of their stunts is not to escape unharmed but to contribute to the downfall of corporations such as Halliburton. Unlike Baron Cohen, therefore, whose performances as characters such as "Ali G." and "Borat" are in many ways more successful the longer they go undetected, the Yes Men's work would seem to depend on their characters' discovery. Those listening to the presentation must become upset, respond, and, ideally, denounce the prank in the media, thereby unwittingly exposing their own immorality to the world. Thus, when the men and women in these audiences fail to recognize the ruse, praising the two presenters for their "progressive" business sense rather condemning their progressive politics, the performance effectively grinds to a halt, leaving Bichlbaum and Bonanno, at least initially, to wonder where they went wrong. One could be satisfied to say, as the pair have, that their audiences simply "came with disbelief pre-suspended. Better, their disbelief had never existed: they knew [the presenters] to be . . . ordinary [Halliburton] representative[s]."[6] But one might also read their failure to provoke a response as an illustration of what Thomas Keenan has described as the contemporary impossibility of "mobilizing shame."

Attempting to mobilize shame for political purposes, Keenan writes, "presupposes that dark deeds are done in the dark, and that the light of publicity—especially of the television camera—thus has the power to strike preemptively on behalf of justice."[7] He recalls, though, that when thieves were caught on camera looting the Albanian town of Mijalic during the 1999 war over Kosovo, the perpetrators, some of whom were Serbian police officers, never attempted to hide their identities. Instead, upon seeing the cameras, they waved. In so doing "these policemen announced their comfort with the camera."[8] Citing Jean Baudrillard, Keenan argues that the potential shame of exposure was rendered anachronistic when we became information, evidence, images. No longer does one hear the classic fetishist's denial "I know very well, but . . . " Keenan argues, for "we all know everything, and there are no second thoughts, no buts. We know, and hence we enact our knowledge, our status, our sense of the complete irrelevance of knowledge."[9] By this logic, those who commit offenses against humanity do not fear the potential "correction" of their identity, to use the Yes Men's terms, because their actions are "done for the camera," they "come into being in a space beyond truth and falsity that is created in view of mediation and transmission."[10] The technologies that would seem to have made the mobilization of shame possible, in other words, have rendered shame itself obsolete. The question of visibility or invisibility is no longer decisive. In an age of mediatized acts and identities, everything is visible. And for this very reason, the significance of concepts such as "exploitation," "oppression," and "genocide," Keenan suggests, remains unintelligible.

As much as I appreciate Keenan's attempt to grapple with the difficulties of politics in the age of spectacle, should we really lay the blame for this failure entirely at the foot of the medium . . . or even the media? In a short piece from the mid-1940s—a time when, it is worth noting, the United States, the Soviet Union, and a number of European nations had all suspended the production of televisions and/or television programming—Theodor Adorno lamented that it had become "difficult to write satire."[11] Satire, he argued, seeks to compare an object with its purported qualities; it measures that object "against its being-in-itself," convicting it without any explicit indication of the satirist's own opinion. Successful satire depends, in other words, on the self-evidence of one's critique. For this reason, historically, the satirist quite predictably sided with authority, with those whose power rendered proof unnecessary. Fixing their sites on marginal or emerging value systems, satirists played repeatedly to their audiences' will to interpret social and historical change as an indication of a general decay of morals. But with the eventual dissolution of these "older strata" so threatened by moral decay, the force that guaranteed the effectiveness of the satirist's critique quickly dissipated. No longer able to appeal to an audience's consciousness of social tension, his/her works lost all traction. Contrary to popular wisdom, therefore, it was not the relativism of values that augured the death of irony but general accord. As Adorno put it, "Agreement itself, the formal a priori of irony, has given way to universal agreement of content. As such it presents the only fitting target for irony and at the same time pulls the ground from under its feet. . . . Today . . . the world, even in its most radical lie, falls back on the argument that things are like this, a simple finding which coincides, for it, with the good."[12]

Before simply applying Adorno's argument to the Yes Men's struggles, it is important to recognize that, looking back on the 1940s, the German political situation would be difficult to describe as one of "universal agreement," or even stability. For this reason, it is absolutely necessary to remember that, just as Adorno and his fellow Frankfurt School theorists were developing these ideas of the general accord underpinning modern society, a group of German economists had begun to formulate a theory in which the guiding principle of capitalism was said to be competition. As Michel Foucault recounted in his weekly lectures at the Collège de France in 1978–79, the free-market theorists of the Freiburg School in 1940s Germany, Walter Eucken, Franz Böhm, Alfred Müller-Armack, and others, argued that the international and interpersonal struggles that resulted from perceived inequality were in fact the engine that powered the development and expansion of the economy. Responding, like Adorno and his colleagues, to Max Weber's theory of the rational irrationality of capitalist society, the Freiburg School extolled competition as the forgotten, synthesizing logic of that society. Where classical liberal economics sought to establish something approaching equilibrium, these neoliberals, or "ordoliberals" as they are sometimes called in reference to their journal, the *Ordo Yearbook*, placed conflict squarely at the heart of their economic theories. Protectionism, state socialism, Keynesian interventionism—for these writers, any attempt by the state to stabilize the market, to curb competition, would inevitably end in disaster. Whether parliamentary Britain, New Deal America, or Soviet Russia, any state that allowed its economic policy to contradict liberal social ideals would invariably be forced to embrace a form of fascism. To be sure, these men had been actively involved in an effort to refute the dominant Keynesian model of economic thought since the early 1930s, but, as Foucault notes, it was not until the late 1940s that these ideas of a market fully freed from the fetters of state regulation began to take root. The reason, of course, was the peculiar difficulty facing postwar Germany, whose citizens, in 1948, were presented with what seemed a previously unthinkable dilemma: how, following the spectacular demise of a state, does one legitimize and give limits to a new form of government prior to its existence? The answer, at least for the Freiburg theorists, was to invert what they saw as the underlying principles of Nazism. As Foucault puts it, "Nazism enabled them to define . . . the field of adversity that they had to . . . cross in order to reach their objective."[13] It should have come as no surprise, therefore, to find them arguing that, in spite of appearances to the contrary, Nazism, a self-contradictory style of right-wing socialism, was the logical outcome of the state's attempt to combine liberal politics and economic interventionism. Where most (the Nazis included) had attributed destructive effects to the free market, the ordoliberals argued that destruction was in fact the result of unchecked state growth. The entire analysis, they asserted, should be reversed; instead of being limited by the state, the market economy should become the principle of the state's internal regulation.

As Foucault traces the development of this nascent form of neoliberal governmentality, he brings us, I believe, quite close to the set of ideas that lie at the heart of the Yes Men's critique of globalization. For the conditions and arguments that he sees attending the "birth of biopolitics" ultimately became, in the hands of Freiburg fellow traveler Friederich von Hayek and his followers in the Mont Pelerin Society, the founding principles of what journalist Naomi Klein has more recently described as "disaster capitalism." As Klein demonstrates, much as we might describe the effects of contemporary free market economics—recessions, mass poverty, and so on—as disastrous, it is important that we also recognize the extent to which capitalist expansion has come to depend on disaster as a tool. Where the collapse of the state provided the Freiburg School with an opportunity to promote their vision of an economy freed from official intervention, Klein argues that disaster has, since the 1970s, been the driving force behind the "new global economy." As Milton Friedman, one of the founding members of the Mont Pelerin Society, wrote in his classic text *Capitalism and Freedom*, "Only a crisis—actual or perceived—produces real change. When that crisis occurs, the actions that are taken depend on the ideas that are lying around. That, I believe, is our basic function: to develop alternatives to existing policies, to keep them alive and available until the politically impossible becomes politically inevitable."[14] For Friedman, in other words, the duty of free market theorists was to formulate utopian visions of a liberated capitalism, visions that would be impossible to realize without a social and political blank canvas. When crises erupt in the form of wars, depressions, or natural disasters, the theorist of the free market must be prepared to act quickly, seizing the opportunity to institute thoroughgoing change before the status quo can be reasserted. As Klein argues, the effects of this "shock doctrine" can be found from late-1970s Chile, where a severe economic crisis provided Augusto Pinochet with the opportunity to institute market reforms (with, of course, the personal advice of Friedman and his students), to Aceh, Iraq, and New Orleans, in which the physical destruction of existing states or cities has provided a clean slate for what is often called "reconstruction": a series of (nation-) building projects undertaken by for-profit consulting firms, engineering companies, and international financial institutions. When one begins to understand this method of exploiting crisis and disaster to generate profits, Klein asserts, it becomes possible to see that "some of the most infamous human rights violations of this era, which have tended to be viewed as sadistic acts carried out by antidemocratic regimes, were in fact either committed with the deliberate intent of terrorizing the public or actively harnessed to prepare the ground for the introduction of radical free-market 'reforms.'"[15]

This is what makes the historical pairing of the Frankfurt and Freiburg thinkers so fascinating as we attempt to understand the failed performances of groups like the Yes Men (one could also think, here, of collectives such as Billionaires for Bush). For Eucken's and Böhm's celebration of competition as the underlying logical premise of capitalism portrayed inequality as utilitarian in the most literal sense. It would, they and their followers believed, produce the greatest good for the greatest number. Perhaps, then, rather than saying, like Keenan, that moral disagreement has been rendered irrelevant by the media—arguably a variation on the all-too-familiar argument that our current predicament is the result of contemporary pluralism—one should think of the Yes Men's performances as doomed by an implicit consensus regarding the virtues of free trade. The problem is not so much the apparent cacophony but the unspoken agreement that lies beneath. No matter how absurd Bichlbaum's and Bonanno's performances seem, the oppression, exploitation, and inequality they attempt to present as part and parcel of globalization never manage to place the general benevolence of that system in question. For the Yes Men's audiences, that is, economic "shock therapy" is not just the best, though regrettable, option available at the moment. To the contrary, it is what it claims to be: the only economic system capable of raising standards of living throughout the world. When Bichlbaum and Bonanno spoke, at another gathering, of employing "a rational, economics-based approach to violence," audience members didn't flinch because they believed that this violence served the greater good. When, confronted by images of cities and villages ravaged by war, natural disaster, or trade imbalances, audiences fail to comprehend the moral implications of their acts, it is not because contemporary imaging technologies have reduced those phenomena to mere simulacra. It is rather, as Adorno might tell us, because those acts have been stripped of any sense of contradiction. Things, the world seems to tell us, are simply like this . . . and that is for the best.[16] Under these circumstances it is not just satire but virtually any critique of the "free market" that becomes in some sense unintelligible. If this is indeed why these gestures of political parody, irony, and caricature fail, then, as they move forward, the Yes Men's efforts to determine just how much exaggeration would have been sufficient to make an audience recognize the critical edge to their performances may ultimately prove futile. Bichlbaum and Bonanno may discover that, at the turn of the millennium, caricature was simply unable to "fix the world."

Given the arguments of the preceding chapters, this, obviously, should not be taken as a reiteration of old assertions that we should eschew questions of style in favor of "real" politics. It is particularly important to make that clear, as, indeed, one hears echoes of this sentiment all too often recently, with activists, journalists, sociologists, historians, and others resurrecting the rhetoric of the early 1960s in discussing the potential power of a movement like Occupy.[17] Virtually reciting the polemics of half a century ago, many of the movement's participants and supporters were eager to sing the praises of a new generation who, awakened by the "Great Recession" and the United States government's attempted solution of "bailing out" the banks that were ultimately responsible for the crisis, had taken up the unfinished work of fighting for social and economic justice. The conditions brought on by the crisis had provided a rare opportunity for the enactment of an authentic resistance—so authentic that many participants refused to speak of any concrete demands, for fear that any effort to simplify this movement, to reduce it to a mere representation, might betray its spirit. In the wake of the greatest financial disaster in generations, in other words, it has come to seem not just possible but logical for hundreds—if not thousands—of individuals to establish an outpost a stone's throw from the New York Stock Exchange and literally call investment bankers and hedge fund managers out for their role in catalyzing a global catastrophe. The bursting of the real estate/mortgage–backed securities bubble had made it necessary to address exploitation and class antagonism in explicit terms. In the fall of 2011, the winner-take-all logic of contemporary political and economic thought no longer seemed so self-evidently moral. Protestors could set up camp in Zuccotti Park, which they renamed "Liberty Square," as an open, unapologetic challenge to those who had for so long profited from the misery of "the 99 percent."

Occupy Wall Street General Assembly, December 1, 2011. Photo by AP.

From the autumn of 2011 to the summer of 2012, we were treated, again and again, to stories of demonstrators drawing on the spirit of "direct, participatory democracy" championed in the sixties by groups such as Students for a Democratic Society and the Movement for a New Society, emphasizing not the *image* of radical political action but an enactment of the ideal of government of all by all. Pulling back from the tactics deployed by groups like the Yippies, the Yes Men, and others, activists had begun to bypass the politics of mass mediation, we were told, in favor of a direct, productive collaboration between individuals. By refusing to offer pithy sound bites, or even to enumerate or discuss specific demands, "Occupiers" were said to challenge both the media and the general public to engage the movement in its own terms rather than in the clichés of contemporary political culture. At the same time, by making strategic decisions in the large, open-forum "General Assembly," where one dissenting opinion could theoretically spell the end of any particular proposal, participants had challenged themselves to enact a form of thought that is, as one discussion "facilitator" (as opposed to leader) explained to historian James Miller, diametrically opposed to the kind of thinking propounded by the present system. "When faced with a decision, the normal response of two people with differing opinions tends to be confrontational. They each defend their opinions with the aim of convincing their opponent, until their opinion has won, or, at most, a compromise has been reached," he said. "The aim of collective thinking, on the other hand, is to construct. That is to say, two people with differing ideas work together to build something new . . . it is the notion that two ideas together will produce something new, something that neither of us envisaged beforehand."[18] The General Assembly, in other words, shunned dialectical confrontations in hopes of engendering a creative dialogue, one in which individual positions and, as a result, the process of collaboration, remained open to improvisation. Not surprisingly, for many observers, this caused as much consternation as it did optimism. Miller, for example, writes that if the participants hoped to realize the true potential of Occupy, they must "avoid fetishizing the demand for consensus, and instead deploy rule by consensus only in situations where it may be both useful and feasible."[19] Only then, he argues, will they be able to forestall the boredom, frustration, and, ultimately, internal divisions that brought about the collapse of those earlier movements that attempted the same things.

Placing these practical questions of the General Assembly's broader political efficacy in abeyance, at least for the moment, I believe it is worth pausing to consider the form of this experiment in "collective thinking." Again, the "facilitator" in Miller's account focuses on the General Assembly's model of nonconfrontational exchange. Rather than aiming for "victory" and accepting a tepid compromise, he explained, Occupiers engaged in dialogical interaction as a potentially creative process. Here it is interesting, at least for my own purposes, to note the way that this language overlaps with a particular strain of contemporary art criticism. Discussing works that treat social interactions as an artistic medium, works that have been labeled "relational," "participatory," "social," and "dialogical," writers such as Nicolas Bourriaud and Grant Kester have outlined the ways in which a great deal of current artistic practice seeks to provide both artists and audiences with the opportunity to experience a radically open, indeterminate, intersubjective experience. In what is probably the most famous attempt to explain this focus on the direct engagement of the artist's interlocutors in works created since the mid-1990s, Bourriaud argues that it is the result, largely, of artists having reconceived the modernist avant-garde project. Leaving behind the vague and often private utopias suggested in earlier work, he writes, the new art takes "as its theoretical horizon the realm of human interactions and its social context."[20] What is at stake when Rirkrit Tiravanija serves guests dinner at a gallery opening, or when Ben Kinmont (or one of his collaborators) hands a random stranger a slip of paper informing the person that "We are the social sculpture," is the creation of a moment, what Bourriaud labels an "interstice," in which individuals might bridge the gap that separates them and collaborate in forging a community in the strongest possible sense. Thus, unlike the traditional work of art, which can only stand in mute opposition to the viewer, the "relational" work seeks to realize a political aesthetic through unscripted personal interaction. "It is not," Bourriaud writes, "a matter of representing angelic worlds, but of producing the conditions thereof."[21] In other words, where the modernist avant-garde only spoke impotently of dissolving the barriers between art and life, relational artists have begun taking actual steps toward that rapprochement. They have recognized that the project of eliminating the fissure separating art from life is inseparable from that of overcoming the distance between individuals.

For Kester, on the other hand, Bourriaud's underlying faith in this traditional avant-gardeist rhetoric causes him to miss a crucial detail. Far from overcoming the modern isolation of the aesthetic, Kester argues, "dialogical" works *depend* on it. To illustrate this point, he recounts a series of performance events organized by artist Suzanne Lacy in cooperation with local teachers and community activists. In the first of these, *The Roof is on Fire* (1994), 220 Oakland high school students sat in cars atop a downtown parking garage and engaged in casual conversations as an audience of over a thousand looked on—community members, as well as local and national journalists and camera crews had received invitations in advance. This initial happening, which enabled the teenagers to present themselves as thinking, feeling individuals rather than as stereotypical delinquents, gang members, teen mothers, and so on, led to further projects aimed at promoting understanding between teens and the representatives of social order, most notably in 1999, when Lacy gathered 100 students and 150 police officers in the same garage. This time, the objective was not simply to provide the students with an opportunity to show themselves as worthy of respect or sympathy but to ask both the teens and the police to set aside their standard conceptions of one another in pursuit of a potentially productive interchange. As Kester explains, Lacy's "goal was to create a 'safe' discursive space . . . in which both police and young people could begin to identify with each other as individuals rather than as abstractions."[22] The ultimate justification for this kind of art, Kester explains, can be found in the writings of the early-twentieth-century Russian philosopher Mikhail Bakhtin, whose theories of "polyphonic dialogue" highlighted the incompleteness of any utterance, its necessary dependence on an interlocutor or a community of speakers.[23] Meaning, for Bakhtin, could only ever be produced through an interaction with others. Thus, Kester argues, in contrast to so many modern art critics, who seemed to "seek indeterminateness and excess in an object that resists classification," Bakhtin offers us the possibility of finding that indeterminateness "in the act of dialogue itself, as the unexpected insights achieved via collaborative interaction produce new forms of subjectivity." For this reason, Kester concludes, "the dialogical artist will find his or her identity 'enriched' or expanded through collaborative interaction, but so, arguably, will his or her collaborators."[24]

I will return to this interest in Bakhtin shortly. For the moment, however, I would like to focus on Kester's suggestion that the creation of these "safe" spaces of dialogue is inconceivable apart from dominant conceptions of the aesthetic as definitively detached from everyday life. As he explains, anticipating the language of Occupy, individuals partaking in events such as Lacy's "would normally take opposite sides . . . attacking and counterattacking with statistics and moral invective. But in the ritualistic context of an art event," participants are "able to communicate outside the rhetorical demands of their official status."[25] I emphasize this point, in part, because it clearly marks Kester's difference from Bourriaud. Where the latter suggests that we have reached the point at which art might finally realize the historical project of the avant-garde, for the former, that type of creative engagement with the everyday is possible only insofar as art remains isolated from life. Eliminating the distance between the two may very well also eliminate the potential for meaningful communication. At the same time, though, Kester's account of contemporary "dialogical aesthetics" echoes, though not precisely, the arguments of Jacques Rancière, one of the most commonly cited philosophers in the contemporary art world. For, as Rancière has asserted repeatedly, the politics of aesthetics lie not, as so many have claimed, in simply dissolving the distinction between art and life, but in the irresolvable tension between artists' desire for social intervention and art's institutional autonomy. Unlike Kester, though, Rancière sees this autonomy as historically determined. In his account, art's isolation from "everyday life" is not to be understood as a tactical decision on the part of individual artists but as a constitutive aspect of our current historical sensibility. In opposition to those who find aesthetics to be obsolete, therefore, Rancière insists that this mode of thought remains valuable, as it invites us to consider that very contradiction, to give real thought to the historical constraints that effectively isolate any attempt to articulate an uncompromising opposition to the status quo. Thus, in a scathing critique of Bourriaud's conception of "relational art," Rancière likens the claim that artists might now truly overcome their isolation and restore a lost social bond to Francis Fukuyama's famous thesis of the "end of history."[26] For Rancière, that is, the idea that we may finally have reached the moment at which art is capable of dissolving itself in a series of relatively modest gestures of interpersonal exchange, comes dangerously close to being an assertion of utopia achieved, a distortion that ignores a great deal not only in its view of our current predicament but also in its analysis of the work. Relational art, he writes, "rejects art's claims to self-sufficiency as much as its dreams of transforming life, but even so it reaffirms an essential idea: that art consists in constructing spaces and relations to reconfigure materially and symbolically the territory of the common."[27]

In using this language of "the common," Rancière brings us, finally, up against the work of two authors who would seem an obvious point of reference in thinking about a movement like Occupy, Michael Hardt and Antonio Negri. After all, in their coauthored *Empire* trilogy, Hardt and Negri frame the project of a contemporary radical politics in terms of a struggle over the configuration of "the common," which comprises not only the "natural world" as traditionally conceived but also virtually every aspect of human society, from languages and codes to gestures and affects. As noted in the introduction, the contemporary experience of the common, for Hardt and Negri, is that of our world as collectively produced and subsequently privatized, an experience that enables us both to become cognizant of exploitation and to begin to recognize the possibility of liberation. This definition of the common, they are careful to note, distinguishes it from other, seemingly similar concepts that have, until now, only served to obscure its characteristics. In one particularly relevant example, they differentiate the common from more traditional ideas of "community," writing that the latter term "is often used to refer to a moral unity that stands above the population and its interactions like a sovereign power."[28] The figure of "the community" alludes to a whole that is greater than the sum of its parts, a whole, therefore, that exists somehow independently of the specific contribution of any individual member. It is, in other words, a vehicle for the exercise of power, authorizing the policing of both its members and its borders. Thus, much as it may suggest communication and commonality, a concept like "community," not unlike "the nation," "the people," and so on, is useful only so long as politics is conceived as a clash of monolithic opponents.

Emphasizing, in contrast, that the common will always be made up of a nonexclusive "multitude" of singularities, Hardt and Negri speak of the radical potential of nondialectical, creative interchange. And, predicting both the language of Occupy's General Assembly and Kester's assessment of contemporary collaborative art, they describe this proposal for a reformulated communication as a call for something like a literal embodiment of the carnivalesque, polyphonic dialogue described by Bakhtin. "The polyphonic character of carnivalesque language," they write,

> has great constructive power . . . there is no center that dictates meaning, but rather meaning arises only out of the exchanges among all the singularities in dialogue. . . . Today's new and powerful movements seem to elude any attempt to reduce them to a monologic history; they cannot but be carnivalesque. This is the logic of the multitude that Bakhtin

helps us understand: a theory of organization based on the freedom of singularities that converge in the production of the common.[29]

Like Bakhtin's notion of polyphonic dialogue, they contend, contemporary grassroots movements tend to be marked by a productive tension between the individual and the collective, each constituting, and being constituted by, the other. It is this relationship, this mutual dependence, that makes these movements so intriguing for Hardt and Negri. Unlike the representative democracy Miller sees as ultimately necessary to Occupy's long-term success, a form of administration that necessarily suppresses the individual in the name of the collective good, they see in "the multitude" the potential for a radical, carnivalesque democracy, one realizing the dreams of liberation that have haunted political theory since the late eighteenth century.

It is important to note, however, that the conclusions Hardt and Negri draw out of this Bakhtinian model differ in at least one important way from those proposed by Kester. For them, establishing a productive dialogue with others will not require a realm of artistic isolation, or even the work of a creative avant-garde. Our current political/social/cultural formation offers opportunities for creative, productive intervention at nearly every turn. Rather than seeing the collapse of an "outside" as the end of any potential for "real" politics, Hardt and Negri insist that it should be understood as a moment of "omnicrisis," in which each and every situation offers the potential for radical action. Unlike Kester and Rancière, that is, Hardt and Negri insist not simply that it is possible to engage in meaningful action but that it is the fact of pervasive crisis as such that makes it virtually nonsensical to speak of an "outside" where critique might find relatively solid footing. One must not retreat in hopes of finding a space that allows or enables meaningful experiments with the "distribution of the sensible," then, but should attempt to recognize and exploit the opportunities that surround us. By extension, as their insistence on dialogue, interpersonal exchange, and the "carnivalesque" convergence of free singularities suggests, it would be a mistake to assume that the interventions to which they allude could unfold merely on the level of imagery. To the contrary, we must recognize that whereas in earlier eras images were restricted because they provided a means for the individual to participate in, imitate, and even identify with the sacred or divine, "today's iconoclasts have also paradoxically usurped the position of the iconophiles." Echoing Keenan, then (not to mention Marcuse), Hardt and Negri suggest that the contemporary formations of power are maintained not through the destruction of images but through their overproduction. Power is now maintained "precisely through the use of images, through the spectacle of the media, and through the control of information. The element of hope and salvation that the Byzantine multitudes found in icons now seems to have been drained from all images."[30]

Yet, quite interestingly, this acknowledgment that the false democratization of imagery has become a standard tool in maintaining the status quo stops short of a call for some new, bottom-up type of iconoclasm. Instead, Hardt and Negri turn, rather surprisingly, to a careful consideration of grassroots political imagery, for "what we need," they write, "are weapons that make no pretense to symmetry with the ruling military power."[31] Refusing to call on "the reality" of oppression and disenfranchisement, to reject style in favor of substance, they instead suggest that contemporary politics will most likely proceed through a creative engagement with representation. Providing examples of some of the many "creative attempts" to forge new political "weapons" in the face of this predicament, they express admiration for the kiss-ins of Queer Nation and the costumes and mimicry that have become staples of counterglobalization protests. The value of these actions lies not, the authors suggest, in their directness or immediacy but in their critical relationship to those very concepts. Through varying degrees of irony, each of these actions, these renderings of political identities, demonstrates that the political tools and strategies of the disempowered, as traditionally conceived, are inadequate. Faced with our particular historical quandary, calls for armed uprisings or adequate representation will, and on some level *must*, seem bizarre. We have not reached a moment at which direct political action is once again possible, as so many of Occupy's supporters insinuate, but one in which the inevitable slippages and failures of representation might be turned to productive ends.

In this sense, Hardt and Negri, when placed alongside Kester, offer a concise illustration of the contemporary dialectic of aesthetics and grassroots politics. The latter focuses on the self-consciously isolated world of art, and the former, casting doubts upon the validity of that isolation, turn instead to the streets, finding the seeds of radical democracy in actions of carnivalesque protest. Both, constructing their critical frameworks on the foundation of Bakhtin's concept of a polyphonic dialogue, arrive at a central paradox, namely, that it is only through an explicit engagement with representation—either by entering the art gallery, a realm explicitly devoted to representational practices, or by engaging in explicitly aestheticized acts of protest— that one becomes capable of casting off the stultifying conventions of self-representation. Personal and political immediacy, it seems, can be approached only by treating identity as plastic. For this reason, we would do well to take the claims, cited earlier, that Occupy embodies an anti- or postrepresentational politics, with a grain of salt. For as Jodi Dean points out, even in naming themselves "the 99 percent," protesters are, quite literally, engaged in the work of formulating representations. Occupy, after all, however much it may express the frustrations of the majority, cannot *actually* claim 99 percent of the population as its members. Why, then, are so many so keen to overlook this obviously figurative gesture in an effort to describe the movement as somehow beyond concerns of representation?

According to Dean, this desire appears to be rooted in a basic denial of the divisions that mark both the self and the movement as a whole. In one sense, the emphasis on creative dialogue and antihi-erarchical decision making rests on the assumption that each par-ticipating individual is fully present to him- or herself, that s/he can know and adequately express his/her positions, wholly conscious of the impulses that motivate them. Rather than the basis for a utopian society, however, Dean argues this notion that we are somehow beyond ideology, that we are fully aware and capable of acting in our best interests, is in fact the governing ideology of our era. Indeed, the power and wisdom of the individual to determine his/her own best plan of action has been used to justify any number of antipopulist measures in recent decades, from anti-union "right to work" laws to the privatization of pensions. To articulate a critique of capitalism using a "neoliberal language of autonomy and a capitalist language of choice" is thus to miss at least some of the point. As Dean puts it, "It's almost as if they fail to get their own critique, stopping it too soon."[32] By the same token, the rhetoric of a unified leaderlessness and horizontal organization serves also to deny significant divisions within the movement, reducing serious disagreements to what Dean labels "forking": "People pursued their own projects, perpetually splitting according to their prior interests and expertise, repeating the patterns dominant in [contemporary] capitalism and failing to keep open the hole in Wall Street even as they dug multiple little ones."[33] The vision of individuals engaged in open discussion feels so right, so appealing, because it is founded in the same fantasies that structure our personal and collective lives as we now know them. By valuing authentic dialogue and valorizing individual difference, that is, Occupy functions in many ways as something like the unsuspecting mirror of a repressively tolerant society. Thus, rather than attempting to deny the aesthetic aspects of Occupy, thereby clinging to the fantasy of difference without antagonism, Dean argues that we should recognize not only the necessity of representation but also its potential power. Protestors should not be ashamed to speak "*in the name of* the 99 percent," for in doing so, they offer a compelling formulation of "the wrong of the gap between the rich and the rest of us."[34]

One wonders, however, if Dean may have stopped her own critique too soon. She stresses repeatedly that the power of Occupy stemmed from its insistence on foregrounding the representation of this wrong in "our space," confronting us with an image of this foundational injustice that would otherwise remain disavowed. Yet it is interesting to note the way in which her language shifts over the course of the account. In the beginning of the essay, she lauds Occupy for formulating "opposition within our setting . . . its energy comes from a vanguard of disciplined, committed activists undertaking and supporting actions in the streets."[35] Later, though, one finds the action unfolding not in the streets but next to them. In emphasizing that it is the figuration of class antagonism that makes Occupy unique, radical, Dean explains that without this element people would be allowed "to assemble in tents on sidewalks" without fear of legal repercussions—think, for example, of ticket lines.[36] And, later still, the site becomes less specific, as much of Occupy's value is said to lie in arranging "the physical presence of large groups of people outside, in visible, urban spaces, in political actions authorized by neither capital nor the state but by the people's collective political will."[37] The way these sites seem to shift—from streets to sidewalks to unspecified urban spaces—is understandable. One might even say it is inevitable. This is because Occupy took shape not in the streets but in Zucotti Park/"Freedom Square," a site chosen not only for its proximity to Wall Street but also for its status as a "privately-owned public space," which meant that demonstrators would not be subject to the curfew laws that applied to New York City parks. Publicly visible as it may have been, therefore, the space "occupied" was not Wall Street but a separate, privately maintained enclave.[38] The act of renaming the space, indicating a change from a site named after an individual to a realm of "true" liberation, does nothing to change this. If anything, the space's new name only underscored the distinctness of this location. Wall Street remained, but a portion of New York City had been marked off as a space of individual autonomy. Thus, the fluctuations in Dean's descriptions of Occupy's sites and spaces may point not to the difficulty of maintaining critical distance from events unfolding in the present—though that is most likely also a factor—but to a more fundamental historical and political dilemma. One might ask, that is, whether the collaborative, creative dialogues of the General Assembly could have taken place without their figurative geographic isolation, the demarcation of a space freed from the competitive compulsions of the "real world." Could these processes have unfolded without somehow isolating/insulating participants from the demands of "everyday life"? Or might Occupy's explicit establishment of a "liberated" space for the staging of the General Assembly instead suggest that, far from embodying, unqualifiedly, a creative engagement with reality, the movement remains bound by the "knot" that Rancière describes as the politics of the aesthetic? Just as it is true that radical movements in our time cannot succeed in bracketing issues of representation, in other words, it may also be true that those same movements cannot avoid being bracketed as "mere representation." As much as Dean was willing to acknowledge the necessary role of aesthetics in political struggle, it seems that her commitment to "real" politics causes her to overlook the realms in which a radical political aesthetic is possible. It may not be so simple as saying that those behind the formulation of Occupy failed to understand their own critique. Rather, it may be that Occupy, like the Yippies, the GAA, and the Black Panthers, finds itself in the difficult position of attempting to articulate dissent while brushing against the limits of historical possibility.

Certainly, a thorough account of Occupy remains to be written. In closing this work dedicated to bringing 1960s theories of art and culture into conversation with the forms of "sixties" activism, my goal here is merely to begin to suggest the ways in which this critical procedure remains essential. In light of the efforts and struggles of grassroots organizers and activists in the last decade, a historical understanding of aesthetic forms may help us not only to recognize the particular difficulties that face groups like the Yes Men but also to ask different, and potentially more productive, questions of a movement like Occupy, as well as of recent engagements with "the common" more generally. After all, the critical debates surrounding both "relational"/"dialogical" art and contemporary activism appear to turn on questions of immediacy and democracy, and the possibility of enacting either without a space explicitly devoted to creative experimentation. For many, it seems all too apparent that progress demands a rededication to direct, unmediated interaction. But, as I have suggested, it is equally clear that any effort to move in this direction will quickly find itself faced with the impossibility of renouncing the aesthetic. In this sense, calls for the resurrection of a lost "social bond," whether in art or in activism, come to feel like the latest in a long line of attempts to deny not only that art remains incapable of overcoming its own isolation but also that politics will inevitably proceed through a complicated negotiation with problems of form. Thus, we should ask not only why the pieces Bourriaud praises seem to engender dialogue only between artists and gallery goers—a question Claire Bishop has already posed quite forcefully—but also why, if what Occupiers wanted was "real" politics, the encampment felt, ultimately, so much like contemporary art?[39] Is it because the average viewer's eyes remain unprepared for the sight of true, living creativity, or because "radical democracy," capable of unfolding only within carefully demarcated sites and taking the means of politics as its content, in the end conforms so nicely to the classic, Greenbergian definition of avant-garde art?

When thinking about Occupy, therefore, rather than rushing to celebrate (or lament) the return of "participatory democracy," it may be more informative and productive to begin from something like a formal, stylistic analysis of the performances we describe as "anti-representational." In light of the preceding case studies, this should seem only reasonable. When hearing praise for artists and activists who seem to have taken it as their mission to create "true" democracy by privileging interpersonal exchange and the possibility of direct action without an institutional safety net, it would be helpful to remember the put-ons of the late 1960s, and to take seriously the predicament that those pranks and hoaxes (and, in some cases, hexes) were attempting to mark. One cannot, as the Yippies, the Panthers, the Gay Activists Alliance, and others clearly recognized, simply will "real politics" into existence. And yet, with each collective expression of outrage, this standard claim resurfaces. In thinking about art and activism in the early twenty-first century, then, our most pressing task may be to address this particular disavowal, to struggle with our desire, as activists, commentators, and critics, to see utopia realized in the present in spite of our knowledge of its historical impediments. Only by doing so might we come to understand, and thus productively utilize, the imbrications of aesthetics and politics.

NOTES

NOTES TO INTRODUCTION

1   Robert Brustein, "Revolution as Theater," *New Republic*, March 14, 1970, 14.

2   Robert L. Gross, "'Revolution' Has Become Giant Put-On of the Era," *Miami Herald*, March 21, 1970, 7A:2.

3   Brustein, "Revolution as Theater," 14. Brustein was hardly alone in his suspicions regarding the "verbal displays" of sixties radicals. David Farber has argued that this discomfort was, ultimately, the motivating force behind the backlash of the "silent majority." See David Farber, "The Silent Majority and Talk about Revolution," in David Farber, ed., *The Sixties: From Memory to History* (Chapel Hill: University of North Carolina Press, 1994), 291–16.

4   This language of "authentic" resistance and/or the search for "authenticity" still surfaces in discussions of grassroots politics, even in those that take theatrical or performative modes of protest as the subject of their investigation. In so doing, however, these authors simply seek to demonstrate that those actions that problematize our very conception of politics are in fact aiming at the same goals. See, for example, Kenneth Tucker, *Workers of the World, Enjoy!: Aesthetic Politics from Revolutionary Syndicalism to the Global Justice Movement* (Philadelphia: Temple University Press, 2010).

5   See, for example, Gavin Butt, "'America' and Its Discontents: Art and Politics, 1945–60, in Amelia Jones, ed., *A Companion to Contemporary Art Since 1945* (London: Wiley-Blackwell, 2006), 19–37; Kelly M. Cresap, *Pop, Trickster, Fool: Warhol Performs Naivete* (Champaign: University of Illinois Press, 2004); and Matthew Tinkcom, *Working Like a Homosexual: Camp, Capital, Cinema* (Durham, NC: Duke University Press, 2002).

6   See Clement Greenberg, "Avant-Garde and Kitsch," in *The Collected Essays and Criticism*, vol. 1, *Perceptions and Judgments, 1939–1944*, ed. by John O'Brian (Chicago: University of Chicago Press, 1988), 5–22.

7   See Michael Hardt and Antonio Negri, *Empire* (Cambridge, MA: Harvard University Press, 2000); and Fredric Jameson, "The Cultural Logic of Late Capitalism," in

Postmodernism, or, the Cultural Logic of Late Capitalism (Durham, NC: Duke University Press, 1990), 1–54.

8   Jonathan Dollimore, *Sexual Dissidence: Augustine to Wilde, Freud to Foucault* (Oxford: Oxford University Press, 1991), 24.

9   Susan Sontag, "Against Interpretation" and "Notes on Camp," in *Against Interpretation* (New York: Dell Books, 1966), 14, 280.

10   Brustein, "Revolution as Theater," 13.

11   Ibid., 14.

12   For more on El Teatro Campesino and the Black Revolutionary Theater, see Harry J. Elam, Jr., *Taking It to the Streets: The Social Protest Theater of Luis Valdez and Amiri Baraka* (Ann Arbor: University of Michigan Press, 1997).

13   Ibid., 14.

14   Ibid., 16.

15   Herbert Marcuse, "Repressive Tolerance," in Herbert Marcuse, Barrington Moore, Jr., and Robert Paul Wolff, *A Critique of Pure Tolerance* (Boston: Basic Books, 1969), 85.

16   Ibid., 90.

17   Marcuse was not the only one to see the media as central to the maintenance of a repressive social order. For other examples of this argument, see Michael Shamberg, *Guerrilla Television* (New York: Henry Holt and Co., 1971); and Norman Fruchter, "Games in the Arena: Movement Propaganda and the Culture of the Spectacle," *Liberation* 16, no. 3 (May 1971): 4–17. For a more recent, and more nuanced, version of this argument, see Jodi Dean, *Democracy and Other Neoliberal Fantasies: Communicative Capitalism and Left Politics* (Durham, NC: Duke University Press, 2009), particularly the chapter "Technology," 19–47.

18   Ibid., 97.

19   Marcuse, "Repressive Tolerance," 94.

20   Ibid., 98.

21   Ibid., 115.

22   Ibid.

23   Herbert Marcuse, *One-Dimensional Man: Studies in the Ideology of Advanced Industrial Society* (Boston: Beacon Press, 1964), ix.

24   Ibid., 10–11 (emphases in original).

25   Ibid., 58.

26   Susan Sontag, "Against Interpretation," in Sontag, *Against Interpretation*, 8.

27   Ibid., 7.

28   Ibid., 11.

29   Ibid.," 9.

30   Sontag, "Psychoanalysis and Norman O. Brown's *Life Against Death*," in Sontag, *Against Interpretation*, 257.

31   For more on *Eros and Civilization* and Marcuse's theory of art and polymorphous perversity, see chapter 2.

32   Ibid., 259.

33   According to Sontag, Surrealism, as a sensibility, looked to shock audiences by

presenting them with the "creative accidents of arrangement and insight," a practice she described as the "collage principle." See Sontag, "Happenings," 269–70.

34 Ibid., 271.
35 Sontag, "Notes on Camp," in Sontag, *Against Interpretation*, 277.
36 Ibid., 279–80.
37 Ibid., 277.
38 Ibid.
39 Ibid., 278.
40 See Charles Baudelaire, "On the Essence of Laughter," in *The Painter of Modern Life and Other Essays*, trans. Jonathan Mayne (New York: Da Capo Press, 1986), 156–58. It should be noted that Sontag's distinction between "naïve, or pure" and "deliberate" Camp virtually replicates Baudelaire's distinction between the "absolute" and "significative comic."
41 Baudelaire, "The Painter of Modern Life," in Baudelaire, *Painter of Modern Life*, 9.
42 Sontag, "Notes on Camp," 290.
43 Ibid.
44 Ibid.
45 In his now-classic essay "Uses of Camp," Andrew Ross makes a similar point. According to Ross, camp was marked not by the "democratic esprit" of Pop Art but by its adherence to the logic of cultural capital. As Sontag wrote in 1964, the "ultimate camp statement" said of its object, "it's good because it's awful." One must also, Ross points out, read this "ultimate statement" "from the point of view of those whom it indirectly patronized, especially those lower middle-class groups whom, historically, have had to bear the stigma of 'failed' taste." Camp, in Ross's account, extracted its cultural capital both from "forgotten forms of labor" and from the sincerity of those who consumed the products of that labor. Just as the "discovered" object of Pop Art could never rid itself of its essential obsolescence, he argues, the resurrected object of camp can "hardly shake off its barbaric associations with the social victimization of its original taste-audience." Thus, where Pop Art claimed to be the result of a passive engagement with/enjoyment of mass culture, the pleasure of camp could only be "the result of the (hard) *work* of a producer of taste, and 'taste' is only possible through exclusion *and* depreciation." See Andrew Ross, "Uses of Camp," in Andrew Ross, *No Respect: Intellectuals and Popular Culture* (New York: Routledge Press, 1989), 153.
46 Ibid., 276.
47 Ibid., 289.
48 Ibid., 277.
49 Fabio Cleto, "Introduction," in Fabio Cleto, ed., *Camp: Queer Aesthetics and the Performing Subject* (Ann Arbor: University of Michigan Press, 1999), 46.
50 Marcuse, "Repressive Tolerance," 115.
51 Marcuse, *One-Dimensional Man*, 14.
52 Ibid., 73.
53 Ibid., 256–57.

54   Ibid., 257.

55   Marcuse, "Repressive Tolerance," 84.

56   Jacob Brackman, *The Put-On: Modern Fooling and Modern Mistrust* (Chicago: Henry Regnery Co., 1971), 17.

57   "Andy Warhol: My True Story," interview with Gretchen Berg, reprinted in Kenneth Goldsmith, ed., *I'll Be Your Mirror: The Selected Andy Warhol Interviews, 1963–1987* (New York: Carroll & Graf Publishers, 2004), 87.

58   See Andy Warhol, *The Philosophy of Andy Warhol (From A to B and Back Again)* (London: Cassell Publishers, 1975), 1.

59   Ibid., 31.

60   Brackman, *Put-On*, 9.

61   See Erving Goffman, *The Presentation of Self in Everyday Life* (New York: Doubleday, 1959); and Pierre Bourdieu, *Photography: A Middle-Brow Art* (Stanford: Stanford University Press, 1990), 83–84.

62   Ibid., 26.

63   Ibid., 9.

64   Ibid., 20.

65   More recent theories of irony have problematized this understanding of it as simply expressing the opposite of that which is said or done. See, for example, Linda Hutcheon, *Irony's Edge: The Theory and Politics of Irony* (London: Routledge, 1995); and Chambers, *Room for Maneuver*.

66   Brackman, *Put-On*, 20 (emphasis in original).

67   Ibid., 90.

68   Ibid., 93.

69   Ibid., 90.

70   Ibid., 92–93.

71   Ibid., 88.

72   Ibid.

73   It is interesting to note that Fredric Jameson, in his classic essay "The Cultural Logic of Late Capitalism," presents a similar critique of postwar American culture, and of the work of Andy Warhol in particular. Instead of the "put-on," however, Jameson refers to what he sees as practices of "blank parody" as "pastiche," "a neutral practice of . . . mimicry, without any of parody's ulterior motives." See Fredric Jameson, "The Cultural Logic of Late Capitalism," in Fredric Jameson, *Postmodernism, or, The Cultural Logic of Late Capitalism* (Durham, NC: Duke University Press, 1991), 17.

74   Brackman, *Put-On*, 88.

75   Robin Morgan, *Going Too Far: The Personal Chronicle of a Feminist* (New York: Vintage Books, 1978), 75.

76   Todd Gitlin, *The Whole World Is Watching: Mass Media in the Making and Unmaking of the New Left* (Berkeley: University of California Press, 1980), 173.

77   Hoffman formulated this perhaps most suggestively in his book *Revolution for the Hell of It*, where he wrote, "Did you ever hear Andy Warhol talk? . . . Warhol

understands modern media." See Free [Abbie Hoffman], *Revolution for the Hell of It* (New York: Dell Publishing Co., 1969), 61.

78 See John D'Emilio, "Placing Gay in the Sixties," in Alexander Bloom, ed., *Long Time Gone: Sixties America Then and Now* (New York: Oxford University Press, 2001), 209–29.

79 See Michelle Wallace, *Black Macho and the Myth of the Superwoman* (New York: Dial Press, 1978).

80 Eldridge Cleaver, *Soul on Ice* (New York: McGraw Hill, 1968), 166.

81 Morgan, *Going Too Far*, 70.

82 See Kobena Mercer and Isaac Julien, "Black Masculinity and the Sexual Politics of Race," in Kobena Mercer, *Welcome to the Jungle: New Positions in Black Cultural Studies* (London: Routledge, 1994), 139; and Leerom Medovoi, "A Yippie-Panther Pipe Dream: Rethinking Sex, Race, and the Sexual Revolution," in Hilary Radner and Moya Luckett, eds., *Swinging Single: Representing Sexuality in the 1960s* (Minneapolis: University of Minnesota Press, 1998), 133–78.

83 Medovoi, "Yippie-Panther Pipe Dream," 146.

84 For Cleaver's discussion of the black male's reduction to mere physicality, see *Soul on Ice*, particularly the essays of part 4, "White Woman, Black Man."

85 One finds many versions of this argument in the popular and academic histories of that decade as well. See, for example, Greg Calvert, *A Disrupted History: The New Left and the New Capitalism* (New York: Random House, 1971); Kirkpatrick Sale, *SDS* (New York: Random House, 1971); Allen Matusow, *The Unraveling of America: A History of Liberalism in the 1960s* (New York: Harper and Row, 1984); Todd Gitlin, *The Sixties: Years of Hope, Days of Rage* (New York: Bantam Books, 1989); James Miller, *Democracy Is in the Streets: From Port Huron to the Siege of Chicago* (New York: Simon & Schuster, 1987); and Tom Hayden, *Reunion: A Memoir* (New York: Random House, 1988).

86 To be sure, in the past decade a number of histories have appeared attempting to problematize this simplistic narrative of declension. This is precisely the narrative D'Emilio, for example, hopes to counter with "Placing Gay in the Sixties." Nevertheless, in spite of a compelling body of work on "the world the sixties made," to quote the title of one recent volume, the dominant understanding of late-twentieth-century America is one in which the political "dreams" of the sixties inevitably fizzled in the 1970s, often referred to as "the me decade." For more on this, see the essays collected in Van Gosse and Richard Moser, eds., *The World the Sixties Made: Politics and Culture in Recent America* (Philadelphia: Temple University Press, 2003).

87 See Gitlin, *The Whole World Is Watching*; Tom Wells, *The War Within: America's Battle over Vietnam* (New York: Henry Holt & Co., 1994); Doug Rossinow, *The Politics of Authenticity: Liberalism, Christianity, and the New Left in America* (New York: Columbia University Press, 1998); and Julie Stephens, *Anti-Disciplinary Protest: Sixties Radicalism and Postmodernism* (Cambridge: Cambridge University Press, 1998).

88 For more on this shift, see, among others, Bradford D. Martin, *The Theater Is in the Street: Politics and Public Performance in Sixties America* (Amherst: University of Massachusetts Press, 2004), 16–19.

89 See Marianne DeKoven, *Utopia Limited: The Sixties and the Emergence of the Postmodern* (Durham, NC: Duke University Press, 2004); and T. V. Reed, *The Art of Protest: Culture and Activism from the Civil Rights Movement to the Streets of Seattle* (Minneapolis: University of Minnesota Press, 2005). For another attempt to reconsider the relationship between performance, public culture, and protest, see Bradford Martin, *Theater Is in the Streets.*

90 Aniko Bodroghkozy, *Groove Tube: 60s Television and Youth Rebellion* (Durham, NC: Duke University Press, 2001). More recently, Stephen Duncombe, using arguments of this sort as the basis for a new manifesto for contemporary radical politics, urges progressive activists to stop thinking in terms of doctrinal purity and "real" politics, and to acknowledge the importance of fantasy, compelling images of alternative social existences, whether possible or absurd, in motivating the behaviors of average citizens. Rather than attempting to avoid being co-opted by the media, he argues, activists should instead learn from mythmakers like Hoffman, and begin to ask just why and how media imagery so effectively resonates with viewers' desires. They should recognize that "everything is theatrical," in the words of organizer David Solnit, and that, in spite of its continued popularity on the left, "traditional protest—the march, the rally, the chants—is just bad theater." Stephen Duncombe, *Dream: Re-Imagining Progressive Politics in an Age of Fantasy* (New York: The New Press, 2007), 24.

91 David Joselit, "Yippie-Pop: Abbie Hoffman, Andy Warhol and Sixties Media Politics," *Grey Room* 8 (Summer 2002): 76.

92 David Joselit, *Feedback: Television Against Democracy* (Cambridge, MA: MIT Press, 2007), 40–41.

93 Ibid., 122.

NOTES TO CHAPTER 1

1 Paul Laikin and Jerry Grandenetti, "Abbie Hoffman's Charm School," *Sick* 10, no. 6 (September 1970): 38.

2 Ibid., 39.

3 Ibid., 42.

4 Nevertheless, in spite of the Diggers' efforts, conditions in the Haight-Ashbury district worsened. Street crime, bad drugs, and venereal disease were rampant. Thus, in frustration, in October 1967, nine months after serving free food to crowds at the first Human Be-In, the Diggers staged a parade proclaiming the death of the hippie. See Michael William Doyle, "Staging the Revolution: Guerrilla Theater as a Countercultural Practice, 1965–68," in Michael William Doyle and Peter Braunstein eds., *Imagine Nation: The American Counterculture of the 1960s and '70s* (New York: Routledge Press, 2002), 80–85.

5   In fact, it was Berg who first described the Diggers as "guerrilla theater," a term
     he coined with Mime Troupe leader Ronnie Davis in 1965. In May 1965, Davis
     delivered an essay titled "Guerrilla Theater," at Berg's urging, to the Mime Troupe.
     The essay was eventually published in the *Tulane Drama Review* (Summer 1966),
     and later reprinted in Ronnie Davis, *The San Francisco Mime Troupe: The First
     Ten Years* (Palo Alto, CA: Ramparts Press, 1975), 149–53.

6   "Trip Without a Ticket," reprinted in Emmett Grogan, *Ringolevio* (New York: Avon
     Books, 1972), 345.

7   Ibid., 345–46.

8   For a description of SDS's goals in calling the "Back to the Drawing Boards" con-
     ference, see Todd Gitlin, *The Sixties: Years of Hope, Days of Rage* (New York:
     Bantam Books, 1993), 226–30. For an account of the contrast between SDS's more
     traditional members and its younger "prairie power" constituents in Austin, Texas,
     see Doug Rossinow, "The Revolution Is about Our Lives: The New Left's Counter-
     culture," in Braunstein and Doyle, *Imagine Nation*, 99–124.

9   The term "straight," as used by the Diggers, suggests not the sexual politics
     of groups like SDS but their cultural and political orthodoxy. Though, as Ian
     Lekus has argued, SDS's position on gay liberation marked it, unmistakably, as a
     "straight" organization. See Ian Keith Lekus, "Queer and Present Dangers: Homo-
     sexuality and American Antiwar Activism During the Vietnam Era," PhD diss.,
     Duke University, 2003.

10   Quoted in Gitlin, *Sixties*, 228.

11   In SDS's founding document, *The Port Huron Statement*, Tom Hayden wrote that
     the "goal of man and society should be human independence: a concern not with
     image of popularity but with finding a meaning in life that is personally authentic;
     a quality of mind . . . which has full, spontaneous access to present and past experi-
     ences, one which easily unites the fragmented parts of personal history." In hopes
     of offering an alternative, he wrote, SDS would provide a vision of "the perimeter
     of human possibility," one that would lead all progressive political movements,
     from Civil Rights struggles to anticolonial revolutions, to see themselves as inter-
     related, and thus to work together to obtain "at least a substantial part of that
     vision in our epoch." Students for a Democratic Society, *The Port Huron State-
     ment*, reprinted in James Miller, *"Democracy Is in the Streets": From Port Huron
     to the Siege of Chicago* (New York: Simon & Schuster, 1988), 332, 367–68.

12   Peter Coyote, *Sleeping Where I Fall: A Chronicle* (Washington, DC: Counterpoint,
     1998), 70 (emphasis in original).

13   Quoted in Gitlin, *Sixties*, 228.

14   Antonin Artaud, "An End to Masterpieces," reprinted in Susan Sontag, ed., *Anto-
     nin Artaud: Selected Writings*, trans. Helen Weaver (Berkeley: University of Cali-
     fornia Press, 1988), 255.

15   Jacques Derrida, "La parole soufflée," in *Writing and Difference*, trans. by Alan
     Bass (Chicago: University of Chicago Press, 1978), 174.

16   Antonin Artaud, "The Theater of Cruelty (First Manifesto)," in Sontag, ed., *Anto-
     nin Artaud*, 242.

17   George Metesky was the name of New York's "Mad Bomber," who perpetrated a series of random, often inept, bombings in New York City from 1940 to 1956. His name was most likely adopted by the Diggers, ironically, because of his outlaw-celebrity status in New York during Grogan's childhood.

18   Grogan, *Ringolevio*, 464.

19   Fourratt ultimately parted ways with the Yippies in 1969, and went on to become one of the founding members of New York's Gay Liberation Front, through which he promoted a profoundly different version of oppositional politics—one based in notions of "sincerity" and "authenticity" rather than "mythmaking." For more on Fourratt and the Gay Liberation Front, see Chapter 2.

20   See Grogan, *Ringolevio*, 395–96; and Peter Coyote, *Sleeping Where I Fall*, 71. Hoffman, on a number of occasions, pointed out the irony of being accused of stealing by a group of individuals who claimed to advocate the destruction of all private property.

21   It should come as no surprise that Wall Street, and the Stock Exchange in particular, were popular targets for political protest and performance in the late 1960s. In addition to Hoffman's action, in February 1967 the Black Mask group paraded down Wall Street wearing black robes and masks, and carrying a skull on a stick, saying that Wall Street would henceforth be known as "War Street." In 1968, on Halloween, a group known as WITCH, headed by former Yippie Robin Morgan, stood on Wall Street and "demanded an audience with Satan, our superior, at the Stock Exchange," placing a hex on the entire financial district for its role in the oppression of women. See *Black Mask and Up Against the Wall Motherfucker: The Incomplete Works of Ron Hahne, Ben Morea, and the Black Mask Group* (London: Unpopular Books, 1993), 26–27; and Robin Morgan, *Going Too Far: The Personal Chronicle of a Feminist* (New York: Vintage Books, 1968), 73.

22   Jezer, *Abbie Hoffman*, 112.

23   Rubin, *Growing (Up) at 37*, 80–81.

24   Quoted in Raskin, *For the Hell of It*, 115.

25   Free, *Revolution for the Hell of It*, 79–80.

26   Marshall McLuhan, *Understanding Media: The Extensions of Man* (New York, 1964), 9. This passage points to an ambiguity and/or contradiction in McLuhan's arguments regarding the essential "coolness" of television as a medium. While he claims that, in fact, a medium's status as "hot" or "cool" depends on the inherent qualities of the medium itself and not on the content of its images, there are, undoubtedly, moments when he argues precisely the obverse. See "Media Hot and Cold," in *Understanding Media*, 22–32. The primacy of the former claim in McLuhan's thinking can be extrapolated from his own research in the effects of media undertaken at his Center for Culture and Technology in Toronto. See Andrew Ross, "Candid Cameras," in Andrew Ross, *No Respect: Intellectuals and Popular Culture* (New York, 1989), 102–34.

27   McLuhan, *Understanding Media*, 28.

28   Free, *Revolution for the Hell of It*, 84.

29   Free, *Revolution for the Hell of It*, 137.

30 Ibid., 137.

31 Ibid., 19.

32 Pierre Bourdieu, *On Television* (New York: The New Press, 1998), 22.

33 Rubin, *Do It!*, 68.

34 Ibid., 69.

35 Ibid.

36 Free, *Revolution for the Hell of It*, 47. The idea of levitating the Pentagon, Hoffman later wrote, originated with Ed Sanders, who, "his eyes redder than a baboon's ass from smoking pipefuls of weed, implored the gods to guide our decision. 'A pentagon is a five-sided symbol of evil,' he assured us. 'Lordy, Lord,' he yodeled, 'suck my pork-pine of inspiration.' The heavens parted. The gods spoke: 'Make it rise you motherfuckers. If you're so gaddam good, make it rise in the air.'" Abbie Hoffman, *Soon to Be a Major Motion Picture* (New York: Perigee Books, 1980), 129.

37 Ibid., 132.

38 Ibid., 133.

39 Ibid.

40 Theodor Roszak, *The Making of a Counter Culture* (Berkeley: University of California Press, 1994), 7.

41 Ibid., 15 (emphasis in original).

42 Herbert Marcuse, *Eros and Civilization: A Philosophical Inquiry into Freud* (Boston, 1966), 39.

43 Ibid., 215.

44. Ibid., 49.

45 Ibid., 50.

46 Roszak, *Making of a Counter Culture*, 42.

47 Ibid., 37.

48 Ibid., 292.

49 *Mademoiselle*, July 1970, 103.

50 Roszak, *Making of a Counter Culture*, 74.

51 In 1970, for example, prosecuting attorney Thomas Foran famously characterized Hoffman, Rubin, and the rest of the defendants in the Chicago Seven conspiracy trial as representatives of the "freaking fag revolution." Quoted in Martin Duberman, *Stonewall* (New York: Plume Books, 1994), 215.

52 Robert J. Corber, *Homosexuality in Cold War America: Resistance and the Crisis of Masculinity* (Durham, NC: Duke University Press, 1997), 11.

53 Ibid., 11–12.

54 Norman Mailer, *The Armies of the Night: History as a Novel/The Novel as History*, 92.

55 Ibid., 92.

56 Free, *Revolution for the Hell of It*, 14–15.

57 Ibid., 66.

58 Ibid., 106–7.

59 See Sally Kempton, "Yippies Anti-Organize a Groovy Revolution," *Village Voice*,

March 21, 1968, 5–6, 30; and Donald Janson, "Coalition Vows Peaceful Protest at Chicago National Convention," *New York Times*, March 25, 1968, 20.

60 Rubin, *Do It!*, 84.

61 Ibid., 84.

62 See Don McNeill, *Moving Through Here* (New York: Knopf Press, 1970), 224–30.

63 *New York Times*, March 25, 1968, 46.

64 Brustein, "Revolution as Theater," 14.

65 From the beginning, the Yippies knew that they had little choice but to negotiate with city officials. If they failed to clear the festival with local authorities, many of the musicians who had agreed to play would refuse to attend, and, as a result, fewer potential Yippies would be willing to make the trip to Chicago.

66 "Revolution Towards a Free Society: Yippie!," reprinted in Free, *Revolution for the Hell of It*, 168.

67 Abe Peck, "A Letter from Chicago," Liberation News Service, August 6, 1968; and "Bay Area Yippies Set to Go No Matter What," *Berkeley Barb*, August 2–8, 1968, 3; both quoted in Farber, *Chicago '68*, 49, 53.

68 Norman Fruchter, "Games in the Arena: Movement Propaganda and the Culture of the Spectacle," *Liberation* 16, no. 3 (May 1971): 10.

69 Ibid., 10–11 (emphasis in original).

70 Ibid., 10.

71 Ibid.

72 Ibid., 8 (emphasis in original).

73 Marcuse, "Repressive Tolerance," 98.

74 Ibid., 115.

75 Ibid.

76 Free, *Revolution for the Hell of It*, 107–8.

77 Quoted in Wells, *War Within*, 262–63.

78 Eugene McCarthy, quoted in Wells, *War Within*, 225. McCarthy was correct to think of himself as an underdog. As Marty Jezer points out, "The rules of the Democratic convention were proof of his campaign's hopelessness. Party regulars, controlled by Johnson, held 60 percent of the delegate votes no matter what McCarthy did in the primaries. Even if he won every primary by a landslide, he would still enter the convention in a minority position." Jezer, *Abbie Hoffman*, 136.

79 Quoted in Wells, *War Within*, 227.

80 Ibid., 227.

81 Free, *Revolution for the Hell of It*, 108.

82 Ibid., 108.

83 For more information regarding the Revolutionary Youth Movement and Weathermen, see Ron Jacobs, *The Way the Wind Blew: A History of the Weather Underground* (New York: Verso Press, 1997).

84 Wells, *War Within*, 273.

85 Free, *Revolution for the Hell of It*, 109.

86 Ibid.

87 Ibid., 109–10.

88   Raskin, *For the Hell of It*, 147.
89   Free, *Revolution for the Hell of It*, 112.
90   Quoted in Raskin, *For the Hell of It*, 148–49.
91   Ibid., 149.
92   David Farber, *Chicago '68*, 218.
93   Ibid., 220–22.
94   Ibid., 218.
95   Jacob Brackman, *The Put-On: Modern Fooling and Modern Mistrust* (Chicago: Henry Regnery Co., 1971), 20 (emphasis in original).
96   Free, *Revolution for the Hell of It*, 30.
97   Ibid., 30–31.

NOTES TO CHAPTER 2

1   Quoted in Toby Marrotta, *The Politics of Homosexuality: How Lesbians and Gay Men Have Made Themselves a Force in Modern America* (Boston: Houghton-Mifflin Company, 1981), 79.
2   Pat Maxwell, "The Emperor's New Clothes," *Come Out!* 5, 10.
3   Ibid., 10.
4   Ibid.
5   See, for example, David Bergman's introduction to the volume *Camp Grounds: Style and Homosexuality* (Durham, NC: Duke University Press, 1993), 1–16; Chuck Kleinhans, "Taking Out the Trash: Camp and the Politics of Parody," in Moe Meyer, *The Politics and Poetics of Camp* (New York: Routledge Books, 1994), 182–201; Sally R. Munt, ed., *Butch/Femme: Inside Lesbian Gender* (London: Cassell, 1998); Judith Butler, *Gender Trouble: Feminism and the Subversion of Identity* (New York: Routledge Books, 1999); Sue-Ellen Case, "Toward a Butch-Femme Aesthetic," in Henry Abelove, Michèle Aina Barale, and David M. Halperin, eds., *The Lesbian and Gay Studies Reader* (New York: Routledge Books, 1993), 294–306; and the essays collected in Fabio Cleto, *Camp: Queer Aesthetics and the Performing Subject: A Reader* (Ann Arbor: University of Michigan Press, 1999).
6   The phrase "the homosexual role" comes from the title of Mary McIntosh's 1968 essay of that name. See Mary McIntosh, "The Homosexual Role," *Social Problems* 16, no. 2 (Autumn 1968): 182–92.
7   Of course, the Mattachine Society was not the first organization dedicated to winning civil rights for gay men and lesbians. As Jonathan Ned Katz points out in his *Gay/Lesbian Almanac*, Chicago's Society for Human Rights, founded by Henry Gerber in 1924, was actually the first American organization formed around the idea of gay and lesbian civil rights and liberties. See Jonathan Ned Katz, *Gay/Lesbian Almanac: A New Documentary History* (New York: Harper & Row, 1983), 418–19.
8   Quoted in David K. Johnson, *The Lavender Scare: The Cold War Persecution of Gays and Lesbians in the Federal Government* (Chicago: University of Chicago Press, 2004), 170.

9   For an account of the 1953 convention of the Mattachine Society, see John
     D'Emilio, *Sexual Politics, Sexual Communities: The Making of a Homosexual
     Minority in the United States, 1940–1970* (Chicago: University of Chicago Press,
     1983), 79–81.

10   "Preamble to Constitution Changed over Objection of Some Members," from *The
     Mattachine Newsletter*, 1953, reprinted in Mark Blasius and Shane Phelan, eds.,
     We Are Everywhere: A Historical Sourcebook of Gay and Lesbian Politics (New
     York: Routledge Books, 1997), 319.

11   For more on the relationship of the Mattachine Society to transvestites and trans-
     sexuals, see Dave King, "Gender Confusions: Psychological and Psychiatric Con-
     ceptions of Transvestism and Transsexualism," in Kenneth Plummer, ed., *The
     Making of the Modern Homosexual* (London: Hutchinson Press, 1981), 155–83.

12   See McIntosh, "Homosexual Role," 182.

13   Jonathan Dollimore, *Sexual Dissidence: Augustine to Wilde, Freud to Foucault*
     (Oxford: Oxford University Press, 1991), 237.

14   This hysteria over the government employment of homosexuals is chronicled in
     great detail in David K. Johnson, *Lavender Scare*. See also *The Employment of
     Homosexuals and Other Sex Perverts in Government* (Washington, DC: Govern-
     ment Printing Office, 1950), reprinted in Mark Blasius and Shane Phelan, eds., *We
     Are Everywhere: A Historical Sourcebook of Gay and Lesbian Politics* (New
     York: Routledge Press, 1997), 241–51.

15   As Robert J. Corber has argued, even "liberal" conceptions of same-sex sexuality
     were shaped, in large part, by the equation of homosexuality and communism. In
     1950s America, Corber explains, racial and sexual minorities fell victim to the broad
     redefinition of liberalism by Cold War intellectuals seeking to distance themselves
     from the more progressive social programs of the New Deal. As Corber puts it, Cold
     War liberals such as Arthur Schlesinger, Lionel Trilling, and Leslie Fiedler sought
     "to preserve the legacies of the New Deal while reclaiming liberalism from the cul-
     tural politics of the Popular Front." The social thought that resulted from these
     efforts, often referred to as the "Cold War consensus," depicted efforts to democ-
     ratize social relations as little more than the remnants of an older, more naïve, and,
     most importantly, socialist-inspired liberalism. By couching their position in terms
     of geopolitical concerns over the global advance of fascism and totalitarianism, Cold
     War liberals sought to preempt the objections of the historically disenfranchised by
     calling upon them to join in creating a united front dedicated to the containment of
     communism. In many cases, in spite of any desire for equal rights these minorities
     may have held, their patriotism and abhorrence of fascism ultimately won the day.
     Thus, rather than being victimized by a pervasive anticommunist hysteria, Corber
     explains, liberal intellectuals were ultimately able to exploit that hysteria to put
     forth "a definition of reality to which Americans consented freely and spontaneously
     because it seemed to correspond to their lived experience." Robert J. Corber, *In the
     Name of National Security: Hitchcock, Homophobia, and the Political Construc-
     tion of Gender in Postwar America* (Durham, NC: Duke University Press, 1993), 3.

16   United States Senate, "Employment of Homosexuals and Other Sex Perverts in the

U.S. Government," in Mark Blasius and Shane Phelan, eds., *We Are Everywhere: A Historical Sourcebook of Gay and Lesbian Politics* (London: Routledge, 1997), 243.

17   D'Emilio, *Sexual Politics, Sexual Communities*, 125.

18   Kenneth Burns, "The Homosexual Faces a Challenge: A Speech to the 3rd Annual Convention of The Mattachine Society," reprinted in Blasius and Phelan, *We Are Everywhere*, 288–89.

19   For example, James Phelan, writing in the *Mattachine Review*, urged his readers who were "sex variants" to "*try* to get cured." James Phelan, "Sex Variants Find Their Own Answers," *Mattachine Review* (September–October 1955), 15–17, quoted in D'Emilio, *Sexual Politics, Sexual Communities*, 125. When the *Mattachine Review* published Allen Ginsberg's poem "The Green Automobile," psychiatrist Karl Menninger wrote a letter to the editors "denouncing the poem and saying they were trying to cure everybody, and here was this terrible poem boasting of those perverted feelings!" "Allen Young Interviews Allen Ginsberg," *Gay Sunshine* 16 (January 1973) and 17 (March 1973), reprinted in Winston Leyland, ed., *The Gay Sunshine Interviews*, vol. 1 (San Francisco: Gay Sunshine Press, 1978), 119.

20   See, for example, David Johnson's account of the short-lived Washington, DC, chapter of the Mattachine Society, which called itself the "Council for the Repeal of Unjust Laws." Founded in 1956 by Buell Dwight Huggins, this chapter was, at least initially, far more concerned with mounting an official challenge to the government's discriminatory employment practices. Huggins's desire to involve his chapter of the society directly in local and federal politics, however, placed him at odds both with the national organization and with a number of his members. When Huggins left Washington at the end of 1957, Johnson explains, the chapter became much more of a "social club," meeting in private homes rather than public spaces, and devoting its newsletter to things like book reviews rather than political analyses. By 1960 the chapter had all but disbanded. See Johnson, *Lavender Scare*, 172–74.

21   For details regarding Kameny's dismissal, see David K. Johnson, *Lavender Scare*, 179–82.

22   Quoted in D'Emilio, *Sexual Politics, Sexual Communities*, 152.

23   Franklin Kameny, "Constitution of the Mattachine Society of Washington," quoted in "Letter to the Members of the U.S. House of Representatives," reprinted in Blasius and Phelan, *We Are Everywhere*, 307.

24   Franklin Kameny, "Speech to the New York Mattachine Society," July 1964, quoted in D'Emilio, *Sexual Politics, Sexual Communities*, 152.

25   Quoted in Johnson, *Lavender Scare*, 201.

26   Ibid.

27   Dennis Altman, *Homosexual: Oppression and Liberation* (New York: New York University Press, 1993), 192.

28   Brian Chavez, "sister," *Gay Sunshine*, October 1970, quoted in Altman, *Homosexual: Oppression and Liberation*, 129.

29   Carl Wittman, "Refugees from Amerika: A Gay Manifesto," reprinted as "A Gay

Manifesto," in Karla Jay and Allen Young, *Out of the Closets: Voices of Gay Liberation* (New York: New York University Press, 1992), 333.

30 Ibid.

31 Ibid., 334.

32 Perry Brass, "From the Men: Games Male Chauvinists Play," *Come Out!* 5 (1970):
22 (emphasis added).

33 Ibid.

34 Ibid.

35 Ibid.

36 Craig Alfred Hanson, "The Fairy Princess Exposed," *Gay Sunshine*, reprinted in
Jay and Young, *Out of the Closets*, 266.

37 Susan Sontag, "Notes on Camp," in *Against Interpretation* (New York: Dell Publishing, 1966), 290.

38 Hanson, "Fairy Princess Exposed," 266.

39 Ibid., 269.

40 Alinder's use of the terms "soul" and "brother" throughout the essay, two words
more commonly associated at the time with the struggle for black liberation, was
quite telling. For Alinder, being gay was virtually the same as being African American. One was indelibly marked by one's sexual identity. No matter how one might
try to hide one's "Gay soul," it could never be completely concealed: "I went to a
small liberal arts college near my home town for two years. . . . Even the lowest
fraternity . . . didn't want me. . . . I was hipper and in some ways more together than
they were. But I couldn't censor myself enough. My Gay self was showing through."
Gary Alinder, "My Gay Soul," in *Gay Sunshine*, reprinted in *Gay Flames* 4 (1970):
3

41 Mark D. Jordan, "Making the Homophile Manifest," in Hillary Radner and Moya
Luckett, eds., *Swinging Single: Representing Sexuality in the 1960s* (Minneapolis: University of Minnesota Press, 1999), 183.

42 Wittman, *Gay Manifesto*, 334.

43 Altman, *Homosexual: Oppression & Liberation*, 38–41.

44 Ibid., 38.

45 Duberman, *Stonewall*, 237.

46 Ibid.

47 Quoted in Duberman, *Stonewall*, 237. These anxieties over cross-dressing, particularly in relation to butch/femme role-playing within the lesbian subculture, were
expressed repeatedly in early lesbian-feminist publications. See, for example, Susan
Helenius, "Returning the Dykes to the Dutch," in *Everywoman* 2, no. 10 (1971): 2;
Radicallesbians, "Woman-Identified Woman," in Jay and Young, *Out of the Closets*,
172–77; and Rita Mae Brown's classic lesbian-feminist novel *Rubyfruit Jungle* (New
York: Bantam Books, 1977). For further discussions of the lesbian-feminist response
both to drag and to the role-playing of butch-femme, see Lillian Faderman, *Odd Girls
and Twilight Lovers: A History of Lesbian Life in America* (New York: Columbia
University Press, 1991), as well as the essays collected in Sally R. Munt, ed., *butch/
femme: Inside Lesbian Gender* (London: Cassel Books, 1998).

48   Laura McAlister, "The Transvestite in America," *Come Out!*, 1, no. 4 (1970): 18.

49   Ibid.

50   This conflation of cross-dressing and homosexuality, a remnant of the myth of gender inversion, still persists today. See Marjorie Garber, *Vested Interests: Cross-Dressing and Cultural Anxiety* (New York: Routledge Press, 1991), 128–31.

51   McAlister, "Transvestite in America," 18.

52   While McAlister correctly points to Harry Benjamin's *The Transsexual Phenomenon* as the only book-length "scientific" study of transsexualism available in 1969 (it served, in effect, as the "transsexual's bible" as Dave King points out) the late 1950s and early 1960s saw a proliferation of scientific studies on transsexualism and transvestism, the writings of David Cauldwell being the most notable among them, as well as the publication of a number of autobiographies and memoirs written by transsexuals such as Christine Jorgenson and the Abbé de Choisy. See Dave King, "Gender Confusions: Psychological and Psychiatric Conceptions of Transvestism and Transsexualism," and Joanne Meyerowitz, *How Sex Changed: A History of Transsexuality in the United States* (Cambridge, MA: Harvard University Press, 2002).

53   McAlister, "Transvestite in America," 18.

54   Maxwell, "Emperor's New Clothes," 10.

55   Garber, *Vested Interests*, 10.

56   Parker Tyler, *Screening the Sexes: Homosexuality in the Movies* (New York: Holt, Rinehart and Winston, 1972), 5.

57   Ibid., x. To be sure, Tyler's unwillingness to acknowledge the political relevance of transsexualism can also be read as an example of what Diane Fuss has described as the "essentializing of essentialism." See Diane Fuss, *Essentially Speaking: Feminism, Nature, and Difference* (New York: Routledge, 1989).

58   Tyler, *Screening the Sexes*, 10.

59   Ibid., 205.

60   Ibid., 219.

61   Ibid., 325.

62   Ibid., 64.

63   Ibid., 21.

64   Ibid., 7.

65   Media historian Steven Capsuto also points out that between 1959 and 1969 the frequency with which gay men and lesbians were represented in the mass media increased dramatically. See Steven Capsuto, *Alternate Channels: The Uncensored Story of Gay and Lesbian Images on Radio and Television, 1930s to the Present* (New York: Ballantine Books, 2000), 37–58.

66   Tyler, *Screening the Sexes*, 46. As Capsuto explains, by the late 1960s, members of homophile organizations such as the Daughters of Bilitis were unruffled by derisive or dismissive accounts of homosexuality in the mass media. Journals such as the Daughters of Bilitis's *The Ladder* and the Mattachine Society's *ONE* never criticized these jokes, interpreting them instead as an indication that the media were growing progressively "gayer." See Capsuto, *Alternate Channels*, 47.

67   Tyler, *Screening the Sexes*, 238.

68   Ibid., 229.

69   Ibid., 238.

70   Ibid., xii.

71   Ibid., 231.

72   Ibid., 104.

73   Altman, *Homosexual: Oppression and Liberation*, 103. See chapter 1 of this volume for a more detailed discussion of *Eros and Civilization*.

74   Ibid., 89.

75   Tom Burke, "The New Homosexual," *Esquire* 72 (December 1969): 316–18, quoted in Marrotta, *Politics of Homosexuality*, 79.

76   This project of embracing a kind of male femininity, as it were, was taken up by a collective that formed within the Gay Liberation Front, the Flaming Faggots, which later became known as the Effeminists, an organization headed by Steven F. Dansky and Kenneth Pitchford. See "Flaming Faggots Collective Poem," *Come Out!* 6 (1970): 22–23; Steven F. Dansky, "Hey Man!," *Come Out!* 4 (1970): 8; and "Gay Men in Consciousness Raising Groups," reprinted in Allen and Jay, *Out of the Closets*, 293–301. Of course, the claims of GLF men to have fully accepted their "femininity" failed to impress the organization's female members, who found this rhetoric insulting at best. See, for example, Martha Shelley, "Subversion in the Womans Movement," *Come Out!* 6 (1970): 9.

77   As Jonathan Dollimore points out, this rhetorical inversion was common both in the gay liberation movement and in the lesbian feminist movement of the early 1970s. See Dollimore, *Sexual Dissidence*, 52–55, 226.

78   Allan Warshawsky and Ellen Bedoz, "GLF and the Movement," *Come Out!* 2 (1969): 4–5 (emphasis in original).

79   For an account of the homophobia experienced by gay men and lesbians attempting to work within the antiwar movement, see Ian Keith Lekus, "Queer and Present Dangers: Homosexuality and American Antiwar Activism During the Vietnam Era" PhD Diss., Duke University, 2003.

80   See Marotta, *Politics of Homosexuality*, 113.

81   Quoted in Marotta, *Politics of Homosexuality*, 112–13.

82   Quoted in Marotta, *Politics of Homosexuality*, 79.

83   Jim Fourratt, "Word Thoughts," *Come Out!* 2 (1969): 15.

84   Ibid.

85   Earl Galvin, Dan Smith, and Mike Brown, "Washington Moratorium: 3 Views," *Come Out!* 2 (1969): 3.

86   Ibid.

87   Lois Hart, "Black Panthers Call a Revolutionary People's Constitutional Convention: A White Lesbian Responds," *Come Out!* 4 (1970): 15. It should be pointed out that Panther leader Huey Newton later issued a formal apology, and pledged the Black Panther Party's official support for the gay liberation movement. See Huey Newton, "A Letter from Huey," reprinted in Len Richmond and Gary Noguera, eds.,

The Gay Liberation Book: Writings and Photographs on Gay (Men's) Liberation (San Francisco: Ramparts Press, 1973), 142–45.

88 The relationship of gay and lesbian oppression to modern capitalism was a common theme in the early writings of GLF members. In addition to the analysis of Bedoz and Warshawsky, an entire subgroup dedicated to what members saw as the intimate links between socialist revolution and gay liberation developed within the GLF, calling itself the Red Butterfly Cell. See "Red Butterfly," in *Come Out!* 2 (1969): 4–5.

89 Quoted in Donn Teal, *The Gay Militants: How Gay Liberation Began in America, 1969–1971* (New York: St. Martin's Press, 1995), 90.

90 Ibid. (emphasis in original).

91 For a more detailed discussion of Theodor Roszak's *The Making of a Counter Culture*, see chapter 1.

92 See chapter 1.

93 See William H. Whyte, Jr., *The Organization Man* (New York: Anchor Books, 1956). Whyte's text was not the only one to describe this post-Fordist model of masculinity. For further examples, see Sloan Wilson, *The Man in the Gray Flannel Suit* (New York: Pocket Books, 1956), and David Riesman, *The Lonely Crowd: A Study of the Changing American Character* (New York: Doubleday Anchor Books, 1953).

94 Martha Shelley, "Gay Is Good," *Rat*, February 24, 1970, reprinted in Jay and Allen, *Out of the Closets*, 34. It is worth noting that Shelley appropriated the title of this essay from the famous homophile manifesto written by Franklin Kameny. See Franklin Kameny, "Gay Is Good," reprinted in Blasius and Phelan, *We Are Everywhere*, 367–76.

95 Ibid., 33.

96 Ibid.

97 Ibid.

98 As Carole-Anne Tyler explains, the transvestic slang phrase "real girl," or "r.g.," "is useful for suggesting that even the 'real thing' needs to be written in quotation marks, since she is only a product of certain gender codes which privilege the body as essential ground of gender identity." See Carole-Anne Tyler, "Boys Will Be Girls: The Politics of Gay Drag," in Diane Fuss, ed., *Inside/Out: Lesbian Theories, Gay Theories* (New York: Routledge Press, 1991), 65.

99 Dollimore, *Sexual Dissidence*, 311–12.

100 See, for example, Marotta, *Politics of Homosexuality*, 94–96, 134–61.

101 David Carter, *Stonewall: The Riots That Sparked the Gay Revolution* (New York: St. Martin's Press, 2004), 243.

102 Evans, "How to Zap Straights," 114.

103 Quoted in Teal, *Gay Militants*, 224.

104 Arthur Bell, *Dancing the Gay Lib Blues: A Year in the Homosexual Liberation Movement* (New York: Simon & Schuster, 1971), 35–36.

105 Ibid.

106 Ibid., 37.

107 "Is ABC-TV Against Us?" *GAY* 10, March 29, 1970.

108 Bell, *Dancing the Gay Lib Blues*, 52.

109 Quoted in Bell, *Dancing the Gay Lib Blues*, 52–53.

110 Carter, *Stonewall*, 245.

111 Bell, *Dancing the Gay Lib Blues*, 56.

112 Quoted in Bell, *Dancing the Gay Lib Blues*, 57.

113 To be sure, debates over the relation of role-playing and visibility hardly ended with the social movements of the late 1960s. As the explosion of writings on performative resistance in the late 1980s and early 1990s—precisely the moment at which a new generation of queer activists had come together once again in opposition to official discrimination—made clear, the question of authentic opposition remains at the heart of discussions of political resistance.

114 Dollimore, *Sexual Dissidence*, 312–13.

115 See Peggy Phelan, *Unmarked: The Politics of Performance* (New York: Routledge Books, 1993).

NOTES TO CHAPTER 3

1   Kobena Mercer and Isaac Julien, "True Confessions: A Discourse on Images of Black Male Sexuality," in Kobena Mercer, *Welcome to the Jungle: New Positions in Black Cultural Studies* (London: Routledge Press, 1994), 139.

2   Ibid.

3   Ibid., 140.

4   Ibid., 141.

5   Cleaver, *Soul on Ice*, 100–102.

6   Ibid., 102.

7   Ibid.

8   Ibid.

9   Ibid., 103.

10 Ibid., 102.

11 James Baldwin, *Nobody Knows My Name: More Notes of a Native Son* (New York: Dell Publishing Co., 1963), 148.

12 Ibid., 151.

13 Ibid.

14 Cleaver, *Soul on Ice*, 107–8.

15 Ibid., 108.

16 Ibid., 106, 108.

17 Ibid., 61, 108.

18 Ibid., 109.

19 Ibid.

20 Ibid., 101.

21 Ibid., 178.

22 Ibid., 177.

23 Ibid.
24 Ibid.
25 Ibid., 179.
26 Ibid.
27 Ibid., 181.
28 Ibid., 182.
29 Ibid.
30 Calvin C. Hernton, *Sex and Racism in America* (New York: Grove Press, 1966), 7.
31 Frantz Fanon, *Black Skin, White Masks*, trans. Charles Lam Markmann (New York: Grove Press, 1967), 165.
32 Ibid., 170.
33 Ibid.
34 LeRoi Jones, *Home: Social Essays* (New York: William Morrow, 1966), 216.
35 Robyn Wiegman, "The Anatomy of Lynching," in *American Anatomies: Theorizing Race and Gender* (Durham, NC: Duke University Press, 1995), 85.
36 Cleaver, *Soul on Ice*, 192.
37 Ibid., 193–94.
38 Ibid., 192–93.
39 Ibid., 194–95.
40 Ibid., 201–2 (emphasis in original).
41 Kathleen Rout, *Eldridge Cleaver* (Boston: Twayne Publishers, 1991), 129.
42 It should come as no surprise that a second group would also have adopted the Black Panther name. After 1965, when the Lowndes County Freedom Organization of Alabama changed its name to the Black Panther Party, a number of local Black Power organizations adopted the moniker as well. See Clayborne Carson, *In Struggle: SNCC and the Black Awakening of the 1960s* (Cambridge, MA: Harvard University Press, 1981).
43 John W. Roberts, *From Trickster to Badman: The Black Folk Hero in Slavery and Freedom* (Philadelphia: University of Pennsylvania Press, 1989), 203–5.
44 Ibid., 206.
45 Ibid., 212.
46 Ibid., 214.
47 Ibid., 179. As psychologists William Grier and Price Cobbs noted in 1968, "The bad nigger in black men no doubt accounts for more worry in both races than any other single factor." See William H. Grier and Price M. Cobbs, *Black Rage* (New York: Basic Books, 1968), 66.
48 Jon Michael Spencer, "Introduction," in Jon Michael Spencer, ed., *The Emergency of Black and the Emergence of Rap* (Durham, NC: Duke University Press, 1991), 7.
49 Eldridge Cleaver, "The Courage to Kill: Meeting the Panthers," in Robert Scheer, ed. *Eldridge Cleaver: Post-Prison Writings and Speeches* (New York: Random House, 1969), 35–36.
50 Quoted in Gilbert Moore, *A Special Rage* (New York: Harper & Row, 1971), 257. Russell Means of the American Indian Movement also indicated the importance

of using the police as something like a dramatic foil. When confronted by park rangers on what became the first night of their occupation of Mount Rushmore, Means recalls telling them, "'We're not coming down until you promise that we'll go to jail.' They looked at one another, not believing what they had heard. The one with the walkie-talkie called down to his boss, 'You're not going to believe this one. These Indians want to be arrested.' I wondered then, and do now, if they had ever watched television or read newspapers—hadn't they heard about protests?" Russell Means with Marvin J. Wolf, *Where White Men Fear to Tread: The Autobiography of Russell Means* (New York: St. Martin's Press, 1995), 169.

51 For more on the pervasive assumption of the revolutionary's hypermasculinity, see Ian Lekus, "Queer and Present Dangers: Homosexuality and American Antiwar Activism during the Vietnam Era," PhD diss., Duke University, 2003.

52 Quoted in Huey Newton, *Revolutionary Suicide* (New York: Harcourt Brace Jovanovich, 1973), 146.

53 Ibid., 147.

54 Ibid.

55 Ibid., 149.

56 Bobby Seale, *Seize the Time: The Story of the Black Panther Party and Huey Newton* (Baltimore, MD: Black Classic Press, 1991), 182.

57 Stew Albert, "White Radicals, Black Panthers, and a Sense of Fulfillment," in George Katsiaficas and Kathleen Cleaver, eds., *Liberation, Imagination, and the Black Panther Party* (London: Routledge Press, 2002), 189.

58 Huey Newton, "The Correct Handling of a Revolution: July 20, 1967," reprinted in *To Die for the People* (New York: Writers and Readers Publishing, 1995), 17.

59 Frantz Fanon, *The Wretched of the Earth*, trans. Constance Farrington (New York: Grove Press, 1968), 130.

60 Huey Newton, "The Correct Handling of a Revolution," in Toni Morrison, ed., *To Die for the People: The Writings of Huey Newton* (New York: Writers and Readers Publishing), 14.

61 As T. V. Reed recently put it, images of the riots appeared to have "awakened countless numbers of Negroes into African Americanness." See T. V. Reed, *The Art of Protest: Culture and Activism from the Civil Rights Movement to the Streets of Seattle* (Minneapolis, MN: University of Minnesota Press, 2005), 51.

62 Newton, "Correct Handling of a Revolution," 17.

63 Malcolm X and Alex Haley, *The Autobiography of Malcolm X* (New York: Grove Press, 1966), 280–81 (emphasis in original). Similar complaints, it is worth noting, were made regarding Abbie Hoffman's appearances on television. As John Brockman quipped, "The revolution ended when Abbie Hoffman shut up for the first commercial." John Brockman, quoted in Michael Shamberg and Raindance Corporation, *Guerrilla Television* (New York: Rinehart and Winston, 1971), 27.

64 Quoted in David C. Carter, *The Music Has Gone Out of the Movement: Civil Rights and the Johnson Administration, 1965–68* (Chapel Hill: University of North Carolina Press, 2009), 107.

65 David Hilliard and Lewis Cole, *This Side of Glory: The Autobiography of David*

Hilliard and the Story of the Black Panther Party (Boston: Little, Brown, and Co., 1993), 3.

66 The coalition between the Panthers and the Peace and Freedom Party (PFP) was largely a marriage of convenience. The PFP hoped that the Panthers could help them secure the 25,000 signatures necessary to place a presidential candidate on the ballot in California; Cleaver, who negotiated the terms of the agreement, hoped that the Panthers' association with the PFP would provide him with a much larger audience. See Earl Anthony, *Picking Up the Gun: A Report on the Black Panthers* (New York: Dial Press, 1970), 80–95.

67 Accounts of this shootout vary greatly, particularly on questions of who was to blame for its occurrence. A few of the Panthers involved blamed Cleaver, saying that he assembled the group that evening with the intention of instigating the battle with the police. Upon their release from prison, however, the party called a press conference in which they repudiated their official statements. For a discussion of the different positions in this debate, see Rout, *Eldridge Cleaver*, 67–73.

68 With the help of the Panthers' lawyer, Charles Garry, Cleaver was released in June, only to have that decision overturned in an appellate court, and a warrant issued for his arrest in September.

69 Eldridge Cleaver, "The Death of Martin Luther King: Requiem for Nonviolence," reprinted in Robert Scheer, ed., *Eldridge Cleaver: Post-Prison Writings and Speeches* (New York: Random House, 1969), 74–75. See also Eldridge Cleaver, "The Fire Now: Field Nigger Power Takes Over the Black Movement," *Commonweal*, June 14, 1968, 375–77.

70 H. Rap Brown, *Die Nigger Die!* (Chicago: Lawrence Hill Books, 2002), 81, 128.

71 Quoted in Rout, *Eldridge Cleaver*, 85.

72 Robert Scheer, "Introduction," in *Eldridge Cleaver: Post-Prison Writings and Speeches* (New York: Random House, 1969), xxii–xxiii.

73 Eldridge Cleaver, speech at Stanford University, October 1, 1968, reprinted in *Eldridge Cleaver: Post-Prison Writings and Speeches*, 114.

74 Eldridge Cleaver, *Post-Prison Writings and Speeches*, 133.

75 Don Schanche, *The Panther Paradox: A Liberal's Dilemma* (New York: David McKay Co., 1970), 19–20.

76 Tom Wolfe, *Radical Chic and Mau-Mauing the Flak Catchers* (New York: Farrar, Strauss and Giroux, 1970), 32.

77 John McGrath, "John McGrath Interviews Eldridge Cleaver," *Black Panther*, October 11, 1969, 17.

78 Cleaver also voiced his support for the Panther 21, whom Newton had expelled, reportedly upon David Hilliard's urgings. A thorough discussion of the trial of the Panther 21 is beyond the scope of this chapter. For a detailed account, see Gail Sheehy, *Panthermania* (New York: Harper & Row, 1971).

79 Huey Newton, "On the Defection of Eldridge Cleaver from the Black Panther Party and the Defection of the Black Panther Party from the Community," reprinted in *To Die for the People*, 48.

80 Ibid., 49 (emphasis in original).

81   Newton, "On the Defection," 51.

82   Newton, *Revolutionary Suicide*, 133.

83   Ibid. (emphasis in original).

84   Huey Newton, "Hidden Traitor Renegade Scab: Eldridge Cleaver," unpublished manuscript, Collected Papers of Huey Newton, Stanford University Library, Special Collections, Box 48, Folders 16–18, 2.

85   Ibid., 4.

86   Ibid.

87   Ibid.

88   Ibid., 2.

89   Ibid.

90   Ibid.

91   Ibid., 6.

92   Ibid., 8.

93   Newton, *Revolutionary Suicide*, 292.

94   See Huey Newton, "A Letter from Huey," reprinted in Len Richmond and Gary Noguera, eds., *The Gay Liberation Book: Writings and Photographs on Gay (Men's) Liberation* (San Francisco: Ramparts Press, 1973), 142–45.

95   Huey Newton, "He Won't Bleed Me: A Revolutionary Analysis of *Sweet Sweetback's Baadasssss Song*," in Newton, *To Die for the People*, 113.

96   Joselit, *Feedback: Television Against Democracy*, 126–31.

97   Newton, "He Won't Bleed Me," 114.

98   Ibid., 118.

99   Henry Louis Gates, Jr., *The Signifying Monkey: A Theory of African American Literary Criticism* (Oxford: Oxford University Press, 1988), 45.

100 Melvin Van Peebles, *The Making of* Sweet Sweetback's Baadasssss Song (New York: Lancer Books, 1972), 15.

101 Michele Wallace, *Black Macho and the Myth of the Superwoman* (London: Verso Press, 1990), 67–68.

102 Ibid., 67.

103 Wallace, *Black Macho*, 69.

104 E. Patrick Johnson, *Appropriating Blackness: Performance and the Politics of Authenticity* (Durham, NC: Duke University Press), 2003, 56–57.

105 Cleaver, *Soul on Ice*, 92.

106 Don Schanche, *Panther Paradox*, 20.

107 Norman Mailer, "The White Negro," *Dissent* 4 (Spring 1957), reprinted as *The White Negro* (San Francisco: City Lights Books, 1970), 2.

108 Ibid., 3.

109 Ibid., 9.

110 Ibid., 15.

111 Ibid., 3.

112 Ibid., 4.

113 Ibid., 16.

114 James Baldwin, "The Black Boy Looks at the White Boy," in James Baldwin,

Nobody Knows My Name (New York: Dell, 1961), 172.

115 Ibid., 181.

116 Ibid., 182.

117 Ibid., 181–82.

118 Ibid., 173.

119 Cleaver, *Soul on Ice*, 98.

120 Ibid., 192.

121 Mailer, "White Negro," 12.

122 Cleaver, *Soul on Ice*, 110.

123 Ibid.

124 Ibid.

125 Ibid., 60.

126 Ibid., 202.

127 Ibid.

128 See, for example, many of the essays collected in the Spring 1991 (vol. 5, no. 1) special issue of *Black Sacred Music: A Journal of Ethnomusicology* on the theme of "The Emergency of Black and the Emergence of Rap," particularly the preface and introduction by editor Jon Michael Spencer (v–7, 1–11), and Michael Eric Dyson, "Performance, Protest, and Prophecy in the Culture of Hip-Hop" (12–24).

129 One of the most famous examples of this position is the work of *New York Times* music critic Jon Pareles, who in the late 1980s and early 1990s wrote repeatedly of the problems with "gangster rap" groups like NWA, the Geto Boys, and others. See, in particular, his article "Gangster Rap: Life and Music in the Combat Zone," *New York Times*, October 7, 1990, http://www.nytimes.com/1990/10/07/arts/pop-view-gangster-rap-life-and-music-in-the-combat-zone.html, accessed April 18, 2014.

130 R. A. T. Judy, "On the Question of Nigga Authenticity," *boundary 2* 21, no. 3 (1994): 216.

131 Ibid., 217.

132 Ibid., 225.

133 Ibid., 227–28 (emphasis in original).

134 Ibid., 228. On this note, Judy quotes Ice-T, who formulated the argument quite succinctly, saying, "Everybody is a nigga to a nigga." Ice-T, "Straight Up Nigga," *Original Gangster*, quoted in ibid., 228.

135 Ibid., 228.

136 Cleaver, *Soul on Ice*, 109.

NOTES TO AFTERWORD

1 See The Yes Men, *The True Story of the End of the World Trade Organization* (New York: The Disinformation Company, 2004), 11. Bichlbaum and Bonanno, of course, are not the real names of the Yes Men. However, as these are the pseudonyms most often used to refer to their characters, I have chosen to use them throughout this paper.

2 Ibid., 115.

3   See, for example, Martha Rosler, "Out of the VOX: Martha Rosler on Art's Activist Potential," *Artforum* 43, no. 1 (September 2004): 218; Yates McKee, "Haunted Housing: Eco-Vanguardism, Eviction, and the Biopolitics of Sustainability in New Orleans," *Grey Room* 30 (Winter 2008): 84–113; and Bridget Hanna, "Bhopal: Unending Disaster, Enduring Resistance," and "The Yes Men in Bhopal: Interview with Andy Bichlbaum, Mike Bonanno, and Satinath Sarangi," in Michael Feher, ed., *Nongovernmental Politics* (Cambridge, MA: MIT Press, 2007), 488–529. A similar enthusiasm for the Yes Men's tactics can also be found in the work of performance studies scholar Amanda Day. Day acknowledges many audiences' failure to get the Yes Men's jokes, but argues that the performances can nevertheless be seen as productive insofar as the Yes Men's films can then reveal this brazenness to a larger audience. See Amanda Day, *Satire & Dissent: Interventions in Contemporary Political Debate* (Bloomington: Indiana University Press, 2011), 170–93.

4   "What Noah Knew: Old Models for New Conditions," Yes Men website, http://theyesmen.org/agribusiness/halliburton/about/hse.html, accessed 10/19/2012.

5   See Augusto Boal, *Theater of the Oppressed* (New York: Theater Communications Group, 1993), 143–47.

6   The Yes Men, *True Story*, 41.

7   Thomas Keenan, "Mobilizing Shame," *South Atlantic Quarterly* 103, no. 2/3 (Spring/Summer 2004): 446.

8   Ibid.

9   Ibid.

10   Ibid., 435.

11   Theodor Adorno, *Minima Moralia: Reflections from Damaged Life* (London: Verso Press, 1974), 209.

12   Ibid., 211.

13   Michel Foucault, *The Birth of Biopolitics: Lectures at the Collège de France, 1978–1979* (New York: Palgrave Macmillan, 2008), 106.

14   Milton Friedman, *Capitalism and Freedom: Fortieth Anniversary Edition* (Chicago: University of Chicago Press, 2002), ix.

15   Naomi Klein, *The Shock Doctrine: The Rise of Disaster Capitalism* (New York: Macmillan Publishing, 2007), 10.

16   A thorough analysis of the contemporary dominance of free market ideology is beyond the scope of this chapter. For more on this, see, among others, Kline, *The Shock Doctrine*; Jennifer Burns, *Goddess of the Market: Ayn Rand and the American Right* (New York: Oxford University Press, 2009); Jeffrey G. Madrick, *Age of Greed: The Triumph of Finance and the Decline of America, 1970 to the Present* (New York: Alfred A. Knopf, 2011); Barbara Ehrenreich, *Bright-Sided: How the Relentless Promotion of Positive Thinking has Undermined America* (New York: Metropolitan Books, 2009); Rakesh Khurana, *From Higher Aims to Hired Hands: The Social Transformation of American Business Schools and the Unfulfilled Promise of Management as a Profession* (Princeton: Princeton University Press, 2007); and Jodi Dean, *Democracy and Other Neoliberal Illusions: Communicative Capitalism and Left Politics* (Durham, NC: Duke Uni-

versity Press, 2009), particularly the chapter titled "Free Trade: The Neoliberal Fantasy," 49–73.

17   See, for example, Astra Taylor et al., eds., *Occupy! Scenes from Occupied America* (London: Verso Press, 2012); Sarah Van Gelder, ed., *This Changes Everything: Occupy Wall Street and the 99% Movement* (San Francisco: Berret-Koehler Publishers, 2011); Writers for the 99%, *Occupying Wall Street: The Inside Story of an Action that Changed America* (Brunswick, Victoria: Scribe Publications, 2012); and John Nichols, *Uprising: How Wisconsin Renewed the Politics of Protest, from Madison to Wall Street* (New York: Nation Books, 2012).

18   Quoted in James Miller, "Is Democracy Still in the Streets?," in Janet Byrne and Robin Wells, eds., *The Occupy Handbook* (New York: Back Bay Books, 2012), 177.

19   Ibid., 183.

20   Nicolas Bourriaud, *Relational Aesthetics* (Paris: Les Presses du Réel, 2002), 14.

21   Ibid., 83.

22   Grant H. Kester, *Conversation Pieces: Community & Communication in Modern Art* (Berkeley: University of California Press, 2004), 116. It is worth noting that, in Kester's account of this performance, the evening was ruined by opportunistic protestors who hoped to use the spectacle of Lacy's work to publicize their own causes.

23   See Mikhail Bakhtin, *The Dialogic Imagination: Four Essays* (Austin: University of Texas Press, 1992).

24   Kester, *Conversation Pieces*, 122.

25   Ibid., 2.

26   See Francis Fukuyama, *The End of History and the Last Man* (New York: Free Press, 1992).

27   Jacques Rancière, *Aesthetics and Its Discontents*, trans. Steven Corcoran (Cambridge: Polity Press, 2009), 22.

28   Michael Hardt and Antonio Negri, *Multitude: War and Democracy in the Age of Empire* (New York: Penguin Books, 2004), 204.

29   Ibid., 210–11.

30   Ibid., 327.

31   Ibid., 346.

32   Jodi Dean, *The Communist Horizon* (New York: Verso, 2012), 227.

33   Ibid., 228.

34   Ibid., 229.

35   Ibid., 215–16.

36   Ibid., 223.

37   Ibid.

38   For more on the choice of Zucotti Park, see Mattathias Schwarz, "Map: How Occupy Wall Street Chose Zucotti Park," *New Yorker* blog, November 21, 2011 http://www.newyorker.com/online/blogs/newsdesk/2011/11/occupy-wall-street-map.html, accessed July 10, 2013.

39   See Claire Bishop, "Antagonism and Relational Aesthetics," *October* 110 (Fall 2004): 51–79.

BIBLIOGRAPHY

Abelove, Henry. *Deep Gossip*. Minneapolis: University of Minnesota Press, 2003.

Abelove, Henry, Michèle Aina Barale, and David Halperin, eds. *The Lesbian and Gay Studies Reader*. New York: Routledge, 1993.

Abu-Jamal, Mumia. *We Want Freedom: A Life in the Black Panther Party*. Cambridge, MA: South End Press, 2004.

Acham, Christine. *Revolution Televised: Prime Time and the Struggle for Black Power*. Minneapolis: University of Minnesota Press, 2004.

Adam, Barry D. *The Rise of a Gay and Lesbian Movement*. Rev. ed. New York: Twayne Publishers, 1995.

Adorno, Theodor. *Minima Moralia: Reflections from Damaged Life*. Translated by E. F. N. Jephcott. New York: Verso Press, 1978.

Albert, Judith Clavir, and Stewart Edward Albert. *The Sixties Papers: Documents of a Rebellious Decade*. New York: Praeger, 1984.

Albert, Stewart Edward. *Who the Hell Is Stew Albert?: A Memoir*. Los Angeles: Red Hen Press, 2003.

Alinder, Gary. "My Gay Soul," *Gay Flames* 4 (1970): 3.

Alonso, Karen. *The Chicago Seven Political Protest Trial: A Headline Court Case, Headline Court Cases*. Berkeley Heights, NJ: Enslow Publishers, 2002.

Altman, Dennis. *Homosexual: Oppression and Liberation*. New York: New York University Press, 1993.

Anthony, Earl. *Picking Up the Gun: A Report on the Black Panthers*. New York: Dial Press, 1970.

———. *Spitting in the Wind: The True Story Behind the Violent Legacy of the Black Panther Party*. Santa Monica, CA: Roundtable Publishing, 1990.

Armstrong, Elizabeth A. *Forging Gay Identities: Organizing Sexuality in San Francisco, 1950–1994*. Chicago: University of Chicago Press, 2002.

212

Austin, Curtis J. *Up Against the Wall: Violence in the Making and Unmaking of the Black Panther Party*. Fayetteville: University of Arkansas Press, 2006.

Baker, Ross K. "Putting Down the Gun." *The Nation*, July 16, 1973, 50.

Balagoon, Kuwasi. *Look for Me in the Whirlwind: The Collective Autobiography of the New York 21*. New York: Random House, 1971.

Baldwin, James. *Nobody Knows My Name: More Notes of a Native Son*. New York: Dell Publishing, 1963.

Barthes, Roland. *Image-Music-Text*. Translated by Stephen Heath. New York: Hill and Wang, 1988.

Baruch, Ruth Marion, and Pirkle Jones. *The Vanguard: A Photographic Essay on the Black Panthers*. Boston: Beacon Press, 1970.

Baruch, Ruth-Marion, Pirkle Jones, and Kathleen Cleaver. *Black Panthers, 1968*. 1st ed. Los Angeles, CA: Greybull Press; distributed by DAP/Distributed Art Publishers, 2002.

Baudelaire, Charles. *The Painter of Modern Life and Other Essays*. Translated by Jonathan Mayne. New York: Da Capo Press, 1986.

Becker, Theodore Lewis, and Anthony L. Dodson. *Live This Book: Abbie Hoffman's Philosophy for a Free and Green America*. Chicago: Noble Press, 1991.

Bell, Arthur. *Dancing the Gay Lib Blues: A Year in the Homosexual Liberation Movement*. New York: Simon & Schuster, 1971.

Bergman, David. *Camp Grounds: Style and Homosexuality*. Amherst: University of Massachusetts Press, 1993.

Berman, Paul. *A Tale of Two Utopias: The Political Journey of the Generation of 1968*. 1st ed. New York: Norton, 1996.

Bishop, Claire. "Antagonism and Relational Aesthetics." *October* 110 (Fall 2004): 51–79.

Black Mask and Up Against the Wall Motherfucker: The Incomplete Works of Ron Hahne, Ben Morea, and the Black Mask Group. London: Unpopular Books, 1993.

The Black Power Mixtape 1967–1975: A Documentary in 9 Chapters. New York: Sundance Selects, 2011.

Blasius, Mark. *Sexual Identities, Queer Politics*. Princeton, NJ: Princeton University Press, 2001.

Blasius, Mark, and Shane Phelan. *We Are Everywhere: A Historical Sourcebook of Gay and Lesbian Politics*. New York: Routledge, 1997.

Bloom, Joshua, and Waldo E. Martin Jr. *Black Against Empire: The History and Politics of the Black Panther Party*. Berkeley: University of California Press, 2012.

Bodrogkozy, Aniko. *Groove Tube: Sixties Television and the Youth Rebellion*. Durham, NC: Duke University Press, 2001.

Boorstin, Daniel J. *The Image: A Guide to Pseudo-Events in America*. New York: Atheneum, 1977.

Bourdieu, Pierre. *On Television*. New York: The New Press, 1998.

———. *Photography: A Middle-Brow Art*. Stanford: Stanford University Press, 1990.

Bourriaud, Nicholas. *Relational Aesthetics*. Paris: Les Presses du Réel, 2002.

Boyle, Kay. *The Long Walk at San Francisco State, and Other Essays*. New York: Grove Press, 1970.

Brackman, Jacob, and Sam Kirshon. *The Put-On: Modern Fooling and Modern Mistrust*. Chicago: H. Regnery Co., 1971.

Brass, Perry. "From the Men: Games Male Chauvinists Play." *Come Out!* 5 (1970): 22.

Bratton, Chris, Annie Goldstein, and Art Institute of Chicago. *Framing the Panthers in Black and White*. Chicago: Video Data Bank, 1990.

Brent, William Lee. *Long Time Gone*. New York: Times Books, 1996.

Brown, Elaine. *A Taste of Power: A Black Woman's Story*. New York: Anchor Books, 1994.

Brown, Howard. *Familiar Faces, Hidden Lives: The Story of Homosexual Men in America Today*. New York: Harcourt Brace Jovanovich, 1976.

Brown, H. Rap. *Die Nigger Die!* Chicago: Lawrence Hill Books, 2002.

Brown, Rita Mae. *Rubyfruit Jungle*. New York: Bantam Books, 1977.

Brustein, Robert. "Revolution as Theater." *The New Republic*, March 14, 1970, 14–17.

Bull, Chris. *Come out Fighting: A Century of Essential Writing on Gay and Lesbian Liberation*. New York: Thunder's Mouth Press/Nation Books, 2001.

Burke, Tom. "The New Homosexual." *Esquire* 72 (December 1969): 316–18.

Butler, Judith. *Gender Trouble: Feminism and the Subversion of Identity*. New York: Routledge, 1990.

Butt, Gavin. "'America' and Its Discontents: Art and Politics, 1945–60." In *A Companion to Contemporary Art Since 1945*, edited by Amelia Jones, 19–37. Oxford: Blackwell Publishing, 2006.

Byrd, Rudolph P., and Beverly Guy-Sheftall. *Traps: African American Men on Gender and Sexuality*. Bloomington: Indiana University Press, 2001.

Capsuto, Steven. *Alternate Channels: The Uncensored Story of Gay and Lesbian Images on Radio and Television, 1930s to the Present*. New York: Ballantine Books, 2000.

Carter, David. *Stonewall: The Riots That Sparked the Gay Revolution*. New York: St. Martin's Press, 2004.

Carter, David C. *The Music Has Gone Out of the Movement: Civil Rights and the Johnson Administration, 1965–1968*. Chapel Hill: University of North Carolina Press, 2009.

Chambers, Ross. *Room to Maneuver: Reading (the) Oppositional (in) Culture*. Chicago: University of Chicago Press, 1991.

Ching, Barbara, and Jennifer Wagner-Lawlor, eds. *The Scandal of Susan Sontag*. New York: Columbia University Press, 2009.

Churchill, Ward, and Jim Vander Wall. *Agents of Repression: The FBI's Secret Wars Against the Black Panther Party and the American Indian Movement*. Boston: South End Press, 1988.

Clavir, Judy, and John Spitzer, eds., *The Conspiracy Trial*. Indianapolis: Bobbs-Merrill Co., 1970.

Clayborne, Carson. *In Struggle: SNCC and the Black Awakening of the 1960s*. Cambridge, MA: Harvard University Press, 1981.

Cleaver, Eldridge. "The Fire Now: Field Nigger Power Takes Over the Black Movement." *Commonweal*, June 14, 1968, 375–77.

————. *Post-Prison Writings and Speeches*. Edited by Robert Scheer. New York: Random House, 1969.

————. *Soul on Ice*. New York: McGraw Hill, Inc., 1968.

Clendinen, Dudley, and Adam Nagourney. *Out for Good: The Struggle to Build a Gay Rights Movement in America*. New York: Simon & Schuster, 1999.

Cleto, Fabio. *Camp: Queer Aesthetics and the Performing Subject: A Reader, Triangulations*. Ann Arbor: University of Michigan Press, 1999.

Commission of Inquiry into the Black Panthers and the Police, Ramsey Clark, and Roy Wilkins. *Search and Destroy: A Report*. New York: Metropolitan Applied Research Center, 1973.

Corber, Robert J. *Homosexuality in Cold War America: Resistance and the Crisis of Masculinity*. Durham, NC: Duke University Press, 1997.

————. *In the Name of National Security: Hitchcock, Homophobia, and the Political Construction of Gender in Postwar America*. Durham, NC: Duke University Press, 1993.

Coyote, Peter. *Sleeping Where I Fall: A Chronicle*. Washington, DC: Counterpoint Books, 1998.

Cruikshank, Margaret. *The Gay and Lesbian Liberation Movement*. New York: Routledge, 1992.

Dansky, Steven F. "Hey Man!" *Come Out!* 4 (1970): 8.

Davis, Ronnie. *The San Francisco Mime Troupe: The First Ten Years*. Palo Alto, CA: Ramparts Press, 1975.

Day, Andrea. *Satire and Dissent: Interventions in Contemporary Political Debate*. Bloomington: Indiana University Press, 2011.

Dean, Jodi. *The Communist Horizon*. New York: Verso Press, 2012.

————. *Democracy and Other Neoliberal Fantasies: Communicative Capitalism and Left Politics*. Durham, NC: Duke University Press, 2009.

de Certeau, Michel. *The Practice of Everyday Life.* Translated by Steven F. Rendall. Berkeley: University of California Press, 1984.

Deitcher, David. *The Question of Equality: Lesbian and Gay Politics in America since Stonewall.* New York: Scribner, 1995.

D'Emilio, John. *Making Trouble: Essays on Gay History, Politics, and the University.* New York: Routledge, 1992.

———. *Sexual Politics, Sexual Communities: The Making of a Homosexual Minority in the United States, 1940–1970.* 2nd ed. Chicago: University of Chicago Press, 1998.

D'Emilio, John, William B. Turner, and Urvashi Vaid. *Creating Change: Sexuality, Public Policy, and Civil Rights.* New York: St. Martin's Press, 2000.

DeKoven, Marianne. *Utopia Limited: The Sixties and the Emergence of the Postmodern.* Durham, NC: Duke University Press, 2004.

Derrida, Jacques. *Writing and Difference.* Translated by Alan Bass. Chicago: University of Chicago Press, 1988.

Dinnstein, Leonard. *The Leo Frank Case.* Athens: University of Georgia Press, 1998.

Dollimore, Jonathan. *Sexual Dissidence: Augustine to Wilde, Freud to Foucault.* Oxford: Clarendon Press, 1991.

Doyle, Michael William, and Peter Braunstein, eds. *Imagine Nation: The American Counterculture of the 1960s and '70s.* New York: Routledge, 2002.

Duberman, Martin B. *Midlife Queer: Autobiography of a Decade, 1971–1981.* New York: Scribner, 1996.

———. *Stonewall.* New York: Plume Books, 1994.

Duncombe, Stephen. *Dream: Re-Imagining Progressive Politics in an Age of Fantasy.* New York: The New Press, 2007.

Elam, Harry Justin. *Takin' It to the Streets: The Social Protest Theater of Luis Valdez and Amiri Baraka.* Ann Arbor: University of Michigan Press, 1997.

Erikson, Erik H., and Huey P. Newton. *In Search of Common Ground: Conversations with Erik H. Erikson and Huey P. Newton.* New York: Norton, 1973.

Faderman, Lillian. *Odd Girls and Twilight Lovers: A History of Lesbian Life in America.* New York: Columbia University Press, 1991.

Fanon, Franz. *Black Skin, White Masks.* Translated by Charles Lam Markmann. New York: Grove Press, 1967.

Farber, David R. *The Age of Great Dreams: America in the 1960s.* New York: Hill and Wang, 1994.

———. *Chicago '68.* Chicago: University of Chicago Press, 1988.

———, ed. *The Sixties: From Memory to History.* Chapel Hill: University of North Carolina Press, 1994.

"Flaming Faggots Collective Poem." *Come Out!* 6 (1970): 22–23.

Foner, Philip Sheldon. *The Black Panthers Speak*. Philadelphia: J. B. Lippincott, 1970.

Foucault, Michel. *The Birth of Biopolitics: Lectures at the Collège de France, 1978–79*. New York: Palgrave McMillan, 2008.

———. *The History of Sexuality*. Vol. 1, *An Introduction*. Translated by Robert Hurley. New York: Vintage Books, 1980.

———. *Power/Knowledge: Selected Interviews & Other Writings, 1972–1977*. Edited by Colin Gordon. New York: Harvester Press, 1980.

Fourratt, Jim. "Word Thoughts." *Come Out!* 2 (1969): 15.

Fuss, Diana. *Essentially Speaking: Feminism, Nature, and Difference*. New York: Routledge, 1989.

———. *Inside Out: Lesbian Theories, Gay Theories*. New York: Routledge, 1991.

Fruchter, Norman. "Games in the Arena: Movement Propaganda and the Culture of the Spectacle." *Liberation* 16, no. 3 (May 1971): 4–17.

Galvin, Earl, Dan Smith, and Mike Brown. "Washington Moratorium: 3 Views." *Come Out!* 2 (1969): 3.

Garber, Marjorie. *Vested Interests: Cross-Dressing and Cultural Anxiety*. New York: Routledge, 1991.

Gates, Henry Louis. *Bearing Witness: Selections from African-American Autobiography in the Twentieth Century*. New York: Pantheon Books, 1991.

———. *The Signifying Monkey: A Theory of Afro-American Literary Criticism*. New York: Oxford University Press, 1988.

Gitlin, Todd. *The Sixties: Years of Hope, Days of Rage*. New York: Bantam Books, 1993.

———. *The Whole World Is Watching: Mass Media in the Making and Unmaking of the New Left*. Berkeley: University of California Press, 1980.

Gramsci, Antonio. *Selections from the Prison Notebooks*. Translated by Quintin Hoare and Geoffrey Nowell-Smith. New York: International Publishers, 1971.

Grier, William H., and Price M. Cobbs. *Black Rage*. New York: Basic Books, 1992.

Goldsmith, Kenneth, ed. *I'll Be Your Mirror: The Selected Andy Warhol Interviews, 1963–1987*. New York: Carroll & Graf Publishers, 2004.

Gosse, Van. *Rethinking the New Left: An Interpretative History*. New York: Palgrave Macmillan, 2005.

———. *Where the Boys Are: Cuba, Cold War America, and the Making of a New Left*. New York: Verso Press, 1993.

Gosse, Van, and Richard R Moser, eds. *The World the Sixties Made: Politics and Culture in Recent America*. Philadelphia: Temple University Press, 2003.

Grogan, Emmet. *Ringolevio*. New York: Avon Books, 1972.

Gross, Larry P. *Contested Closets: The Politics and Ethics of Outing*. Minneapolis: University of Minnesota, 1993.

Gross, Robert L. "'Revolution' Has Become the Giant Put-On of the Era." *The Miami Herald*, March 21, 1970, 7A:2.

Halberstam, Judith. *Female Masculinity*. Durham, NC: Duke University Press, 1998.

———. *In a Queer Time and Place: Transgender Bodies, Subcultural Lives*. New York: New York University Press, 2005.

Hardt, Michael, and Antonio Negri. *Commonwealth*. Cambridge, MA: Harvard University Press, 2009.

———. *Empire*. Cambridge, MA: Harvard University Press, 2000.

———. *Multitude: War and Democracy in the Age of Empire*. New York: Penguin Press, 2004.

Harry, Joseph, and William B. DeVall. *The Social Organization of Gay Males*. New York: Praeger, 1978.

Hart, Lois. "Black Panthers Call a Revolutionary People's Constitutional Convention: A White Lesbian Responds." *Come Out!* 4 (1970): 15.

Haskins, James. *Power to the People: The Rise and Fall of the Black Panther Party*. New York: Simon & Schuster Books for Young Readers, 1997.

Hay, Harry. *Radically Gay: Gay Liberation in the Words of Its Founder*. Edited by Will Roscoe. Boston: Beacon Press, 1996.

Heath, G. Louis, and Black Panther Party. *Off the Pigs! The History and Literature of the Black Panther Party*. Metuchen, NJ: Scarecrow Press, 1976.

Hebdige, Dick. "The Function of Subculture." In *The Cultural Studies Reader*, edited by Simon During. 2nd ed. New York: Routledge, 1999.

———. *Subculture: The Meaning of Style*. New York: Routledge, 1981.

Heineman, Kenneth J. *Put Your Bodies Upon the Wheels: Student Revolt in the 1960s*. Chicago: I. R. Dee, 2001.

Helenius, Susan. "Returning the Dykes to the Dutch," *Everywoman* 2, no. 10 (1971): 2.

Hennessy, Rosemary. *Profit and Pleasure: Sexual Identities in Late Capitalism*. New York: Routledge, 2000.

Hernton, Calvin C. *Sex and Racism in America*. New York: Grove Press, 1966.

Hilliard, David, and Lewis Cole. *This Side of Glory: The Autobiography of David Hilliard and the Story of the Black Panther Party*. Boston: Little, Brown, 1993.

Hocquenghem, Guy. *Homosexual Desire*. Translated by Daniella Dangoor. London: Allison & Busby, 1978.

Hoffman, Abbie. *Revolution for the Hell of It*. New York: Dial Press, 1968.

———. *Soon to Be a Major Motion Picture*. New York: Putnam, 1980.

Hoffman, Abbie, Nancy Cohen, MDWA Productions, and Cinema Guild. *My Dinner with Abbie*. New York: MDWA Productions, 1989.

Hoffman, Abbie, Jerry Rubin, and Ed Sanders. *Vote!* New York: Warner Paperback Library, 1972.

Hoffman, Abbie, and Jonathan Silvers. *Steal This Urine Test: Fighting Drug Hysteria in America.* New York: Penguin Books, 1987.

Hoffman, Anita, and Abbie Hoffman. *To America with Love: Letters from the Underground.* 2nd ed. Los Angeles: Red Hen Press, 2000.

Hoffman, Jack, and Daniel Simon. *Run Run Run: The Lives of Abbie Hoffman.* New York: Putnam's, 1994.

Humphreys, Laud. *Out of the Closets: The Sociology of Homosexual Liberation.* Englewood Cliffs, NJ: Prentice-Hall, 1972.

Hunt, Linda. *Out of the Past the Struggle for Gay and Lesbian Rights in America.* New York: A-Pix Entertainment, 1997.

Hutcheon, Linda. *Irony's Edge: The Theory and Politics of Irony.* London: Routledge, 1994.

———. *The Politics of Postmodernism.* 2nd ed. London: New York: Routledge, 2002.

———. *A Theory of Parody: The Teachings of Twentieth-Century Art Forms.* New York: Methuen, 1985.

"Is ABC-TV Against Us?" *GAY* 10, March 29, 1970.

Jacobs, Ron. *The Way the Wind Blew: A History of the Weather Underground.* New York: Verso Press, 1997.

James, Joy. *Imprisoned Intellectuals: America's Political Prisoners Write on Life, Liberation, and Rebellion.* Lanham, MD: Rowman & Littlefield, 2003.

Jameson, Fredric. *The Ideologies of Theory: Essays, 1971–1986.* Vol. 2, *Syntax of History.* Minneapolis: University of Minnesota Press, 1988.

———. *Postmodernism, or, The Cultural Logic of Late Capitalism.* Durham, NC: Duke University Press, 1991.

Janson, Donald. "Coalition Vows Peaceful Protest at Chicago National Convention." *New York Times* March 25, 1968, 20.

Jay, Karla. *Tales of the Lavender Menace: A Memoir of Liberation.* New York: Basic Books, 1999.

———. *Out of the Closets: Voices of Gay Liberation.* Twentieth-anniversary edition. New York: New York University Press, 1992.

Jay, Karla, and Allen Young. *Lavender Culture.* New York: Jove Publications, 1979.

Jeffreys, Sheila. *Unpacking Queer Politics: A Lesbian Feminist Perspective.* Cambridge: Blackwell Books, 2003.

Jeffries, J. L. *Huey P. Newton: The Radical Theorist.* Jackson: University Press of Mississippi, 2002.

220   BIBLIOGRAPHY

———, ed. *Black Power in the Belly of the Beast*. Urbana: University of Illinois Press, 2006.

Jezer, Marty. *Abbie Hoffman, American Rebel*. New Brunswick: Rutgers University Press, 1992.

Johansson, Warren, and William A. Percy. *Outing: Shattering the Conspiracy of Silence*. New York: Haworth Press, 1994.

Johnson, David K. *The Lavender Scare: The Cold War Persecution of Gays and Lesbians in the Federal Government*. Chicago: University of Chicago Press, 2004.

Johnson, E. Patrick. *Appropriating Blackness: Performance and the Politics of Authenticity*. Durham, NC: Duke University Press, 2003.

Jones, Amelia, and Andrew Stephenson, eds. *Performing the Body/Performing the Text*. New York: Routledge, 1999.

Jones, Charles E. *The Black Panther Party (Reconsidered)*. Baltimore: Black Classic Press, 1998.

Jones, LeRoi. *Home: Social Essays*. New York: William Morrow, 1966.

Joselit, David. *Feedback: Television Against Democracy*. Cambridge: MIT Press, 2007.

———. "Yippie Pop: Abbie Hoffman, Andy Warhol, and Sixties Media Politics," *Grey Room* 1:8 (2002): 62–79.

Joseph, Peniel E. *The Black Power Movement: Rethinking the Civil Rights-Black Power Era*. New York: Routledge, 2006.

———. *Neighborhood Rebels: Black Power at the Local Level*. New York: Palgrave Macmillan, 2010.

———. *Waiting 'til the Midnight Hour: A Narrative History of Black Power in America*. New York: Henry Holt and Company, 2006.

Judy, R A T. "On the Question of Nigga Authenticity." *boundary 2* 21, no. 3 (Autumn 1994): 211–30.

Katara, Aiyada Asya, Eldridge Cleaver, Revolutionary Peoples' Communications Network, and Black Panther Party. "Right On! Black Community News Service." Bronx, NY: Black Panther Party, 1971.

Katsiaficas, George, and Kathleen Cleaver, eds. *Liberation, Imagination, and the Black Panther Party*. New York: Routledge, 2002.

Katz, Jonathan Ned. *Gay/Lesbian Almanac: A New Documentary History*. New York: Harper & Row, 1983.

Keating, Edward M. *Free Huey!* Berkeley: Ramparts Press, 1971.

Keenan, Thomas. "Mobilizing Shame." *South Atlantic Quarterly* 103, no. 2/3 (Spring/Summer 2004): 435–49.

Kellner, Douglas. *Television and the Crisis of Democracy*. Boulder, CO: Westview Press, 1990.

Kempton, Sally. "Yippies Anti-Organize a Groovy Revolution." *Village Voice* March 21, 1968, 5–6, 30.

Kester, Grant. *Conversation Pieces: Community and Communication in Modern Art.* Berkeley: University of California Press, 2004.

Krafft-Ebing, Richard von. *Aberrations of Sexual Life: The Psychopathia Sexualis.* Translated by Arthur Vivian Burbury. London: Staples Press, 1959.

Krassner, Paul. *Confessions of a Raving, Unconfined Nut: Misadventures in the Counter-Culture.* New York: Simon & Schuster, 1993.

———. *Who's to Say What's Obscene?: Politics, Culture and Comedy in America Today.* San Francisco: City Lights Books, 2009.

Laclau, Ernesto, and Chantal Mouffe. *Hegemony and Socialist Strategy: Towards a Radical Democratic Politics.* New York: Verso Books, 1985.

Laikin, Paul, and Jerry Grandenetti. "Abbie Hoffman's Charm School." *Sick* 10, no. 6 (September 1970): 38–42.

Lazerow, Jama, and Yohuru R. Williams. *In Search of the Black Panther Party: New Perspectives on a Revolutionary Movement.* Durham, NC: Duke University Press, 2006.

Leahy, Michael P. T., and Dan Cohn-Sherbok. *The Liberation Debate: Rights at Issue.* New York: Routledge Press, 1996.

Lehman, Peter. *Masculinity: Bodies, Movies, Culture.* New York: Routledge Press, 2001.

Lekus, Ian. "Queer and Present Dangers: Homosexuality and American Antiwar Activism during the Vietnam Era." PhD diss., Duke University, 2003.

Leyland, Winston, ed. *The Gay Sunshine Interviews.* Vol. 1. San Francisco: Gay Sunshine Press, 1978.

Lockwood, Lee. *Conversation with Eldridge Cleaver: Algiers.* New York: McGraw-Hill, 1970.

Luckett, Moya, and Hilary Radner, eds. *Swinging Single: Representing Sexuality in the 1960s.* Minneapolis: University of Minnesota Press, 1998.

Lule, Jack. *Daily News, Eternal Stories: The Mythological Role of Journalism.* The Guilford Communication Series. New York: Guilford Press, 2001.

Mailer, Norman. *The Armies of the Night: History as a Novel/The Novel as History.* New York: Penguin Books, 1994.

———. *Miami and the Siege of Chicago: An Informal History of the American Political Conventions of 1968.* New York: Penguin Books, 1968.

———. "The White Negro." San Francisco: City Lights Books, 1970.

Marable, Manning. *Black American Politics: From the Washington Marches to Jesse Jackson.* London: Verso Press, 1985.

Marcus, Eric. *Making History: The Struggle for Gay and Lesbian Equal Rights, 1945–1990: An Oral History.* New York, NY: Harper Collins Publishers, 1992.

Marcuse, Herbert. *Eros and Civilization: A Philosophical Inquiry into Freud*. New York: Vintage Books, 1962.

———. *Negations: Essays in Critical Theory*. London: Free Association Books, 1988.

———. *One Dimensional Man: Studies in the Ideology of Advanced Industrial Society*. Boston: Beacon Press, 1964.

Marcuse, Herbert, and Douglas Kellner. *The New Left and the 1960s*. New York: Routledge Press, 2005.

Marine, Gene. *The Black Panthers*. New York: New American Library, 1969.

Markson, Morley, Timothy Francis Leary, Fred Hampton, John Sinclair, Deborah Johnson, Don Cox, Allen Ginsberg, Jerry Rubin, Abbie Hoffman, William Moses Kunstler, Morley Markson & Associates, and First Run/Icarus Films. *Growing Up in America*. New York: First Run/Icarus Films, 1988.

Marotta, Toby, and Edwin Clark Johnson. *The Politics of Homosexuality*. Boston: Houghton Mifflin, 1981.

Martin, Bradford D. *The Theater Is in the Street: Politics and Performance in Sixties America*. Amherst: University of Massachusetts Press, 2004.

Maxwell, Pat. "The Emperor's New Clothes." *Come Out!* 5 (1970): 10.

McAlister, Laura. "The Transvestite in America." *Come Out!* 4 (1970): 18.

McCarthy, Timothy Patrick, and John Campbell McMillian. *The Radical Reader: A Documentary History of the American Radical Tradition*. New York: New Press, 2003.

McIntosh, Mary. "The Homosexual Role." *Social Problems* 16, no. 2 (Autumn 1968): 182–92.

McLuhan, Marshall. *The Mechanical Bride: Folklore of Industrial Man*. New York: Vanguard Press, 1951.

———. *Understanding Media: The Extensions of Man*. New York: McGraw-Hill, 1965.

McLuhan, Marshall, and Quentin Fiore. *The Medium Is the Massage*. New York: Bantam Books, 1967.

McNeill, Don, and Allen Ginsberg. *Moving through Here*. New York: Knopf, 1970.

Mercer, Kobena. *Welcome to the Jungle: New Positions in Black Cultural Studies*. New York: Routledge, 1994.

Messner, Michael A. *Politics of Masculinities: Men in Movements*. Gender Lens Series in Sociology. Thousand Oaks, Calif.: Sage Publications, 1997.

Metcalf, George R. *Black Profiles*. New York: McGraw-Hill, 1971.

Meyer, Moe. *The Politics and Poetics of Camp*. London: Routledge, 1994.

Meyerowitz, Joanne. *How Sex Changed: A History of Transsexuality in the United States*. Cambridge, MA: Harvard University Press, 2002.

Miller, James. *"Democracy Is in the Streets": From Port Huron to the Siege of Chicago*. New York: Simon & Schuster, 1988.

Mohr, Richard D. *Gay Ideas: Outing and Other Controversies.* Boston: Beacon Press, 1992.

Moore, Gilbert. *A Special Rage.* New York: Harper & Row, 1971.

Morgan, Robin. *Going Too Far: The Personal Chronicle of a Feminist.* New York: Vintage Books, 1978.

Muñoz, José Esteban. *Disidentifications: Queers of Color and the Performance of Politics,* Minneapolis: University of Minnesota Press, 1999.

Munt, Sally R., ed. *Butch/Femme: Inside Lesbian Gender.* London: Cassell Books, 1998.

Newton, David E. *Gay and Lesbian Rights: A Reference Handbook, Contemporary World Issues.* Santa Barbara, CA: ABC-CLIO, 1994.

Newton, Huey P. "Hidden Traitor Renegade Scab: Eldridge Cleaver." Unpublished manuscript. Collected Papers of Huey P. Newton. Stanford University Library Special Collections, Box 48, Folders 16–18.

———. *To Die for the People.* New York: Vintage Books, 1972.

———. *Revolutionary Suicide.* New York: Harcourt Brace Jovanovich, 1973.

———. *War Against the Panthers: A Study of Repression in America.* New York: Harlem River Press, 1996.

Newton, Huey P., David Hilliard, and Donald Weise. *The Huey P. Newton Reader.* New York: Seven Stories Press, 2002.

Nordquist, Joan. *Queer Theory: A Bibliography, Social Theory, No. 48.* Santa Cruz, CA: Reference and Research Services, 1997.

Ogbar, Jeffrey Ogbonna Green. *Black Power: Radical Politics and African American Identity, Reconfiguring American Political History.* Baltimore: Johns Hopkins University Press, 2004.

Olsen, Jack. *Last Man Standing: The Tragedy and Triumph of Geronimo Pratt.* New York: Doubleday, 2000.

O'Neill, Daniel J. *Speeches by Black Americans.* Encino, CA: Dickenson Pub., 1971.

Orphan of America. New York: First Run/Icarus Films, 1981.

Owens, Craig. "Posing." In *Beyond Recognition: Representation, Power, and Culture,* edited by Scott Bryson, Barbara Kruger, Lynne Tillman, and Jane Weinstock, 201–17. Berkeley: University of California Press, 1994.

Pearson, Hugh. *The Shadow of the Panther: Huey Newton and the Price of Black Power in America.* Reading, MA: Addison-Wesley Pub. Co., 1994.

Peck, Abe. "A Letter From Chicago." Liberation News Service, August 6, 1968.

———. "Bay Area Yippies Set to Go No Matter What." *Berkeley Barb,* August 2–8, 1968, 3.

Phelan, Peggy. *Unmarked: The Politics of Performance.* New York: Routledge Press, 1993.

Plummer, Kenneth, ed. *The Making of the Modern Homosexual.* London: Hutchinson Press, 1981.

Raskin, Jonah. *For the Hell of It: The Life and Times of Abbie Hoffman*. Berkeley: University of California Press, 1996.

Rancière, Jacques. *Aesthetics and Its Discontents*. Translated by Steven Corcoran. Cambridge: Polity Press, 2009.

Rayside, David Morton. *On the Fringe: Gays and Lesbians in Politics*. Ithaca: Cornell University Press, 1998.

The Red Butterfly Cell. "Red Butterfly." *Come Out!* 2 (1969): 4–5.

Reed, T. V. *The Art of Protest: Culture and Activism from the Civil Rights Movement to the Streets of Seattle*. Minneapolis: University of Minnesota Press, 2005.

Richmond, Len, and Gary Noguera. *The Gay Liberation Book*. San Francisco: Ramparts Press, 1973.

Riesman, David. *The Lonely Crowd: A Study of the Changing American Character*. New York: Doubleday Anchor Books, 1953.

Riggle, Ellen D. B., and Barry L. Tadlock. *Gays and Lesbians in the Democratic Process: Public Policy, Public Opinion, and Political Representation, Power, Conflict, and Democracy*. New York: Columbia University Press, 1999.

Roman, David. *Acts of Intervention: Performance, Gay Culture, and AIDS*. Bloomington, IN: Indiana University Press, 1998.

Ross, Andrew. *No Respect: Intellectuals and Popular Culture*. New York: Routledge, 1989.

Roszak, Theodor. *The Making of a Counter Culture*. Berkeley, CA: University of California Press, 1994.

Rout, Kathleen. *Eldridge Cleaver*. Boston: Twayne Publishers, 1991.

Rubin, Jerry. *Growing up at Thirty-Seven*. New York: M. Evans, 1976.

———. *We Are Everywhere*. New York: Harper & Row, 1971.

Rubin, Jerry, Eldridge Cleaver, and Quentin Fiore. *Do It: Scenarios of the Revolution*. New York: Simon and Schuster, 1970.

Rudd, Mark. *Underground: My Life with SDS and the Weathermen*. New York: William Morrow, 2009.

Sale, Kirkpatrick. *SDS*. New York: Random House, 1973.

Scanlon, Jennifer. *The Gender and Consumer Culture Reader*. New York: New York University Press, 2000.

Schanche, Don A. *The Panther Paradox: A Liberal's Dilemma*. New York: D. McKay Co., 1970.

Scott, Wilbur J., and Sandra Carson Stanley. *Gays and Lesbians in the Military: Issues, Concerns, and Contrasts, Social Problems and Social Issues*. New York: Aldine de Gruyter, 1994.

Seale, Bobby. *A Lonely Rage: The Autobiography of Bobby Seale*. New York: Times Books, 1978.

BIBLIOGRAPHY 225

---. *Seize the Time: The Story of the Black Panther Party and Huey P. Newton.* New York: Random House, 1970.

Sedgwick, Eve Kosofsky. *Between Men: English Literature and Male Homosocial Desire.* New York: Columbia University Press, 1985.

---. *Epistemology of the Closet.* Berkeley: University of California Press, 1991.

Shamberg, Michael. *Guerrilla Television.* New York: Henry Holt and Co., 1971.

Shames, Stephen, and Charles E. Jones. *The Black Panthers.* New York: Aperture Foundation, 2006.

Sheehy, Gail. *Panthermania: The Clash of Black against Black in One American City.* New York: Harper & Row, 1971.

Shelley, Martha. "Subversion in the Women's Movement." *Come Out!* 6 (1970): 9.

Shepherd, Simon, and Mick Wallis. *Coming on Strong: Gay Politics and Culture.* London: Unwin Hyman, 1989.

Signorile, Michelangelo. *Queer in America: Sex, the Media, and the Closets of Power.* New York: Random House, 1993.

Sloman, Larry. *Steal This Dream: Abbie Hoffman and the Countercultural Revolution in America.* New York: Doubleday, 1998.

Smith, Jessie Carney. *Black Heroes.* Detroit: Visible Ink Press, 2001.

Sontag, Susan. *Against Interpretation, and Other Essays.* New York: Farrar, Strauss & Giroux, 1966.

---, ed. *Antonin Artaud: Selected Writings.* Translated by Helen Weaver. Berkeley: University of California Press, 1988.

Stein, David. *Living the Revolution: The Yippies in Chicago.* New York: Bobbs-Merrill, 1969.

Stone, Willie, and Chuck Moore. *I Was a Black Panther.* Garden City, NY: Doubleday, 1970.

Sycamore, Matt Bernstein. *That's Revolting! Queer Strategies for Resisting Assimilation.* Brooklyn: Soft Skull Press, 2004.

Teal, Donn. *The Gay Militants.* New York: Stein and Day, 1971.

Thompson, Mark. *Long Road to Freedom: The Advocate History of the Gay and Lesbian Movement, Stonewall Inn Editions.* New York: St. Martin's Press, 1994.

Tinkcom, Matthew. *Working Like a Homosexual: Camp, Capital, Cinema.* Durham, NC: Duke University Press, 2002.

Tischler, Barbara L. *Sights on the Sixties.* New Brunswick: Rutgers University Press, 1992.

Trager, Oliver. *Sexual Politics in America: An Editorials on File Book.* New York: Facts on File, 1994.

Tucker, Kenneth H. *Workers of the World, Enjoy!: Aesthetic Politics from Revolutionary Syndicalism to the Global Justice Movement.* Philadelphia: Temple University Press, 2010.

Tyler, Parker. *Screening the Sexes: Homosexuality in the Movies*. New York: Rinehart and Winston, 1972.

Van Peebles, Melvin. *Panther: A Novel*. New York: Thunder's Mouth Press, 1995.

Walker, Daniel. *Rights in Conflict: The Violent Confrontation of Demonstrators and Police in the Parks and Streets of Chicago During the Week of the Democratic National Convention of 1968*. Washington, DC: National Commission on the Causes and Prevention of Violence, 1968.

Wallace, Michelle. *Black Macho and the Myth of the Superwoman*. New York: Dial Press, 1978.

Warhol, Andy. *The Philosophy of Andy Warhol (From A to B and Back Again)*. London: Cassell Publishers, 1975.

Warshawsky, Allan, and Ellen Bedoz. "GLF and the Movement." *Come Out!* 2 (1969): 4–5.

Washington, Albert Nuh. *All Power to the People*. Toronto: Arm the Spirit/Solidarity, 2002.

Wells, Tom. *The War Within: America's Battle Over Vietnam*. New York: Henry Holt and Co., 1994.

Whyte, William H. *The Organization Man*. New York: Anchor Books, 1956.

Wiegman, Robyn. *American Anatomies: Theorizing Race and Gender*. Durham, NC: Duke University Press, 1995.

Williams, Raymond. *Marxism and Literature*. Oxford: Oxford University Press, 1978.

———. *Television: Technology and Cultural Form*. London: William Collins Sons & Co., 1974.

Wilson, Sloane. *The Man in the Gray Flannel Suit*. New York: Pocket Books, 1956.

Wolfe, Tom. *Radical Chic and Mau-Mauing the Flak Catchers*. New York: Farrar, 1970.

Wolff, Robert Paul, Barrington Moore, and Herbert Marcuse. *A Critique of Pure Tolerance*. Boston: Beacon Press, 1965.

The Yes Men. *The True Story of the End of the World Trade Organization*. New York: The Disinformation Company, 2004.

INDEX

Page numbers in italic refer to illustrations.

McGrath, John, 141

McIntosh, Mary, 83, 197n6

McKenzie, Scott, 64

McLuhan, Marshall, 46–48, 194n26

McNeill, Don, 61

mechanical reproduction, 14, 44, 46

media zaps. *See* zaps

Medovoi, Leerom, 115

Mercer, Kobena, 115–17

Metesky, George, 44, 194n17

Mobe. *See* National Mobilization to End the War in Vietnam

monkey theater, 49–50, 59, 73–74. *See also* guerilla theater; Hoffman, Abbie

Monterey Pop Festival, 59

Morgan, Robin, 27, 115, 194n21

Motherfuckers, 61

Movement for a New Society, 174

Mulford, Donald, 129–30

Müller-Armack, Alfred, 169. *See also* Frieburg school

multitude, 179–80. *See also* Hardt, Michael; Negri, Antonio

Muñoz, José, 7

N

National Mobilization to End the War in Vietnam (Mobe), 50–51, 69; and Youth International Party, 59-60, 62. *See also* antiwar movement; Dellinger, David; New Left

Negri, Antonio, 5–6

Newton, Huey P., 4, 116, 126–38, 141–50, 157, 159, on Eldridge Cleaver, 141–45; and Panther Patrols, 26–27, 129, 141, 142; on *Sweet Sweetback's Baadasssss Song*, 145–47

New Left, 33, 67, 69, 70–71, 76–77; and Diggers, 42–43, and gay liberation, 88, 101–6. *See also* Students for a Democratic Society

New York Newsreel, 64. *See also* Fruchter, Norman

New York Radical Women, 27. *See also* Women's International Terrorist Conspiracy from Hell

O

Occupy, 32, 173–75, 180–85

Occupy Wall Street. *See* Occupy

Ochs, Phil, 64–65

Oglesby, Carl, 69. *See also* Students for a Democratic Society (SDS)

ordoliberals, 170

Owens, Craig, 7

Owles, Jim, 105, 107–8. *See also* Gay Activists Alliance

Panther 21, 207n78

Papp, Joseph, 9

Parks, Gordon, 148

Peace and Freedom Party (PFP), 137, 207n66

Phelan, Peggy, 7, 114

Pinochet, Augusto, 171

Pitchford, Kenneth, 202

polyphonic dialogue, 177, 180, 182. *See also* Bakhtin, Mikhail

Pop Art, 15–17, 189n45

Presley, Elvis, 125, 156

P

Put-On, the, 8, 23. *See also* Brackman, Jacob

put-on, 3, 8, 22–26, 56, 62, 75–77; and irony, 24–25, 190n65; Yippies and, 28, 35–36, 52–53

Q

Queer Nation, 181

R

racial death-wish, 117–20

racial oppression, 21–22, 124

Rackley, Alex, 137

Rafferty, Max, 31, 116, 140

Ramos, Mel, 5

rap music. *See* hardcore rap